Roller Derby

TERRY AND JAN TODD SERIES ON PHYSICAL CULTURE AND SPORTS

Edited by Sarah K. Fields, Thomas Hunt, Daniel A. Nathan, and Patricia Vertinsky

Also in the series:

Ronald A. Smith, *The Myth of the Amateur: A History of College Athletic Scholarships*

Andrew R. M. Smith, *No Way but to Fight: George Foreman and the Business of Boxing*

Jason P. Shurley, Jan Todd, and Terry Todd, *Strength Coaching in America: A History of the Innovation That Transformed Sports*

Kevin Robbins, *Harvey Penick: The Life and Wisdom of the Man Who Wrote the Book on Golf*

John Hoberman: *Dopers in Uniform: The Hidden World of Police on Steroids*

John D. Fair, *Mr. America: The Tragic History of a Bodybuilding Icon*

Thomas Hunt, *Drug Games: The International Olympic Committee and the Politics of Doping, 1960–2008*

ROLLER DERBY
The History of an American Sport

MICHELLA M. MARINO

University of Texas Press
Austin

Copyright © 2021 by the University of Texas Press
All rights reserved
Printed in the United States of America
First edition, 2021

Requests for permission to reproduce material from this work should
    be sent to:
    Permissions
    University of Texas Press
    P.O. Box 7819
    Austin, TX 78713-7819
    utpress.utexas.edu/rp-form

♾ The paper used in this book meets the minimum requirements of
ANSI/NISO Z39.48-1992 (R1997) (Permanence of Paper).

LIBRARY OF CONGRESS CATALOGING-IN-PUBLICATION DATA

Names: Marino, Michella M., author.
Title: Roller derby : the history of an American sport / Michella M.
    Marino.
Other titles: Terry and Jan Todd series on physical culture and sports.
Description: First edition. | Austin : University of Texas Press, 2021. |
    Series: Terry and Jan Todd series on physical culture and sports |
    Includes bibliographical references and index.
Identifiers:
    LCCN 2021008774
    ISBN 978-1-4773-2382-3 (cloth)
    ISBN 978-1-4773-2383-0 (library ebook)
    ISBN 978-1-4773-2384-7 (ebook)
Subjects: LCSH: Roller derby—United States—History—20th century. |
    Roller derby—United States—History—21st century. | Roller
    derby—Social aspects—United States. | Roller derby—Political
    aspects—United States.
Classification: LCC GV859.6 .M37 2021 | DDC 796.21—dc23
LC record available at https://lccn.loc.gov/2021008774

doi:10.7560/323823

CONTENTS

Acknowledgments

I try to quote the movie *A League of Their Own* for any situation in life, and I abide by the statement "anything worth doing is worth doing right." This includes giving credit where credit is due. I have been filled with gratitude along the way for all the help I have received, and the thanks given here are not enough, but they are a start.

Since this is an offshoot of my dissertation, I want to begin with my UMass Amherst folks. My dissertation committee — Chris Appy, Joyce Berkman, Brian Bunk, Jennifer Fronc, and Pat Griffin — were all-stars. I could not have asked for a better team, and they were critical for my getting the project off the ground in its earliest phase. My dear and brilliant friend Laura Miller was a constant support during the writing of my dissertation and has remained so throughout the process of turning it into a book. Our friendship transcends the miles that separate us.

As I state in the introduction, the project would not have been possible without my teammates at Pioneer Valley Roller Derby (PVRD). You inspired me on and off the track, and I have never known a more remarkable, athletic, fun, and dedicated group of people, and I am thankful for all the lessons you taught me about being a teammate, the DIY ethic, skating, and roller derby.

Through my relationship with the folks at PVRD, I was able to form critical roller derby networks that helped me meet the old guard of the sport as well as skaters from other parts of the country, and these contacts were invaluable for my project. Thank you to all the skaters, past and present, that took the time to talk with me in person or over the phone. You were incredibly generous with your time and memories. Talking with you was hands down my favorite part of this project. I learned so much, and was constantly inspired by your passion for the sport. Thank you also to Gary Powers with the National Roller Derby Hall of Fame and Museum, who graciously allowed me to spend time in the Hall of Fame collection and to use some of its photographs for this book.

A highlight of my travels and meeting roller derby stars occurred in 2011 when my sister and I flew cross-country to California to interview Jerry Seltzer. He graciously opened his home to us and served as host and tour guide in Sonoma. It was a pleasure visiting with him and really piecing together the nitty-gritty history of the sport founded by his father and continued under his management. For years after the interview, Jerry continued to answer my roller derby questions as they came up. It is a great regret of mine that I was unable to finish this book before he passed, but I hope he knew how thankful I was to know the Commissioner.

Although I no longer teach at Hastings College, it will always hold a special place in my heart. My colleagues were incredibly supportive of my research and this project, especially Rob Babcock and Glenn Avent, both of whom valued sports history and always encouraged me to carve out research and writing time amid our heavy teaching loads. They kept me fed with a good supply of dangerously strong coffee and cheap Chinese food. Hastings College also provided financial support for the project and provided stipends for me to hire Grace Rempp and Joe Prickett as research assistants. Although just undergraduates, Grace and Joe functioned as graduate students and really provided the help I needed to get over a few key hurdles. Thanks, you two. My other students frequently asked about my research, and occasionally pictures of Coors Lightning would make their way into the office. You all were the best. And finally to my J-term students who took the first-ever college course on the history of roller derby—we were a part of history even as we studied it.

I also want to extend my deepest thanks to my Indiana Historical Bureau colleagues. I could not ask to work with a better group of dedicated and fun historians and have learned so much about public history from each of you. I enjoy my work at IHB exponentially more because of you all!

And now to my family. My parents, Phil and Rosemary Nigh, have always encouraged my athletic career, even when that became academic. I inherited an innate sense of competitiveness and a dry sense of humor from them, and I am always thankful for such great parents. My in-laws, Mike and Cindy Marino, are the best family I could have acquired through marriage — fun and supportive even when I dragged their son for years at a time to the East Coast and then the Plains. My sister, Erin Flynn, served a brief stint as research assistant on our big California adventure, but more than that, she is also my best friend. Although it took Sara Crafton and I until second grade to become best friends, there is something grounding about having a friend who has been with you for every stage of your life and will, you know, be there for the rest of them as well. You provided unwavering support throughout this tedious project and encouraged me when I needed it.

Last but never ever least, I want to thank my husband, Tony, and my son, Matthan. This project pre-dates Matty, but in finishing this book, I hope to instill a valuable lesson in him: "The hard is what makes it great." Also, you are my best boy. Tony has been through this with me every step of the way. He has contributed his time and skills by editing, transcribing, proofreading, analyzing, and serving as a constant sounding board. Ultimately, "He's seen enough to know he's seen too much." But he always has my back, and I know I would not have been able to start or finish this project without his generous help and complete support. This is for you, Tony. I love you, and thank you.

ROLLER DERBY

INTRODUCTION

On a chilly November night in western Massachusetts, I sat with my husband, Tony, in our car with the heater blazing. I cannot remember where we had been, but if history is a guide, it mostly likely involved burritos. He was getting ready to get out of the car to walk back to our apartment on the other side of town, about a mile or so away. I was getting ready to drive to an event called "Fresh Meat Night."

To be honest, I was pretty terrified. Who in their right mind willingly goes to an event with that title unless she is studying to be a butcher, which I most certainly was not. Instead, I was studying to be a professional historian, but currently held the title of poor history graduate student. I was heading out of my comfort zone in the name of academic research. Tony looked at me with a wry grin and said jokingly, "Godspeed." I, less jokingly and more anxiously, replied, "If I'm not back in three hours, come looking for me." He was gone, and off I drove to Interskate 91, the local roller-skating rink in Hadley, Massachusetts, tucked in on the second floor of the mall right above the Subway and overlooking the movie theater. I headed in to where, I could only assume, I was to meet my untimely demise via quad skates. Instead, that evening marked the beginning of a completely new personal and professional journey that, at the risk of sounding overly dramatic, changed my life.

My decision to attend "Fresh Meat Night" had not been made on a whim. It was the culmination of about a year's worth of research into the sport of roller derby. As a doctoral student in the History Department at the University of Massachusetts Amherst and a lifelong athlete, I knew I wanted to study some aspect of women's sports for my dissertation, and as a longtime basketball player, I wanted to explore the gender dynamics related to that sport. But my advisor, Chris Appy, suggested the project would be more viable if I used a comparative framework. He sagely advised me to pick another sport that had a long history of women's participation but that maybe was less "mainstream" than basketball. I distinctly remember the moment when he said, "How about roller derby?" And I tentatively responded, "What about roller derby?" In my mind, I saw vague images of spandexed Rollerbladers on cable television, maybe TNT or TNN, about the time when *American Gladiators* was briefly popular. (I still recalled those bronzed, muscular, and hair-sprayed competitors with their clearly made-up names — Diamond, Blaze, Nitro, and Gemini.) Other than those random snippets, I really had no other frame of reference. He explained that roller derby, which had been around for a long time, had recently made a resurgence and that the sport's complex gender dynamics might be interesting to explore. With very little real interest except a graduate student's need to please, I agreed. "Sure, I'll look into it," I heard myself saying.

So I did. Appy was right (as he always is). I became fascinated and, furthermore, hooked. The same tensions I had long recognized while playing and studying basketball were inherent in roller derby, except they were amped up in an in-your-face, totally unapologetic way — or at least that was how it seemed to me at first. Long history of female participation? Check. Conflict over sexuality? Check. Intentional and unintentional mandates of white middle-class femininity? Check, check. I distinctly remember being fascinated by how the Gotham Girls Roller Derby described its brand of skater as "an amalgam of athlete, pin-up girl, rocker and brute rolled into one badass derby girl."[1] "What were their skaters really like," they asked. "Pretty? Hell, yeah! Tough? Of course! Badass? Always! These ladies are taking all the action and excitement of the roller derby you remember and doing it with a modern twist to keep you on your toes." This was my introduction to the modern version of roller derby, which emerged in early 2001.

I heeded Appy's advice and continued researching the sport. Roller derby had a long history in America and was in fact born out of the struggles of the Great Depression. It had a long history of female participation. Indeed, it was founded as a co-ed sport. Men and women had been skating alongside one another as teammates since 1935. The sport evolved from its origins as a kind of skating marathon into a full-contact sport. Roller derby faded from the limelight in the 1970s, had brief periods of revival in the 1980s and 1990s, and reemerged with a no-holds-barred feminist DIY ethic in the early 2000s. By late 2009, roller derby seemed to be teetering on the brink of cutting ties with its countercultural roots and perhaps pushing its way into the mainstream spotlight. The sport's renewed emphasis on athleticism over showmanship and the recent star-packed Hollywood version of modern roller derby featured in the Drew Barrymore film *Whip It*, starring Elliot Page, Drew Barrymore, Kristen Wiig, and Jimmy Fallon, made a younger generation aware of and interested in this badass contact sport for women, even if the movie's portrayal was not exactly accurate.[2]

Whip It, for all its glory and faults, marked an important transition in modern roller derby. Numbers surged in roller derby leagues across the nation. People were talking about roller derby again, the new version and the old. It was as if a collective amnesia had lifted about this longtime cultural mainstay in American society, one that the famous sportswriter Frank Deford described as nothing short of a slice of Americana.[3] Everyone now had a roller derby story, or was interested in making their own.

I began playing roller derby during this post-*Whip It* phase, and was just assumed to be a part of the wave of interest generated by the film. I finally worked up the courage to attend "Fresh Meat Night" the month after *Whip It* premiered, but the movie had not actually influenced my decision to try the sport, as if I somehow thought it looked fun or interesting as Elliot Page, aka Babe Ruthless, got slammed around the banked track. What the movie signaled to me was that modern roller derby was on the cusp. On the cusp of what, I am not sure I knew, but when I picked up the October 2009 *Cosmopolitan* issue, with Elliot Page and Drew Barrymore on the cover in their Riedell skates, I sensed that it was a big moment—this sport was going public. In fact, I felt as though my research on the sport was being exposed—that this thing existed, that it had a long history worth investigating, and that it was now out there in a very real way. This was a bizarre feeling, since I had no claims on the sport. I had been researching it, but not playing it. I had not even seen a bout in person. I knew there was a local league, and a woman with pink hair had helped start it, and it was about time I got serious about figuring out the ins and outs of the sport. So I found myself at Interskate 91, awkwardly strapping on a rented pair of unforgiving quad skates with bright orange rubber wheels.

To some extent, roller derby moved through several distinct eras marked by the big stars who were skating at the time, the base location of the sport, the type of game played, and media coverage, particularly the derby's stints on television. Yet it lacked a clear, linear history, one that could easily be followed, organized, and understood chronologically. Roller derby as an idea, as a sport, and as entertainment cannot be easily categorized or analyzed. One must embrace the whole to understand the parts and to fully comprehend how roller derby worked as a sport and a business. Though the Seltzer family's Roller Derby was the main entity, understanding its history, difficult in itself, does not encompass the whole of the tale. Leo Seltzer may have organized the most popular and structurally cohesive version of roller derby, along with trademarking the name "Roller Derby," but skaters constantly moved between Seltzer's Roller Derby, short-lived outlaw units, and the longest-lasting competitor organization, Roller Games. Thus, if you talk to skaters, they can often, but not always, tell you whom they were skating for and when. Their stories about the roller derby past are usually about roller derby itself, and not always firmly grounded in one specific organization or another. Both the constancy and the fluidity of the sport were what kept it going, but that dynamic makes it difficult to firmly pin down as well.

I naively wanted to show that roller derby in the earlier era was somehow purer and more legitimate, more a sport, than its later incarnations, in part because this was what the sport's founder, Leo Seltzer, wanted, even if it was never fully achieved. In some ways, my initial inclinations generally proved correct. In the last decade of the Seltzer Roller Derby, it became showier and more theatrical than its earlier version, although never to the extent that its competitor Roller Games did. Drawing fans has always been the foremost concern of professional roller derby, from its nascent, Transcontinental marathon days. To mix sports metaphors and borrow a line from the film *A League of Their Own*, "If we don't have fans, we don't have a league." Fans want to see sport *and* entertainment. It is what they pay for. The question then becomes, how do you strike a perfect balance? In individual games and series and seasons, that perfect balance was struck: all skaters skated fully legit and true sport emerged. Yet sometimes fans hated it, and in fact thought it was rigged! In some seasons and series, the balance was out of whack. The hometown favorite always won, and plenty of action occurred on the track. A brilliant move in Chicago might be seen again in St. Louis. The die-hard fans knew it and loved it. The occasional fan did not question it. In general, it is very difficult to keep a record of what was what. All one can do is embrace the entire scope of roller derby for what it was—an incredibly popular sport-entertainment combo featuring athletic skaters, showmen, and showwomen—a veritable hell on wheels.

It is my intention, after fully embracing roller derby in all its forms, controversies, and incarnations, to provide an in-depth, contextual history of the sport through a critical feminist perspective. An analysis of the history of roller derby can begin to show what Americans have considered a real sport as well as what they have embraced as a beloved institution even while not always taking it seriously. A feminist academic study of roller derby showcases an alternative sporting model that emphasizes gender equality while grappling with the constricting social restraints of the mid-twentieth century. This analysis highlights gender relations within a co-ed sport while offering a comparison with more traditional sex-segregated sports. Furthermore, it reveals the changing nature of women's access to contact sports and the ways in which the reproductive lives of athletes were harnessed to conform to and simultaneously challenge social norms about parenthood.

As previously mentioned, roller derby has been a co-ed venture from its inception. How roller derby athletes made sense of their sporting endeavors and how their experiences were packaged and presented to the American public are themes woven throughout the text. Gender was constantly structured and negotiated within roller derby and the larger society. But I do not give as much time and analysis to masculinity and manhood as I do to the presentation, manipulation, and performance of femininity and womanhood. Instead, I explore more fully the gendered aspects of roller derby as they pertain to women, femininity, and athleticism. Focusing on the experiences of female skaters as part of the larger history of roller derby helps unpack the deep-seated gender tensions that have plagued sports in modern America.

Several central questions frame my research into the long of history of roller derby. First, how did the inclusion of female athletes affect the popularity of roller derby in the masculine sporting world and the larger American culture? How did roller derby balance its general gender, sexual, and racial egalitarianism with its need to keep afloat as a business operation? How did this balance evolve over the course of the twentieth and twenty-first centuries? How did women skaters navigate the complications stemming from juggling multiple, and often supposedly conflicting, identities while also succeeding professionally? How did Roller Derby create and support a family model within a professional sporting organization? Finally, does the twenty-first-century incarnation of the sport exemplify a feminist revolution, or even as it pursues a feminist agenda, does it continue to grapple with the issues that have plagued female athletes from the sport's inception? In essence, is the long history of roller derby a story about change or continuity?

The answers to these questions are complicated. Ultimately, I argue that roller derby is an important cultural institution due to its gender integration, which required constant negotiations around femininity, masculinity, and sexuality as well as debates over what constitutes a "real" sport. Throughout its history, roller derby has existed as an on-going contradiction. Indeed, it has skated a thin line between challenging the dominant culture of mid-twentieth-century America on the one hand and, on the other, embracing and reinforcing normative social practices and mainstream beliefs in order to survive as a commercial endeavor. It was roller derby's constant juxtaposition of sport and spectacle, counterculture and mainstream, male and female, and sexy and family-oriented, that allowed it to defy easy categorization and ensured its longevity.

Chapter 1, "From Spectacle to Sport," traces the origins of the sport from the roller marathons of the late nineteenth century to the concept of the modern roller derby in the early twentieth century. Leo Seltzer popularized the idea of the roller derby with the addition of bodily contact in the late 1930s. He also trademarked the name "Roller Derby," which effectively prevented any would-be competitor from organizing an event with that name. This chapter explores the constant evolution of the sport through the mid-twentieth century as it strove to shift from spectacle to legitimate sport while combating stereotypes about Roller Derby skaters and their fans.

Chapter 2, "Skating through the Boundaries of Identity," begins by using a 1938 *Ladies Home Journal* story as a metaphor for how equality in Roller Derby undercut the male hold on the larger masculine sports world. Roller Derby skaters, particularly the women, had to reconcile their feminine identities with their athletic careers in ways that men were (and still are) never asked to do. The sport of Roller Derby provides insight into the complicated negotiations female skaters had to make between their personal identities and society's expectations. These negotiations both mirrored and diverged from those undertaken by other male and female athletes of the twentieth century.

In Chapter 3, " 'A Very Handsome King for a Very Beautiful Queen,' " I explore how Roller Derby reflected mid-twentieth-century social and cultural trends while simultaneously complicating them. Roller Derby used beauty contests to showcase the femininity of its female skaters and tried to adhere to white, heterosexual, middle-class standards of beauty. Yet Roller Derby emphasized equality, so it held a men's king contest too. While the male competition was mainly about popularity, looks played a role. The Seltzers tried to show that their female skaters were not roughnecks and that their male skaters were respectable athletes, regardless of their association with female skaters. Despite the outward emphasis on white middle-class ideals, Roller Derby was accepting of racial and sexual minorities within its ranks, although it did not always openly market that inclusivity.

Chapter 4, "Diaper Derbies," demonstrates how the Seltzer Roller Derby embraced parenthood because of the importance of its female skaters and the business's reliance on them. It provided an alternative model to most female sports organizations, which forced women to choose between being a mother and being an athlete. Furthermore, male skaters were celebrated for being fathers, and Roller Derby allowed parents to bring their children with them on road trips. Children of Roller Derby skaters often grew up with Roller Derby and participated in such events as halftime Diaper Derbies. This chapter further explores the accommodation of Roller Derby to family life and the effects growing up with the derby had on the skaters' children.

Chapter 5, "California or Bust," follows the Seltzer Roller Derby's love-hate relationship with television, which ultimately forced the organization to relocate from New York to California in the mid-1950s. Leo Seltzer handed over the reins of Roller Derby to his son Jerry in 1959. Jerry revitalized the fledging sport, and under his guidance, Roller Derby evolved into yet another version of itself, one remembered for its brilliant use of television syndication and flashy skating theatrics. It was also an era of stiff competition from the rival skating organization best known as Roller Games. After both businesses collapsed in the mid-1970s, a variety of roller derby incarnations continued to pop up, mostly on the West Coast, through the 1980s and 1990s, but none had the lasting power of the Seltzer family's Roller Derby.

Chapter 6, "DIY Roller Derby," takes the reader up to the modern version of the sport, which emerged early in the new millennium in Austin, Texas. Like roller derby of the past, this new, mostly female flat-track roller derby has continually evolved over the past two decades and, with this evolution, has spread across the globe like wildfire. This chapter examines the twenty-first-century revolution of roller derby, particularly the modern gender politics, organizational growth, and governance conflicts still unfolding in the larger derby world. These issues showcase advances in women's sports as well as lasting struggles.

I was lucky to skate among the women and men of the Pioneer Valley Roller Derby (PVRD) for about three years as the ever-classy Coors Lightning. I could have never completed my dissertation or this book without those skating experiences. I did not really understand roller derby until I became a skater myself. Those who participate in the sport in a variety of capacities are the experts, and thus it was important to rely on oral histories to help tell the history of roller derby. The power of using oral history as a methodological tool for sports history lies, as Susan Cahn notes, in its ability "to broaden historical knowledge, to force us to rethink existing understandings, and, ultimately, to blur the outmoded distinction between 'popular' and 'professional' scholarship"; in addition, "it permits us to establish valuable links between popular, public, and academic history."[4] Furthermore, oral history is critical for understanding how women have defined themselves in relation to complicated questions about sports, motherhood, power dynamics, and sexual and gender identity.[5] Oral history interviews provide extraordinary insight into how people make historical meaning of their life experiences.[6]

Oral histories, however, cannot be read naively as offering unmediated access to reality; no historical sources do that. As in all historical research, oral histories are checked against other sources whenever possible. But oral history is invaluable for uncovering women's experiences, since the narrator has the opportunity to "tell her own story in her own terms."[7] This is particularly crucial for women athletes, since their stories have generally been told by male journalists and in relation to male athletes.[8] Women's sports have never received equal media or historical coverage, and the minimal coverage they have received has not always been preserved because of the marginalization of women's sports, and of roller derby as a whole.[9] Oral histories can reshape the historical narrative by giving voice to those whom the historical record has long silenced.[10]

The selection process and criteria for oral history interviews serve as an integral part of any oral history undertaking and undoubtedly shape the larger project in both intended and unintended ways. I began my research with the goal of interviewing roller derby skaters, coaches, administrative personnel, and fans of diverse socioeconomic, racial, ethnic, generational, and sexual backgrounds, in order to highlight the complexity that these factors give to a singular and static experience, narrative, and identity. I succeeded in amassing a wide variety of interviewees from across the country. I interviewed people of Jewish, Italian American, and African American backgrounds. I interviewed athletes, coaches, managers, children of skaters, and fans. I talked with skaters from different eras, and I interviewed both women and men involved with roller derby in a variety of capacities and across time.

Despite my best efforts to diversify my interviewees, I experienced difficulties gathering a representative sample. Outside factors, often beyond my control, occasionally prevented me from interviewing important athletes, which could have greatly aided my research. For instance, the daughter of one of the most famous Roller Derby skaters initially agreed to an interview with me, but became skittish after our discussion of the standard oral history consent and release form. She had recently been burned by some smooth-talking Hollywood men trying to make a quick buck off her mother's story, which led to a lost opportunity for me. I also faced difficulties in gathering a representative sample of Black skaters from the mid-twentieth century. Only a handful of Black women skated for Roller Derby during its golden era. The most prominent African American woman skater, although sympathetic to my project, was working on her own research at the time and declined to be interviewed. Another popular Black female skater initially talked with me on the phone, but I was unable to procure an actual interview. Fortunately, I was able to interview three of the top Black male skaters of the 1960s and 1970s, who provided deep insight to the sport and its racial dynamics.

Race was not the only problematic issue I encountered. When conducting oral history interviews, I had to take into account interpersonal relations and tensions within the roller derby community. At times, contentious disputes between former skaters, their families, former management, and the National Roller Derby Hall of Fame had me toeing a fine line in order to avoid any interpersonal feuds. Conflict between skaters and fans of the Seltzer Roller Derby era and the modern roller derby revival has also emerged. There is a level of mistrust between older skaters and fans and the modern roller derbyists. Neither side fully understands the other, and neither side knows how to bridge the gap, or even whether it wants to. Some Roller Derby skaters from decades past have reached out in the new millennium and offered their skating and organizational expertise to local roller derby leagues. In most cases, this has turned out to be a mutually beneficial relationship. But some modern

FIGURE 0.1. *Pioneer Valley Roller Derby skaters, 2011. Photo by Lesley Arak.*

leagues want nothing to do with the old game or its participants, leading to tension between the two communities. Many modern leagues associate Roller Derby with the antics of 1970s Roller Games and the late-1990s *RollerJam* (broadcast on TNN), as opposed to the skillful and more strategic game of the 1940s, '50s, and '60s. And many former roller derby skaters associate the new leagues with the Austin revival, which originally hyped the skaters' alter egos, fishnets, and hot pants over their skating skills and game strategy.

I attempted to position myself as both an insider and an outsider regarding the roller derby community. I initially attended the "Fresh Meat Night" in November 2009 in an effort to understand the game better, but I stayed because I am competitive. I did not know how to skate. I did not know the basic rules of the modern game. But as an athlete at heart, I like to be challenged, and I wanted to be good. I started going to practices with PVRD regularly and soon became a league member. I continued to play because I grew to love the sport. This project was never intended to be an exposé of any sort. One of the first scholarly studies of modern roller derby was conducted as a "covert participant observation."[11] This subterfuge upset the revival derby community and made its members wary of outside researchers moonlighting as one of their own. Therefore, I was forthright about both my personal athletic interests and my historical interest in the sport.

My involvement in modern roller derby essentially provided me with the insight, understanding, commitment, and networks to complete this project. My experiences with skating, the rules of the game, and team dynamics helped inform questions for my interviewees. I knew what to ask, and I could relate. I understood their answers, and I could sympathize. I understood the differences between what had been and what currently is—most skaters do not have this appreciation. But my insider status could hinder the interviewing process, particularly with the old guard. I had to let them know I was familiar with the rules of the game and the dynamics of skating. I had seen their footage, I had read their publications, and I knew the big names. I had to gauge their feelings about the most recent revival, not all of which were positive, as well as indicate my awareness of the differences between the past and present versions of the sport.

As a conscientious oral historian, I believe in sharing the fruits of my labor with other scholars and hope that my interviews can be of use for future works on women athletes and the sport of roller derby. All my interviews and transcripts have been (or are in the process of being) donated to the Special Collections and University Archives at the W. E. B. Du Bois Library of the University of Massachusetts Amherst and are available to researchers, subject to conditions set by my interviewees.[12] To my knowledge, no other such collection of oral history interviews of roller derby skaters and related athletic personnel is housed in an academic institution, but I hope that will change.

Roller derby has enticed athletes and fans for over eighty-five years now and is still going strong. Americans from all walks of life have been attracted by the uniqueness of what the sport offers. As David Ketchum, a longtime fan and current skater, explained, "The moment I saw it, I was addicted to it. I couldn't wait until the next week to watch it again. . . . [I was drawn to] the speed, the color of it, the kind of roles the skaters took on, the fighting, the fact that there were both men and women playing. And the characters are bigger than life."[13] Roller derby has been and continues to be a beloved, slightly offbeat cultural and sporting phenomenon that deserves and indeed demands to be taken seriously without being solely defined and limited by traditional parameters and expectations. Jerry Seltzer, Roller Derby's owner from 1959 to 1973, understood that people loved Roller Derby even if they could not fully understand why. "They can relate to it," he philosophized. "In many senses Roller Derby is a sport that's bigger than life. . . . The people's sport, that's what we are."[14] In this book, I endeavor to tell the history of the people's sport.

1 | FROM SPECTACLE TO SPORT

I have dedicated twenty-eight years of my life to bringing forth a sport which I feel is destined to become the greatest contact sport of all—Roller Derby. I do not mean for it to be an exhibition or a show but a true sport.

LEO A. SELTZER, FOUNDER OF ROLLER DERBY

In 1929, Josephine "Ma" Bogash, a stocky Chicago wife and mother who worked in the mail-order department at Sears, Roebuck, received unfortunate news from her doctor: she had diabetes. Her doctor, concerned for her health, ordered the forty-one-year-old to begin exercising to help control her weight, and suggested she go to a local gymnasium. Bogash, more interested in the pastime of roller skating, decided to hit the local roller rink instead. From that fateful day forward, Bogash became a "roller rink buff" in order to help combat her diabetes, and she managed to keep her symptoms under control as long as she was skating.[1] In August 1935, Bogash learned about an exciting new skating marathon that was opening at the nearby Chicago Coliseum. Bogash, her husband, her son, and a group of friends paid a nickel each to attend the first Transcontinental Roller Derby, presented by Leo A. Seltzer. Surrounded by band music and her family and friends, Bogash sat in the packed audience and watched the male and female skaters whir round and round the long flat oval track as competitors tried to outlast one another in a marathon-style skating race similar to the six-day bicycle races that were also popular at the time.[2]

The female skaters in the Transcontinental Roller Derby failed to impress the avid roller-skating Bogash. As her son later recalled, "My mother looked at my dad and said, 'I can skate as good as or better than

FIGURE 1.1. *Josephine "Ma" Bogash, 1938. Courtesy of Gary Powers and the National Roller Derby Hall of Fame and Museum.*

those girls are doing here.'"[3] In response, Bogash's husband, Richard, a longtime worker on the Wabash Railroad, dared her to try out for the next derby. When tryouts were announced in Chicago the following week, Ma Bogash dragged her eighteen-year-old son, Billy, with her. Roller Derby personnel were thrilled with Bogash's skating ability but were relatively unimpressed with young Billy, who failed to pass the required time trials. The loyal mother refused to join unless they took Billy as well, and Derby officials gave in to her demands. Bogash and Billy joined the Roller Derby on September 6, 1935, and were immediately sent to Kansas City for the second Transcontinental Roller Derby.[4]

Ma Bogash and Billy skated as a mother-son duo and took the new sport by storm. The crowds loved Ma, and she and Billy became the first real gate attraction.[5] Ma was nothing like the young, petite, and beautiful skater Ivy King, a popular competitor whom fans aspired to be like. Ma was much closer to fans' reality: a "stockily built" wife and mother with diabetes trying to improve her health while proving something to her husband. The fans could relate to her, saw themselves in her, and lived vicariously through her. She was everywoman. And if she could be a successful professional athlete, what did that indicate about the sport

FIGURE 1.2. *Billy Bogash, 1938. Courtesy of Gary Powers and the National Roller Derby Hall of Fame and Museum.*

of Roller Derby? What did that say about women's athletic capabilities and the women and men who participated side by side in the derby? What type of sport was this, and where did it belong?

The media, the male-dominated sports world, social critics, and sports fans grappled with these questions as Leo Seltzer, the owner of Roller Derby, sought to make Roller Derby the next big sport and a profit-generating business. From Roller Derby's beginnings, the skaters, both male and female, blatantly challenged ideas about women's relationship to and participation in sports. By allowing women to compete on par with men, Roller Derby had to fight for legitimacy and, ultimately, inclusion in the wider world of sports. Despite this battle, or perhaps because of it, fans—particularly female fans—were drawn to Roller Derby more strongly than to other sporting events of the era, because of its relatability. The nature of the co-ed contact sport highlighted tensions between genders, social classes, and sports, which marginalized Roller Derby in the sports pages but endeared it to Hollywood elites, famous athletes, and its working-class fan base.

Leo Seltzer's Transcontinental Roller Derby drew on a long history of roller skating as a leisure activity. The invention of the roller skate is attributed to a Belgian named John Joseph Merlin, who sported a pair of skates in London in the 1760s. Apparently, Merlin was not steady on his newfangled wheels. He wore his skates to a masquerade party but "could not control his speed or direction and crashed into a large mirror, severely injuring himself and possibly setting back the sport of roller skating for years."[6] The activity did not take off until a century later when James L. Plimpton, an American from Massachusetts, improved the skate design in 1863 with his "rocker skate," which removed the wheels from the plate of the skate, allowing skaters a greater range of movement, including the ability to make more fluid turns.[7] The next major skate improvement emerged in the 1880s with the creation of the Richardson ball-bearing skate, equipped with metal casters, which increased the durability of the skate and allowed skaters to go faster without the fear of wooden rollers cracking. The revolutionary addition of ball-bearing wheels led to a roller-skating "rage" across Europe and North America in the early 1880s. The sport went through dramatic cycles of boom and bust, exciting vast interest only to be forgotten. A resurgence of roller skating occurred in the 1930s when the "pastime picked up enthusiasts by the hundreds and then the thousands."[8] It was this enthusiasm for skating that drew Seltzer's interest.

Besides roller skating as a popular pastime, roller-skating races and skating marathons have a long history in the United States. These races drew public attention as early as 1883 in Boston, Fall River, and Salem, Massachusetts; Providence and Newport, Rhode Island; and New York City.[9] By the mid-1880s, roller skating had entered a "craze" phase that spread rapidly across the nation. Reporters compared the enthusiasm for skating to other crazes such as that for tobogganing, teas, and progressive euchre (a card game).[10] In early March 1885, an "international" six-day skating tournament and marathon was held at Madison Square Garden in New York City along with a number of other spectator events.[11] The event drew large crowds, leading to planning for future marathon races; roller skating seemed on its way to being a permanent fixture in American life.

But only two months after the March 1885 races, the popularity of roller skating, particularly roller races, declined after a series of skating-related deaths and "social transgressions" occurred.[12] Two young men, including the winner of the Madison Square Garden race, died as a result of their participation in the skating marathon.[13] A few weeks later, marathon skating claimed the lives of a young woman from Brooklyn and a young man from Philadelphia.[14] In Connecticut, two teenage girls ran away from their homes because they were "infatuated with roller skating" and had been banned from the local rink by their parents.[15] Besides the potential health risks of skating, detractors charged that the activity was leading America's youth to misbehave and intermingle in inappropriate and unchaperoned facilities, preparing "the way for long lives of wretchedness."[16]

The National Roller Skating Congress maintained that skating was "a healthful recreation and an exceptionally moral enjoyment,"[17] but the *New York Times* took an opposing view, reporting on a failed roller-skating match at Madison Square Garden that "by many it will be regarded with great satisfaction as an indication that the mania for roller skating will soon become a thing of the past."[18] Perhaps unsurprisingly, the activity and sport were popular among teenagers and young adults but "[had] not won the approval of thoughtful and sensible fathers and mothers." "Almost every day," the *Times* writer claimed, "stories in which the dangers that beset the young in the rinks were shown. Elopements, betrayals, bigamous marriages, and other social transgressions were traced to the association of the innocent with the vicious upon the skating floor." Even the National Roller Skating Congress spoke out against the marathon skating contests, labeling them "injurious."[19] As with any craze, its popularity waned, attendance at races dropped, rinks went out of business, and moralists found other social ills to denounce.[20] Roller skating did not die, though. Some rinks managed to survive the ebb and flow of skating's popularity and keep their doors open, while skating races, tournaments, and championships continued to be held at least sporadically throughout the late nineteenth and early twentieth centuries.[21]

The entertainment businessman and promoter Leo A. Seltzer owned several movie theaters in Portland, Oregon, throughout the 1920s. During the Great Depression, he became interested in the potential value of live entertainment and sporting events. He hosted a series of popular walkathons in the early 1930s and took his shows on the road, traveling across the country. Dancing, bicycling, and walking marathons provided just the type of cheap, mindless, and lighthearted entertainment that struggling Americans craved as diversions from the difficult reality of the Depression. These marathons offered a spectacle without requiring participants to have particularly specialized skills; endurance was everything. They promoted an everyday, workingman's (or workingwoman's) sort of hero, one unlikely to achieve superstar status. The ordinary skill of dancing, walking, or riding a bike evolved into a type of sport when done in a marathon style. Anyone could dance, walk, or ride a bike, but could they do it for twenty-four hours straight? Could they do it for days on end?[22] The promoters challenged participants to outlast their opponents in these ferocious competitions, which could drag on for days or even weeks as dancers, walkers, or riders collapsed in exhaustion one by one. The prize money for winners was not much—usually about $1,000, split between couples for over a thousand participation hours—but it was enough to attract a Depression-beleaguered field.[23]

Seltzer's marathons were particularly entertaining, since he added popular emcees such as Red Skelton to provide humorous commentary and amuse the audience with jokes during the event. Seltzer transformed the marathons into full-scale productions to ensure that audiences became repeat customers. To entice the audience, he added a different side event each night, such as a cellophane wedding in which the bride wore a dress and veil of cellophane, ice-sitting contests, ladies' nights, south-of-the-border evenings, and Indian powwow celebrations. The marathons were sometimes broadcast live on the radio to increase interest, and listeners could enjoy the entertainment from the comfort of their own homes, although hosts would encourage fans to "come on down, there's still plenty of room."[24]

In 1933, at age thirty, Seltzer moved his base of business operations to Chicago, Illinois, where he became the main leaseholder on the historic and colossal Chicago Coliseum on South Wabash Avenue.[25] He continued hosting walkathons and similar attractions in the Coliseum but decided to investigate more profitable, affordable, and exciting events after a series of disappointing walkathons. Walkathons, Seltzer concluded, were a temporary novelty: "They'll buy it once, twice maybe—but a third time is pressing your luck."[26] He needed something that would attract long-term fans. During this search, he claims to have stumbled across a *Literary Digest* magazine article with a surprising statistic. According to Seltzer, the article stated that over 90 percent of Americans roller-skated at some point in their lives. Roller skating, it seemed, appealed to practically everyone—from young children to matronly women like Ma Bogash, and it cut across class lines. With skating enjoying such a high participation rate among Americans, surely, Seltzer figured, some sort of sport on skates would draw an enthusiastic—and, more importantly, paying—audience.[27]

Supposedly drawing inspiration from this magazine article, Seltzer conceived the idea of Roller Derby. Yet Seltzer's idea was not as original as he claimed or as was commonly reported. An early Transcontinental Roller Derby program from a 1936 race at the New York Hippodrome stated that in June 1934, Seltzer attended a marathon-style roller race in Chicago that lasted six days.[28] Apparently, "he was so enthused over the race that he sat there hour after hour marveling at the speed and thrills that these racers were presenting the public in their many jams."[29] There was no mention of the *Literary Digest* article that supposedly inspired Seltzer to create the sport from scratch. The program claims that Seltzer combined components of the Chicago roller race with the popular six-day bike race and the transcontinental race idea to form the Transcontinental Roller Derby.[30] The 1934 race was not even the first roller-skating derby in Chicago. The *Chicago Tribune* had provided coverage of the National Roller Skating Derby, which took place in April 1922.[31] The National Roller Skating Derby consisted of a one-mile race for amateurs, a series of sprint races for professionals, and a six-day twenty-five-mile roller-skating marathon, which was for professional skaters who had their eye on the "fat purse."[32] Indeed, the term "roller derby" was used in the 1920s and early 1930s to describe various male and female roller-skating races and marathons held by skating and sports clubs. Roller derbies had been held from coast to coast: for instance, a twenty-one-day roller-skating derby was held in Newark, New Jersey, in February 1934, and another was held in the streets of Los Angeles—skaters intended to skate along the Pacific Coast Highway from Canada to Mexico in April 1935.[33]

Leo Seltzer's true inspiration was mostly likely a combination of events and ideas, but sources claim that Seltzer and his sports buddies and associates worked out his version of roller derby while dining at the Johnny Ricketts restaurant, a "sports hangout" then located on Chicago Avenue. He hastily scribbled notes on a tablecloth that outlined a roller-skating marathon-type race among a field of co-ed teams. The race would occur on a flat track where men and women would test their endurance and speed simultaneously on wooden wheels.[34]

Leo Seltzer's Transcontinental Roller Derby debuted on August 13, 1935, on a hot Chicago afternoon. Twenty-five two-person male-female teams skated before a crowd of twenty thousand curious, enthused, and paying spectators (including Ma Bogash and her family), jam-packed into the cool air-conditioned Chicago Coliseum. The goal of the derby was simple in principle: the winners would be the first team to skate the approximately 3,000-mile distance from New York to San Diego, the equivalent of 57,000 laps on the flat track sprawled across the center of the coliseum.[35] Teams, denoted by jerseys with the same number, were required to skate for eleven to fourteen hours a day, and one of the two team members had to be on the track at all times, or else the team faced elimination.[36] If a team did not meet a specified mileage each day, it was disqualified. A giant map of the United States showed the route across the country, and small lights on the map were lit as skaters advanced along the replicated path, marking their distance and mileage as they progressed city by city. Staying true to the crowd-pleasing antics in walk and dance marathons, sprints (later renamed "jams") provided opportunities for skaters to gain an advantage by lapping their competitors. Crowds loved the fast-paced action of the sprints, which broke up the monotony of the endurance race.[37] Skaters who fell, collapsed, or were injured at any point were replaced on the track by their partners. These substitutions incurred a one-lap penalty.[38]

The teams skated continually from approximately one thirty in the afternoon to twelve thirty in the morning.[39] A member of each team had

More than 20,000 people packed the Chicago Coliseum for the Transcontinental Roller Derby

FIGURE 1.3. *"More than 20,000 people packed the Chicago Coliseum for the Transcontinental Roller Derby," August 13, 1935. Courtesy of Gary Powers and the National Roller Derby Hall of Fame and Museum.*

to be skating throughout the entire monthlong derby when audiences were present. While one team member skated, the other slept on a cot in the infield portion of the track, read, cheered for his or her teammate, ate, or provided the crowd with other forms of entertainment. After weeks of skating, exhaustion and injuries, despite safety prevention and on-site medical care, quickly reduced the number of teams. On September 11, 1935, Bernie McKay and Corrisse Martin pulled ahead on the giant lit map tracking their eight-wheeled voyage to the West Coast, and they maintained a steady lead for the next week and a half. On September 22, the duo defeated the nine remaining teams by completing the 57,000 laps, winning the first ever Transcontinental Roller Derby.[40] Despite the victory, McKay never skated again, saying he saw no real future with the derby.[41]

Others were less pessimistic than McKay. Despite the limited financial rewards, and the dedication and tough training required of skaters, Seltzer's Transcontinental Roller Derby provided unparalleled opportunities during the bleak times of the Great Depression. During Roller

Derby's early years, Seltzer offered modest salaries but also opportunities for prize money. First-place teams won the grand prize of $1,000.[42] A little extra cash could be made during special sprinting jams when the worn-out skaters would stop midstride and take off in a hard sprint around the track with "quick bursts of speed," getting in a few more laps in order to win instant prize money.[43] In addition to a base salary, skaters were given housing, food, clothing, and medical care.[44]

Many of the early skaters in the Transcontinental Roller Derby joined for financial reasons. They had been unemployed, or their families had been hard hit by the Great Depression, and they saw no other opportunities on the horizon.[45] A former skater named Gene Vizena Nygra remembered how these factors played a role in her skating career. A recent high school graduate, she was attempting to get hired at Sears, Roebuck, but experienced a string of bad luck. She recalled, "I had been hunting for a job, and I would take the test at Sears, Roebuck, and the next morning they'd call me when I'm out looking for a job, so I lost it."[46] When presented with the opportunity to try out for Roller Derby, she decided to give it a whirl, even though she did not know how to skate. "I was the fourth-worst skater there," she lamented about her tryout. "I would barely go round the track. I knew nothing about skating, except I had put skates on before . . . But you gotta remember, this was the Depression. Nobody had jobs. And we were guaranteed twenty-five dollars a week."[47]

Seltzer, a savvy businessman, hurried to copyright his version of roller derby, most likely to combat competition and corner the market on the potentially moneymaking enterprise. It is unlikely Seltzer would have been granted a patent, since his version of roller derby was not a particularly new invention, so he got creative. He applied for a copyright on the "Transcontinental Tour" (detailed in a pamphlet) and the "Roller Derby" (in a book).[48] The "stories" described the setting for Seltzer's Roller Derby, the nature of the competition, and the rules and regulations of the sport. An excerpt from the pamphlet reads as follows: "So far the boys of the teams have held the track, and now the fellow with the skate trouble retires, and his girl teammate takes up the grind. She is greeted with a hand from the crowd. Soon, other feminine members take to the track until the field is mixed with the male and female characters of the drama."[49]

The "Transcontinental Tour" received its copyright on September 21, 1935, and the "Roller Derby" received its on November 2, 1935.[50] Seltzer then gave his Indiana-based company, the Transcontinental

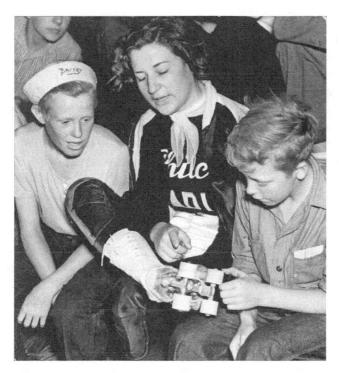

FIGURE 1.4. *Two* Minneapolis Tribune *carriers looking at the skates of Gene Vizena at the municipal auditorium, August 6, 1937. Minneapolis Newspaper Photograph Collection, Hennepin County Library.*

Roller Derby Association, Inc., "an exclusive license to stage this competitive event."[51] In a shrewd move, Seltzer attempted to copyright the Roller Derby programs sold at his events by reproducing them in books and pamphlets and rewording passages in more flowery, dramatic prose. He clearly wanted to use copyright law as a way to prevent other promoters from reprinting the rules of roller derby in their event programs; the logic seemed to be that if rival promoters couldn't legally print the copyrighted rules, which clarified the intricacies of the competition, they would be deterred from putting on their own roller derbies.[52]

Seltzer put this idea to the test when he sued another promoter, Larry Sunbrock, as well as the managers of the Pan-Pacific Auditorium in Los Angeles, for copyright infringement in 1938 after they attempted to host a roller derby. But the judge ruled that the pamphlet and the book that Seltzer had copyrighted had "no fixed plot or story . . . [and]

no distinct characters"; in fact, "All we have here is a set of regulations for running a race."[53] The judge did not believe that Seltzer's publications deserved copyright protection. Furthermore, according to the judge, Seltzer's concept of roller derby was not particularly original, even if Seltzer had added a few novel features such as a penalty box and the "open house, or free for all." The judge stated, "Defendants' program bears strong internal evidence of having been derived, not from plaintiffs' protected works, but from the sources common to both authors. The exhibits disclose that such roller-skating races have been staged under similar rules, at least since 1929; and that many of the features, more recently introduced, have been used in bicycle racing and in other sports for many years."

The ruling set an important precedent in copyright law pertaining to sports and games (essentially, they are uncopyrightable), especially since the 1938 ruling was upheld in an almost identical case, *Seltzer v. Corem*, which was appealed in November 1939 in Gary, Indiana, in the Seventh Circuit Court of Appeals. This appellate case reversed a ruling by an Indiana district court in March of that year, in a case in which Seltzer attempted to again test his copyrights. This second case was most likely prompted by the unfavorable ruling in Los Angeles in 1938. In the original trial of *Seltzer v. Corem*, the judge ruled unequivocally for Seltzer and upheld his copyrights, contradicting the 1938 California ruling. From the trial record, it appears that the district court judge was unaware of the *Seltzer v. Sunbrock* judgment in California. Immediately after the district court's ruling, Corem's lawyers filed exceptions to the ruling and decided to appeal.[54]

The appeal of *Seltzer v. Corem* took an odd turn. The appellate court judges suspected that Leo Seltzer and Henry Corem were in collusion. The judge wrote, "This is an exceedingly friendly suit. Indeed it is so much so that our suspicion is somewhat aroused. . . . We are interested, of course, in knowing whether there is a good faith controversy between these parties, and whether the appellant [Henry Corem] has really committed the acts which he has admitted in his stipulation."[55] In fact, the court suspected Seltzer of providing funds to Corem to pretend to put on a roller derby so Seltzer could pretend to stop him: "In other words, if this law suit is being instigated and financed by the appellee [Seltzer], or if in fact there is no good faith controversy before us, these parties have no business in this court or any other court, and such conduct ought not to be passed without mention."[56] Furthermore, neither Seltzer's nor Corem's lawyers had mentioned the California case to either the district court or the appellate court, which the appellate judges deemed a "significant fact" when they discovered it on their own. They noted that the cases were virtually the same: "Every question presented here was presented there [in California] and decided adversely to the appellee [Seltzer] in this case. . . . It is sufficient to say that we approve that court's conclusions in every respect. We adopt its rulings and hold that the copyrights here involved were invalid and not infringed."

Even though the copyrights failed (twice), Seltzer was able to prevent other promoters from holding official roller derbies. In 1936, he received a trademark on the name "Roller Derby," which prevented anyone else from hosting a roller derby and calling it such.[57] Throughout most of the twentieth century, the Seltzer family used the trademark effectively to prevent other organizations from using the term "Roller Derby," even if not the rules or the idea itself. The Roller Derby Skate Company, which was owned by Leo Seltzer and his brother Oscar, was the only organization other than Leo's skating business that was allowed to use the term and thus host a Roller Derby or produce official merchandise.[58]

The early Transcontinental Roller Derby that Seltzer promoted as a skating variant of the dance marathons, walkathons, and bike races of the early 1930s was in fact just a more extreme version of roller-skating races and marathons that had been around since the 1880s.[59] Nonetheless, Roller Derby came to resemble an original concept as it evolved to include team play, physical contact, and a unique rule set by the end of the 1930s.[60] This evolution was Leo Seltzer's unique contribution. Within a year or two of the sport's debut, Seltzer reorganized the partner and scoring format to make the Transcontinental Roller Derby into a more traditionally organized team sport. Skating couples were placed onto either a black or a white team. Each team consisted of ten skaters, five females and five males, but the skaters were still partnered with a member of the opposite sex and shared a uniform number (as they had in the past), effectively creating five couples on each team. The score was tallied by adding up each couple's laps for a total team score.[61] The team with the highest lap total won the Roller Derby. Because of the popularity of the sprints and jams, the endurance race with skaters' progress tracked between cities on a giant lit map was "gradually phased out in favor of a pass-for-points system," which rewarded skater and team competition.[62] Endurance was still important, but this shift meant that speed became a bigger factor in game play. Emphasis was placed on team scoring and intense competition, which was fueled by the excitement of skaters vying to pass and lap each other on the sprints.[63]

Seltzer replaced the large oval flat track with a track banked at forty-five degrees early on, because when skaters tired or lost control, they often skidded off the track and ended up sprawled onto fans' laps, which perhaps delighted some audience members but was ultimately a safety hazard.[64] Seltzer knew the banked track would also increase the speed of the race, which would appeal to the audience as well.[65]

Seltzer targeted his marketing to the specific communities where the Roller Derby performed. In the late 1930s, Seltzer had a traveling derby troupe that would split into two teams for each extended competition. Skaters would be picked up via try-outs in one location or another and might train until they were ready to play, but he had a core group of skaters on which he would draw to skate in the approximately month-long competitions. Before the roller derby arrived at its destination, advance men would create hype in an area by claiming that the Roller Derby teams were from rival cities or that a traveling team was playing a "local" team. This ploy created the appearance that dozens of teams were spread out across the country. In the postwar era, the Seltzer operation did expand to include multiple traveling units, and some teams were based in specific locales across the country, including New York, Hollywood, and Chicago. But in the early days of the Seltzer Roller Derby, the same skaters generally traveled together across America, competing against one another but creating the illusion of local rival teams. This was an intentional move by Seltzer, who firmly believed that unless fans were invested in an event, they would not keep paying to see it.[66]

After initially taking advantage of a popular trend, Leo Seltzer transformed the roller races and marathons of the past with his emphasis on several important aspects: the novelty of professional female athletes, female fans, and spectacle.[67] As an entertainment promoter, although he disliked the term for its less-than-reputable connotations, Seltzer "understood the value of a good hook and angle."[68] In the early years of the sport, participants who demonstrated crowd-pleasing talents such as singing, dancing, joke-telling, or even juggling were often hired over those who could merely skate.[69] Thus, Seltzer intentionally created a spectacle that combined sport and entertainment to ensure audiences of paying spectators.[70] He also realized that a large audience demographic was for the most part ignored in the male-dominated sports world. He figured that by including women as competitors in Roller Derby, as they had been in dancing, walking, and roller marathons, he could expand his audience. Female skaters would attract female fans, since Roller

Derby was one of the few opportunities for women to see other women compete on a team and in such a way that highlighted their athleticism, toughness, and strength; men, on the other hand, would be drawn to a sport that featured pretty women roughing each other up. What Seltzer failed to foresee was that the inclusion of women in Roller Derby would continually raise doubts in the mainstream sports world about the seriousness of the sport and the type of people who participated in it. In the eyes of some, the mere participation of women alongside men relegated the sport to a "sideshow novelty."[71]

Seltzer's Roller Derby quickly developed into a highly organized co-ed sport that garnered large crowds, interested skaters, and media attention as he scheduled his derbies in city after city across the country. Skaters would try out in one city during the derby's monthlong stint, and if lucky, they would be traveling with the troupe when the derby headed out to the next location, barnstorming-style. From the beginning, Roller Derby was a flexible and evolving sport and business, pursuing what worked and what pleased the audience while discarding rules and regulations that hindered its popularity. In some cases, rules added to a race or a game on Monday might be removed for the Wednesday game, depending on fans' reactions. Seltzer continually adjusted the game based on audience feedback and informal surveys of spectators. He explained, "There was no AAU, no NCAA for me to worry about. If I saw something that looked good, or if someone said, 'Seltzer, I like that,' why, I would put it in for good the next night."[72]

The creation of larger squads, in particular, added a "more lasting appeal," but as the sport struggled to stay afloat in the early years of the Great Depression, prize money was reduced and eventually eliminated.[73] At the lowest point, "salaries became an informal sort of thing."[74] Skaters did not abandon the fledgling operation, since they enjoyed skating, liked the camaraderie, and needed the work, even if the sport's continued existence was sometimes in doubt. Plus, if the derby earned a profit, Seltzer gave the players a cut. Toward the end of the 1930s, both the United States and the Roller Derby pulled out of the Depression, but even then the top skaters still earned only around eighty dollars for a solid month of skating.[75] That wage was nonetheless an improvement over what they could earn in other fields.

Yet the money issues that plagued Roller Derby were not what almost led to its early demise. After the first race, in Chicago, Seltzer took the Transcontinental Roller Derby on the road, playing in Kansas City,

Louisville, Detroit, New York, San Francisco, and Minneapolis.[76] This cross-country, barnstorming travel brought national exposure to Roller Derby, but in a most unwanted manner.[77]

On March 24, 1937, twenty-three members of Seltzer's Transcontinental Roller Derby were traveling on a private bus on Highway 50 west of Salem, Illinois, en route from St. Louis to Cincinnati, when the front-right tire blew out. The bus was going downhill at about forty miles per hour when the blowout occurred, causing the bus to career wildly across the highway. It crashed into a concrete bridge abutment fifty feet away before flipping violently on its side, which smashed the gas tanks.[78] The bus struck the abutment so hard that the engine was torn loose and thrown through the air, landing two hundred feet away.[79] According to one newspaper report, "Flames from its exploding gasoline tanks immediately enveloped the bus and reduced it to twisted junk."[80] The flames reached forty feet into the air and "turned the bus into a funeral pyre for those trapped in it when it crashed and overturned. The bus smoldered for an hour after the accident."[81]

According to the Associated Press, the bus accident was considered "one of the worst disasters in the history of motor-bus transportation." Twenty of the twenty-three persons on board perished in the accident or died later of burn-related injuries.[82] Many of the victims' bodies were burned beyond recognition, according to reports. A four-year-old child, the daughter of Mrs. Emma Caldwell, the skaters' dietitian, was "so badly burned [that] determination of its sex was difficult."[83]

Don Flannery, a surviving skater from Kansas City, described the awful scene to Chicago reporters: "I can still hear my pals' screams of terror. They were trapped in a regular mass of fire. The boys as well as the girls were hysterical and all fought like mad to get out."[84] Flannery escaped by crawling out a window, but realizing that his fiancée, Ruth Hill, also of Kansas City, was still trapped inside, he attempted to rescue her, receiving first-degree burns and other injuries in the process. "She called to me twice," Flannery told hospital attendants. "I finally found her. I tried to pull her out, but she was pinned and I couldn't move her." The hospital staff "reported he wept as he asked, 'I did the best I could for her, didn't I?'"[85]

Even at Roller Derby's lowest point, a little bit of its crazy humor was able to survive. The nonskating Roller Derby master of ceremonies, Ted Mullen, was one of the few travelers to escape the bus before it exploded in flames. Nonetheless, Mullen sustained life-threatening injuries and was rushed to a hospital. As the story goes, "near death the next day, Mullen beckoned to a doctor and, through blistered lips, asked: 'Do you think I'll ever be able to skate?' The doctor quickly assured him he would. 'Funny,' Mullen whispered in agony, 'I never was able to before.' . . . He died shortly thereafter."[86]

From that awful date in March 1937, an honorable and "lasting if bittersweet legacy"[87] of Roller Derby emerged. The jersey number "1" was officially retired, never again worn in Roller Derby, as a tribute to those who died in the tragic bus accident. The famous skater Ann Calvello once stated, "If you see the number '1' on a skater, you're not watching Roller Derby."[88] This legacy has continued into the twenty-first century with the modern revival of the sport.

The bus accident killed the majority of Seltzer's skaters and almost demolished Roller Derby, yet Seltzer scrambled to keep the sport alive and to fulfill existing commitments, partly in response to the few remaining dedicated skaters, who "convinced him to go on."[89] Seltzer called back skaters who had not been on the bus, and recruited skaters from roller-skating rinks in Chicago, sending them to Cincinnati to skate.[90] Seventeen-year-old Mary Youpelle had joined Roller Derby only a month before the bus accident and had skated in her first marathon in St. Louis. In an ironic twist of fate, Youpelle's brother had broken his hip in a car accident, so her parents drove to St. Louis to take her home to Chicago to be with her injured brother during his recovery. Since Youpelle did not get on the team bus heading to Cincinnati, she assumed her Roller Derby career was over. Instead, she narrowly escaped death. After the accident, Seltzer traveled to Chicago to beg her parents to allow her to rejoin the derby, which they did. Youpelle traveled to Cincinnati and remained with the derby, becoming one of the sport's top skaters over the next few decades.[91]

As the remaining skaters regrouped, Seltzer instituted a change that permanently altered the history of Roller Derby. In late 1937, he amended the rules to allow physical contact between skaters, which transformed the nature of the sport and officially severed its ties with the marathon races of the past. Apparently, at least one skater had flirted with doing this as early as 1936. At a race in Louisville, Kentucky, the champion skater Joe Laurey threw a couple of male skaters over the railing. He stated, "They fined me $25 and disqualified me, so I threw my skates on the track and left. Everyone else was pushing, so I thought, 'What the hell?' People loved it."[92]

Although Laurey claimed to be the first to add contact and melodrama to Roller Derby, no official changes were made until 1937, during a successful race series held in the Miami, Florida, area.[93] In those days, according to the derby fan and author Keith Coppage, "the speedier, shorter, more lithe skaters had always been able to maneuver around the larger skaters for laps, a fact of the game that vexed the taller, beefier players but seemed to entertain crowds to no end."[94] During one of the men's races in Miami, the larger skaters became increasingly frustrated as the smaller, quicker skaters kept breaking away and lapping them, resulting in more points for their team. The bigger skaters began pushing, shoving, and elbowing the speedsters, pinning them in the pack behind them, despite rules forbidding any sort of physical contact. The referees ended the sprinting jams and started penalizing and fining the bigger skaters, eliciting loud boos and hisses from the excited crowd. Seltzer, as usual, was attuned to the audience reaction. Curious to see what might develop, he ordered the referees to allow skater contact.[95]

During the race, Seltzer sat with the famed New York sportswriter and essayist Damon Runyon, who was intrigued by the illegal scuffle between the players as well as by the audience's reaction to it. Seltzer vividly recalled his conversation with Runyon: "So Runyon leaned over after a while, and he said: 'You know, Seltzer, you ought to incorporate that into the game.'"[96] Over dinner that evening in Miami, Seltzer and Runyon scribbled out details modifying the rules of the game to allow contact, which changed the sport forever and established Runyon as an important figure in roller derby history.[97]

The updated version of Roller Derby called for five players of the same sex from each team to start on the track together. Upon the referee's whistle, all ten players would begin to skate counterclockwise around the track and would group closely together to form what was called a pack. Each team consisted of two jammers, skaters who could score points, and three blockers. Once the pack was formed, jammers, who began in the back of the pack, attempted to work their way through the pack to break free from the blockers. The blockers' job was twofold: prevent the other team's jammers from breaking away from the pack, and helping their own jammers break out as quickly as possible—a complicated mission of simultaneous offense and defense. This was accomplished through strategic maneuvering and blocking. As soon as the first jammer broke away from the pack, the jam clock began. This meant that the jammers had two minutes to lap the pack and attempt to score as many points as possible before the jam time ran out.[98] Jammers scored points for each member of the opposing team they passed after lapping the pack once. Jams did not have to last the full two minutes. As Coppage explains, "The lead jammer (the one out in front of the others attempting to score) has the option to stop the play by placing the hands on the hips."[99] A jam could also be called off if the lead jammer fell down or exited the track. Each Roller Derby game consisted of eight periods, each lasting approximately fifteen minutes, with a half-time after the first four periods. The women skated first, followed by the men, and then the sexes alternated every other period. Although a few modifications occurred over the years, the basic premise of the sport created that evening on a napkin in Miami remained throughout Roller Derby's existence.[100]

While the added physical contact separated Roller Derby from other co-ed sports, women's participation in Roller Derby as equal competitors on a mixed team both drew in audiences and made people question its legitimacy. Leo Seltzer's Roller Derby provided a venue for America "to see women compete on an equalized playing field,"[101] or, rather, track. Both male and female skaters played under the same set of rules, skated the same amount of time, and contributed equally to the score and, thus, the success of their team, a rare opportunity for female athletes in midcentury America. Even the few other professional female sports organizations at the time, such as the All-American Girls Professional Baseball League (AAGPBL), were sex segregated—indeed, were put into a league of their own. The AAGPBL was created by the Chicago Cubs' owner, Philip K. Wrigley, in 1943 as a replacement for men's baseball, since the fear was that the men's professional game would be postponed for the duration of World War II. When it was discovered that men's baseball would not be shut down, Wrigley "fashioned the [AAGPBL's] objectives to compliment [*sic*] the war effort in the mid-sized industrial communities that supported its teams,"[102] as opposed to having the women's league stand in for the men's game. By the end of the AAGPBL's tenure, AAGPBL athletes were playing baseball with rules mirroring those of the men's game. The league had evolved from professional women's softball, an "appropriate" sport for women, to baseball over the course of the first couple of seasons. The women's league's structure and organization were intentionally different from those of Major League Baseball, and the AAGPBL was not in direct competition with men's major- or minor-league baseball teams.[103]

In Roller Derby, after the shift to team play, men and women did not usually compete against one another directly on the track. This did happen occasionally, however, if a skater was injured. In the early years of the sport, if a male player got hurt and no male alternates were available, the player's female counterpart would take his place on the track, skating against the men. The reverse was true as well. If a female player was injured, her male partner would skate against the women.[104] Men and women were on the same team, were paid the same, and were held to the same expectations. Yet despite this early and generally unprecedented version of athletic equality, some traditional gender roles remained. The female skaters, for instance, washed their uniforms as well as the men's and mended all uniforms, and the men ground the women's skate wheels and were responsible for setting up and breaking down the track. Both sexes were generally compensated with extra money for performing their traditional tasks.[105]

In the early years of the sport, female skaters were expected to dress like ladies when not on the track. They wore skirts and dresses, since that was common clothing for women at the time. When traveling, the women sported brown and blue traveling suits that matched the men's in color and material but were fitted for women's bodies; "the purpose of the outfits [was] to give the skaters a well-tailored, distinctive appearance during their hours off the track."[106] It was generally expected that at some point, the female skaters would get married and have children, although that eventuality did not necessarily end their derby careers. Many gender roles were so deeply entrenched in society that even Roller Derby, which practiced equality in unparalleled measure in the sports world, could not escape them and at times furthered them. That conformity clearly reflected the times in which the skaters lived, and it highlights the contradictions of the era. Roller Derby afforded women opportunities to compete in ways that other sports did not, but there was a limit to its brand of progressivism. The entire social system could not be bucked. Seltzer worked to find the sweet spot between offering an enticing novelty and offending the social sensibilities of average citizens, who might then stop buying tickets.

Roller Derby did not just provide professional sporting opportunities for female skaters. Female fans were drawn to the sport early on and consistently made up more than half the audience throughout the sport's existence.[107] In 1950, Seltzer claimed that women composed 70 percent of the Roller Derby audience.[108] He found women more receptive to the new sport. Bert Wall, a skater who partnered with Leo Seltzer in organizing some Roller Derbies, explained that Seltzer fervently believed that men were reluctant fans at first but that women were all-in from the start. According to Wall, female fans brought the men with them.[109] Seltzer reflected in the 1960s on this issue: "It took years for me to realize the hardest thing to do was sell a new sport to men. They would only accept those sports with which they had grown up. Instead of being tolerant, they refused it. But, on the other hand, women readily accepted Roller Derby."[110] That favorable reception might have been due in part to women in the mid-twentieth century not being socialized to think of sports as an inherent part of the female sphere, and thus they did not have deeply ingrained ideas about particular sports. As one sportswriter put it, "Many women love to yell, but modern civilization hasn't offered them much of a chance. [Leo Seltzer] has given them something to yell at."[111] Seeing women participate in a full-body contact sport made "teen-age bobby soxers and staid old grandmothers whoop for blood when the racing feminine skaters tangle and maul and spill each other on the shin-shredding track."[112] Seltzer capitalized on female enthusiasm for the sport by catering to average women's roles and routines: he sold tickets in places that women frequented, such as grocery stores, department stores, beauty salons, and fabric shops.[113] Seltzer knew that women provided the key to keeping the sport alive: "Women spend the entertainment dollar, and where they want to go the men will follow."[114]

The mother-son team of Ma and Billy Bogash has been credited with drawing in a large portion of the female audience, particularly housewives and middle-aged or older women.[115] Ma's determined drive and outstanding ability turned housewives into long-term fans.[116] Many women of the era could not relate to football or baseball stars, but they could relate to Ma, who was their own age, a wife, and a mother.[117] If an unlikely diabetic athlete like Ma Bogash could do it, maybe they could too, or they could at least live vicariously through her, channeling their pent-up aggressions and releasing them through wild cheers for their favorite skaters.[118] Other sorts of entertainment available to women did not provide the temporary escape they desperately needed during the difficult times of the Depression, or later during their ordinary lives, but Roller Derby did.

The idea that everyone could relate to and live through Roller Derby was, in fact, a large part of the sport's appeal. "It's hard to visualize you being a football player, or a basketball player or anything else, unless, you know, you're nine feet tall and weigh 400 pounds," explained Bert Wall. "But with roller derby . . . we try to make the team up so that you had a big, tall hero . . . and then you have a little buddy . . . the small fast little guy that could skate."[119] Basically, Roller Derby offered a hero for every type of person — male, female, big, small, tall, or short. Fans would watch Roller Derby and say, "He's a lot like me. If I hadn't a got married. I could be out there skating."[120] And Roller Derby, unlike many other sports featured on television in the mid-twentieth century, appealed to women because women were competing on par with men. As Wall explained, "It gave [women] a chance to be equal to the guys. . . . In fact, they were more popular than the men were."[121]

Leo Seltzer viewed women's "blood-curdling enthusiasm" for the game as a natural reaction to the performed violence on the track.[122] "Let's face it—women aren't the weaker sex," the progressive Roller Derby owner stated in 1950. "Nature made them stronger. They are far sturdier than men," he declared. Seltzer attempted to capitalize on his female skaters by presenting them as ordinary women, but ordinary women who were not, in fact, a weaker sex. Furthermore, expressing hostility during a derby provided women with a healthy emotional outlet, one that Seltzer believed prevented them from taking it out on their poor husbands.[123] Still, sometimes the female fans grew rowdy and got out of hand.[124] At a Roller Derby game in the Chicago Coliseum in early April 1940, eggs flew from the balcony where 3,000 women were seated; directed at the two male officials, they landed on the track infield. Ushers raced up to the balcony to "stop the barrage."[125] The women were not easily subdued, though. A mere hour later, more female fans began hurling lemons and ice cream cones at the officials and the opposing (New York) team. Chairs, vegetables, staples, purses, hammers, and ball bearings hurled with slingshots were used as missiles by audiences across the country.[126]

When Seltzer's son Jerry took over the enterprise in 1959, he found that female fans still used Roller Derby as an outlet for their anger. Like the supporters of Ma Bogash years before, the new crowd of fans channeled their aggression through the play of one of derby's biggest stars, in this case, Joanie Weston. The sportswriter Frank Deford noted about Weston, "It is almost eerie how strongly a whole arena of women attaches to her. It seems as if the aggressions of every woman in the house have been willed to Joanie Weston, so that she might expend them on behalf of those in the crowd."[127] Jerry Seltzer shared similar feelings with Deford: "Sometimes, I think we must be doing a service. I think we must be keeping that woman from going home and killing her husband tonight. And every night, there is some woman like that."

One practically unbelievable story of fanatical fan behavior has grown into a Roller Derby urban legend. The story's participants change depending on who was asked and when, but the story line remains the same. As the tale goes, an infuriated and annoyed female fan caught up in the drama of the game chucked her baby at a skater on the track, who, fortunately, caught it. In a version told by Joanie Weston, the fan hurled the baby at Toughie Brasuhn, who was, luckily, alert enough to catch the infant.[128] As reported in a March 1950 article in the *Chicago Daily Tribune*, the baby tossing occurred in Columbus, Ohio. According to the journalist's interviews with skaters, who swore to the story's truth, "Russ Baker of the Chicago Westerners had just bumped a rival Roller Derby skater into a track post when he heard a woman fan screaming imprecations at him. Baker, now at the rail, turned just in time to catch the woman's baby, which she had hurled at him in absentminded wrath. The baby was unhurt. The woman fainted."[129] But in an early-1970s television interview, Ann Calvello claimed to have been the target of the baby-throwing episode. Calvello insisted that a lady threw her baby at her, but luckily a referee caught it.[130]

In another instance of seemingly temporary insanity, most likely caused by drunkenness, "an irate woman armed with a handbag holding a partly drained fifth of whiskey" attacked the Roller Derby skater Jack Walker.[131] Calvello claimed that a crazed female fan in Stockton, California, tried to sneak up behind her and hit her in the back with a chair. Another time, three little girls about ten or eleven years old apparently started kicking and hitting Calvello when she went over the rail. She kicked them back. Calvello believed that people did not intend to be vicious, but rather it was a part of human nature for spectators to want to see blood and to see the skaters get hurt.[132] Mirroring and occasionally enacting the performed violence on the track, fan aggression and intimidation were a real concern. Fans wildly waving scissors in their hands regularly threatened Bobbie Mateer, who was known for her flowing ponytail, as she skated off the track. Mateer recalled, "I had a long ponytail. It used to swish around . . . and people used to bring scissors to the game and go 'click-click' and if you had to go off the track, you had to go through the audience to get to the dressing rooms. . . . You had to be careful. I used to take a jacket and put it over our heads."[133] Loretta Behrens, a Roller Derby skater from 1949 to 1959, remembers needing police escorts to get off the track. She stated, "When you get into these vicious crowds, they'll kill you."[134]

Whether all these instances are completely true or veer into folklore territory is in many ways irrelevant.[135] Roller Derby served as one of the first sporting endeavors to draw female spectators as its primary fan base, and plenty of evidence shows that it riled up female fans in ways that other sports and entertainment activities of the time did not. For instance, neither journalists nor female basketball players ever reported such fan violence, intimidation, or loss of control at women's basketball games in the mid-twentieth century. Despite basketball being one of the most popular sports for women, its ties to official institutions like colleges, civic centers, or local businesses perhaps prevented players and fans from acting on their emotions in public. In contrast, the rougher nature of the full-contact sport seen on the Roller Derby track, which had no lasting attachments to such organizations or particular communities, allowed women to let loose. As with the supposed baby-throwing incident, female fans could not be seen as completely acting outside gender boundaries, even in this untraditional sport. The baby is never injured in any of the tales, and often the woman is described as having lost control over her emotions only temporarily. She would surely never behave in such a manner under "normal" circumstances. It is Roller Derby that forces her to mimic acts of violence and behave in such an aggressive, masculine way.

Although Roller Derby became a very popular sport and entertainment attraction, perhaps even a quintessential bit of Americana,[136] not everyone was sold on its value and excitement, including some American women. Their dislike of Roller Derby, sometimes amounting to disgust, highlighted class issues and the social respectability of different sports in the mid-twentieth century. Laura Elizabeth Kratz, a doctoral candidate at Ohio State University in the late 1950s, wrote her dissertation on women's participation in sports and the social implications of their participation. She investigated how the "motives of the American people for participating or not participating in a sport, and how they participate, give an indication of the national character" of America.[137] Kratz raises the important question, "What creates a social capsule around the lady wrestler and the roller skating derbyist?"

Ultimately, Kratz's purpose was to investigate the behavior patterns and concepts behind women's participation in sports and to place them in the larger context of the contemporary American society.[138] To conduct her study of women's participation in sports, Kratz interviewed a sample of 150 female athletes between the ages of twenty-one and forty-five. Their participation levels ranged from very active to slightly active in their sporting endeavors. She did not interview any professional athletes, current female physical educators, or college students. Her interviewees were white middle-class women, and all but two lived in or near

Columbus, Ohio, which was described as a "typical fast-growing Midwestern city."[139]

Many of the women who participated in Kratz's study gave Roller Derby one of the lowest marks of acceptability, but often ranked it "a notch or two above wrestlers," who were continually placed at the bottom of the lists.[140] Kratz contends that the sports ranking lowest in respectability were given such marks because the larger society failed to endorse them. She notes that the sports' high risk of bodily injury may have influenced social disapproval. In direct contrast to Seltzer's beliefs, Kratz states, "In American society, the concept prevails which demands the protection of women from bodily harm, and assumes that women, as the 'weaker sex,' are not capable of absorbing as much physical stress and strain. Going back further, the 'danger rationale' may be founded on outright fear and avoidance of any situation which would cause physical discomfort."[141] In essence, the fact that Roller Derby was a contact sport for women gave it a negative connotation, because it directly challenged the idea of women as a weaker sex, and the kind of rough women who would choose to participate in such an activity likewise had lower-class connotations.

While Columbus, Ohio, may have been a typical midwestern city as far as sports participants were concerned, that fact does not necessarily explain the opinions of women concerning Roller Derby. The cities and parts of the country that embraced Roller Derby did not follow a discernible pattern, especially in its early years. For instance, Roller Derby drew huge crowds in Cincinnati, Ohio, but in Louisville, Kentucky, a mere 100 miles to the southwest, it was generally a flop. Both cities had large working-class populations. In Los Angeles and San Francisco, Roller Derby was a hot and trendy event, but that was not the case in the large southern city of Atlanta. Sometimes Seltzer would lose a great deal of money in one area, such as Colorado, but would make it up in places such as Seattle, where the derby was well received.[142] So although Columbus might have been an "average" city, that representativeness did not necessarily mean that these midwestern athletic women's generally negative reaction to Roller Derby was typical.

Many of Kratz's interviewees claimed that Roller Derby skaters were rough and tough, which some seemed to view negatively and others positively.[143] This labeling of the sport as "rough" indicates a class bias.[144] The interviewees' use of the terms "rough" and "tough" could indicate moral issues as well. Throughout the first half of the twentieth century, women not exhibiting traditional female characteristics or looks were often referred to as rough. The word was frequently used to describe women as masculine, lower class, or possibly lesbian. Kratz notes that "many of the respondents volunteered the observation that sports participation sometimes depends on economic status."[145] Sports such as roller skating, Roller Derby, wrestling, and bowling had a stigma attached to them based on class values and "the company they [the participants] keep."[146] All of Kratz's interviewees who mentioned this stigma "claimed that there was usually nothing wrong with a sport per se, but that many activities were spoiled by the 'roughness' of the 'crowd' that took part in them," that is, the type of lower-class women who would hurl lemons or babies at skaters on the track, "or the location of the place of participation in some 'questionable' district."[147] In many cases, the respondents judged Roller Derby participants as belonging to a lower, unworthy class of people: "Socially, I look down on them"; "Roller-derby is not a sport; tough class of people"; "The clientele is bad; ice-skating is better"; "Don't admire that kind of person"; "These are rough women"; "They do this unfairly. A lower class of people."[148] Kratz used these examples to conclude that "social approval is an important factor in the acceptability of sports as appropriate for women's participation."[149]

While Kratz's observations rang true for some women, Roller Derby was the most popular television show on the ABC network in 1949, indicating that it had broad appeal across social classes. From 1949 to 1952, Roller Derby was telecast live, fifty-two weeks a year. ABC treated Roller Derby as a "prime-time TV show, not a Saturday afternoon staple like college football."[150] Roller Derby continually earned higher ratings than the few sports, such as boxing, wrestling, and the occasional college sporting event, that were broadcast on TV, which indicates that it had a wide American fan base.[151] According to Keith Coppage, these other sports were never broadcast in prime time.[152]

The dismissal of Roller Derby by Kratz's interviewees as a lower-class activity leads into a larger conversation about the reception of the sport itself. Roller Derby offered multiple meanings to the American public, and unsurprisingly, these meanings have changed as the sport itself evolved. For instance, many mainstream sportswriters and male sports fans claim that women's participation in Roller Derby made it an illegitimate sport. Most newspapers refused to cover Roller Derby, unlike other men's and women's professional sports, or relegated it to the entertainment section as a form of spectacle.[153]

The *Indianapolis Star* provides a good example of this type of coverage. When Roller Derby traveled to Indianapolis in late September 1937, an article titled "They Go 'Round and 'Round and Have the Darnedest Time—At the Roller Derby" appeared in the first section of the paper, along with general news stories, marriage announcements, and radio programming, not in the "Sports, Financial, and Classifieds" section.[154] In February 1940, the sports editor of the *Star* explained the paper's stance on covering—or rather, not covering—Roller Derby in the sports section: "When it came to the roller derby here we said, 'Nay, nay' for the sports pages—purely amusement. There was a squawk from the promoters, but the 'front office' backed us up in our contention."[155] Roller Derby did appear in the *Star*'s sports pages from time to time over the years, but usually when local skaters were highlighted or when the paper felt compelled to explain why it still viewed derby as an illegitimate sport. For instance, a 1954 article in the sports section describes Roller Derby as "a mechanized morality play . . . [that has] dusted off an old wrestling script"; furthermore, it was viewed as sexually ambiguous and disruptive: "It's quite difficult to determine when the sex of the competition changes off. If anything, the girls are the more nasty."[156] Yet huge numbers of female and male fans embraced Roller Derby in Indianapolis and across the country for decades; most often, it was the female skaters who drew in male fans.[157] The longevity and popularity of the sport indicate that no real social backlash or opposition to women's involvement occurred at a national level.

Many Roller Derby skaters did come from working-class backgrounds—as did athletes in most professional sports—but during the golden years of the late 1930s through the 1950s, the derby appealed to all social and economic classes. Fans included high-profile celebrities such as Joe DiMaggio, Jack Benny, George Burns, and Kate Smith, as well as a Chicago church group that purchased a sixteen-inch TV so that congregants and their children could watch television programs, including Roller Derby.[158] When Roller Derby played Los Angeles in May and June 1938, the *Los Angeles Times* reported that there was not a single "night that hordes of film, sport, and civic personalities do not attend en masse."[159] In fact, the Hollywood starlet Betty Grable agreed to "start the field . . . in the first lap of the roller derby" at the Pan-Pacific Auditorium.[160] Eddie Cantor, a famous singer, dancer, and comedian, attended the same Roller Derby series every night it was in town. According to the newspaper, Cantor procured a "permanent box and [cheered] and [booed] as wildly as the kids up in the stands."[161]

Jerry Seltzer, Leo's son, recalled meeting many of the famous stars attending Roller Derby when he was six or seven. "[My dad] set up these kind of boxes, and all the Hollywood stars would come out," recalled Seltzer. "And, you know, I got to meet them, and I got kissed by Eleanor Powell, who danced with Fred Astaire in the movies, and Clark Gable and Betty Grable and, you know, W. C. Fields."[162] Seltzer reminisced about a particularly exciting yet mortifying encounter with a celebrity when he was sitting with his father in one of his "Hollywood" suites with a few of the most famous comedians of the era:

And suddenly Mickey Rooney came in with his entourage and sat there. Now, Mickey Rooney was *the* biggest Hollywood star, top box office draw with the Andy Hardy series and all of those movies. And he turned to me, and he said, "Jer, I haven't seen you for a while. How you been?" I . . . turned red and crawled under the seat. And of course my father had set that whole thing up.[163]

Like the Hollywood elite, famous athletes were often spotted in the audience at Roller Derby games. The boxing crowd in Los Angeles frequently attended, and many baseball players in New York came out to watch. As Jerry Seltzer explained, "People like to go to a place where there's excitement and there's a lot of people. . . . The atmosphere of derby was charged."[164] During its midcentury golden era, Roller Derby was something to see and a place to be seen.

While the Hollywood stars were great to have in attendance and provided extra publicity, Leo Seltzer was more interested in appealing to the masses in order to create a solid and lasting fan base. He attempted to draw crowds by offering discounted tickets, a classic promotional gimmick on which he frequently relied. To court the working and middle classes, Roller Derby actively sought sponsors to help subsidize ticket costs so that fans could buy tickets at much cheaper, discounted rates.[165] These tickets were placed in grocery stores, department stores, beauty salons, and other places where women were likely to shop, to tempt them to purchase discounted tickets for their families.

Contemporary observers such as Laura Kratz and the women involved in her study, as well as some journalists, often lumped Roller Derby fans in with wrestling fans, but Jerry Seltzer insists that it was a completely different crowd. According to him, Roller Derby fans tended to not like other sports, traditional or not. They were not the die-hard football fans, nor were they drawn into the "personality and the story line" of wrestling. "Everybody always says, you know, [Roller Derby fans were] the same as wrestling fans, but they weren't," explained Seltzer. "And out [in California], wrestling could be at the Cow Palace on Friday night and we'd be there on Saturday, and we'd both sell out, and it wasn't to the same crowd at all."[166] Roller Derby fans belonged to a different crowd, at least during Jerry's tenure as owner. "[Roller Derby] was counterculture at a time when nobody knew what counterculture was. And once [fans] could get to a game, most of them just pretty much got hooked," he stated. Arena owners often asked Jerry where his fans came from: "Who are these people? . . . They're never here for any other sporting event."[167]

Lenny Berkman, a Jewish boy growing up in a working-class neighborhood of Brooklyn during the late 1940s and early 1950s, was one such fan. Berkman corroborated Seltzer's description of the countercultural or at least partly stigmatized nature of Roller Derby. Berkman fell in love with Roller Derby because he identified as a social outsider and thus related to derby's marginal status in the sports world.[168] "As a Roller Derby fan, I felt like a freak," explained Berkman, but when he was in the sixth grade, Berkman found a kindred spirit: "Discovering Alan Dietz was a Roller Derby fan made our friendship, because he was the one person I could talk to about it, and the one! I mean there just was nobody else."[169] Berkman and Dietz established a friendship based solely on their love of Roller Derby. Berkman's experience exemplifies the accessibility of Roller Derby to the masses but simultaneously highlights the stigma of openly associating with the sport. Roller Derby was widely popular and universally acknowledged, but not accepted in the mainstream sports world and thus was often relegated to the sidelines, again as spectacle.

Roller Derby's fan demographics, based on weekly telecasts in the 1960s and 1970s, indicate that the sport's viewers largely ranged in age from eighteen to forty-nine and were either split equally across the sexes or with women occasionally edging men out by a percentage point or two, "a statistic no other sport [could] claim."[170] Most were deemed " 'blue collar' with rather significant purchasing and political power."[171] "They feel relaxed with the Derby, and certainly many of them even identify with it, for it is the one celebrated thing that appears tough and obvious, like their lives," observed Frank Deford. "It is easy for them to relate to the players, who are working class, like them, carpenters and laborers and bartenders."[172] "By contrast," Deford notes, "football and baseball and basketball players are all college men and stockbrokers who shoot golf off-season at some country club."

The working-class, "solid home folks," as Deford described them, were not the sole fans of the sport, even if they were the base. As previously mentioned, Roller Derby was the in thing with the Hollywood and New York elites in the 1940s and 1950s, but in the 1960s and 1970s, the college crowd took to the sport. Roller Derby increasingly booked dates to play on college campuses, often on Sunday afternoons. According to Deford, colleges preferred the Sunday-afternoon time slot, "when the students have free time and the faculty kids can drag their curious fathers to see the phenomenon."[173] As the former skater, manager, and coach Hal Janowitz described this newfound popularity, "It is just all cycles, good and bad. These new people come along, a whole new generation, I guess. There have always been cycles in the Derby."[174]

Some observers, usually referring to Roller Derby of the 1960s and 1970s, insist that it was spectacle or show as opposed to a sport. Yet many derby players swear that nothing was staged, or that at least no outcomes were fixed. Any set plays or repeated acts were done in response to positive fan reactions. Deford claimed that choreographed action did not negate the sporting aspects of Roller Derby.[175] He described it as a "very physical sport": "It involves not only the balance and the speed of skating but also the roughness of banging into one another. . . . I don't think anybody couldn't call it a sport." At the same time, Deford acknowledged that by the late 1960s, a level of staged performance had become characteristic: "To say that it was the equivalent to a major league baseball game, that is suitably not true. There was a certain amount of choreography that took place."

If Roller Derby is viewed as a theatrical event, as all sports are on some level, the skaters performed a play that many Americans understood, related to, and embraced. Through the common scenarios of good guys versus bad guys, heroes versus villains, or locals versus outsiders, fans could relate to their favorite skaters and cheer on the side they wanted to win. In many instances, fans connected with and supported "red shirt" skaters as much as they did the so-called heroes or "good guys."[176] By providing background on the skaters' "ordinary" lives or by highlighting a particular aspect of their road to success in Roller Derby, the culture of the sport allowed average Americans to identify with, relate to, and empathize with the skaters in ways they could not with other professional athletes. The drama of the sport was reflected in the skaters' and fans' lives.

Roller Derby continually evolved in its rules, regulations, and structure throughout the twentieth century as it wavered between spectacle and sport. Roller Derby was a co-ed team sport from its outset, and any changes influenced both sexes equally. It evolved from bottom-up changes driven by the sport's fans; the majority of changes implemented by Leo and Jerry Seltzer were generally prompted by fans' reactions to the game. While the sport was at the mercy of the Seltzer family's management, they usually gave in to fans' whims, desires, and demands. Roller Derby was a popular sport concerned with athletic performance, but it was equally a business and an entertainment venture. The Seltzers did whatever it took to put paying people in the seats: discounting tickets, adding antics that excited or riled up the fans, or removing whatever dismayed them.[177] Leo Seltzer, in particular, wanted Roller Derby to be "the next major professional sport."[178] But he was always a sports promoter, and his responsibility was to generate revenue for his business. John Hall, a former skater, explained, "Every skater relied on his reputation, his image as a skater. But they also realized that this was a business and that the income they made depended upon the income of the operation they were skating in."[179]

Roller Derby athletes largely belonged to the working and middle classes. Young women often joined the derby immediately after graduating high school, and some skaters left high school early to pursue their skating careers. As a professional sport, Roller Derby met the athletic needs of the skaters, but it also provided career opportunities that they could not find elsewhere, particularly during the Depression. By the 1940s and 1950s, Roller Derby had emerged as one of the most popular sports in America. Games drew large crowds, filling up venues ranging from 3,000-seat armories to a 16,000-person audience at Madison Square Garden for the annual playoffs.[180] The derby played in New York and Los Angeles but traveled to smaller cities as well. As a nationally syndicated television program in the 1960s and 1970s, it earned high ratings, attracted new fans, and entertained those who could not see the games in person.

Although athletics became a more accepted pastime for women over the course of the twentieth century, an emphasis on femininity was still commonplace. Beauty was an inherent part of a woman's identity, whether she was an athlete or not, and the beauty of female athletes was often emphasized to counter any associations with the masculine attributes of a sport. Roller Derby skaters participated in a completely unmodified, full-contact sport after 1937, which blatantly challenged doubts about women's athletic capabilities. Because women were competing on par with men, the Roller Derby's management and the media emphasized the female skaters' femininity in an attempt to justify their athleticism and to appeal to the average woman and to middle-class notions of respectability. But by directly confronting gender norms, female skaters paid a price: they were relegated, by both the sports media and middle-class arbiters of propriety, to the level of "spectacle" or "show" performers rather than being accepted as legitimate athletes. Roller Derby, it was believed, could not be a true sport if women competed on the same level as men. These skating athletes challenged ideas about women's relationship to and participation in sports, yet throughout the century, they could not fully overcome the larger society's emphasis on traditional white middle-class gender norms.

2 | SKATING THROUGH THE BOUNDARIES OF IDENTITY

The important meanings of dance, sport, and exercise are not found in the writings of philosophers. . . . Rather, they are found in the lives of the millions of people who find their own involvement in dance, sport, or exercise meaningful.

ELEANOR METHENY, *MOVEMENT AND MEANING*

Thirty years before the 1968 Eleanor Metheny remark used as this chapter's epigraph, the popular women's magazine *Ladies' Home Journal* published a short story titled "Don't Beat Your Husband." The narrative follows the budding romantic relationship between Winifred, a fit, confident, and accomplished athlete, and Hartley, a successful businessman who loves and respects Winifred for the self-sufficient, competitive athlete she is, at least at the beginning of the tale. After a brief, weeklong engagement, Hartley and Winifred marry at city hall and jet off to Bermuda for their honeymoon. There the couple spends their time riding bicycles, going for swims, and playing tennis, shuffleboard, and golf. Winifred continually challenges Hartley in these sporting activities and begins to threaten his masculinity by competently competing alongside him and even beating him in direct competition. Hartley starts to begrudge Winifred her "ability [and] resourcefulness."[1] He reflected, "It never used to irritate me. Rather impressed me when she would beat me at something. Now I resent it."

The rising tension culminates in a blowup between the newlyweds that almost dissolves their marriage. Tired of continually coming in second to his wife, Hartley lashes out, "You ought to have . . . some idea of the normal relationship of a man and wife, and make an effort to restrain yourself. . . . Do you think a man likes to have his wife constantly trying to show him she's just as good as he is?"[2] Hartley not only feels that his masculinity is at stake but also attacks Winifred's femininity: "When a woman acts the way you do it's because she has some lack. Compensation, that's what. Afraid you haven't enough natural, feminine appeal to attract men so you have to assume every male prerogative trying to impress them."

When the two were merely friends, Hartley appreciated Winifred's competitive nature and athletic ability. It did not threaten him in any real way, since he was not romantically tied or legally bound to her. But in a marriage, with its clear gender boundaries, rules, and expectations, Hartley felt his manhood challenged by his wife's athletic prowess. He lashed out at Winifred's essence, her femininity, in an attempt to protect his own masculinity. Hartley's accusations devastated Winifred. All she ever intended was to meet Hartley on his own terms, simply "trying to please him by being proficient doing the things he did."[3]

Winifred realizes that she must allow Hartley to care for her, protect her, and uphold a traditional masculine position in their marriage if she wants their relationship to work. She solves her marital troubles by letting Hartley rescue her from a runaway horse-drawn carriage. As the carriage careens wildly over a hill leading down to the ocean, Winifred screams for Hartley to save her, which he does. He pulls her to safety from the carriage as she frantically clings to him. He asks, "'Why didn't you grab [the reins]?' 'I don't know,' Win said lamely. 'I don't know what to do with horses. I'm scared to death of them.'"[4] He holds her tightly until she calms down, and then he not so modestly declares, "I just happen to know how to handle horses. Used to ride with the national guard when I was in college."[5] Winifred further boosts his ego by pleading female incompetence: "Oh, but there are so many things only a man can do — think fast in an emergency, not lose his head, like a woman."[6] Her comment underscores her feigned weakness and vulnerability while boosting Hartley's sense of his own masculinity. "I really love you," he whispered. "Forget all that nonsense. I don't know what I was driving at."[7]

The story ends with Winifred and Hartley settling into their new city apartment. Cheerfully listening to music, they unpack their belongings as a fire blazes in the hearth. Winifred stops to leaf through a photo album in which she runs across an "old picture of herself, a lanky child in a derby, mounted on a long-legged horse and easily clearing a hurdle."[8] Winifred quickly removes the photograph from the album and drops it onto the burning logs. She resumes singing along with her husband as the song and the story come to a close.[9] By destroying the only evidence of her equestrian proficiency, Winifred dramatically subsumes herself to Hartley and his needs. She tossed her natural athleticism aside when it threatened her husband's masculinity and contemporary standards of femininity. The story makes clear that Winifred was a capable athlete who could have easily saved herself from a runaway carriage.

In many ways, this *Ladies' Home Journal* story serves as a metaphor for the relationship between the male-dominated sports world, the mainstream sports media, and the identity of female athletes. Hartley and Winifred's platonic relationship represents the sex-segregated sports world. From the late 1930s through midcentury, women made some gains in playing sports, and men grudgingly accepted them. It was fine for women to play sports so long as they played only with women and were viewed as inferior athletes — for example, basketball and women's basketball, golf and women's golf, and so forth. Clear, persistent gender rules labeled sports a predominantly male preserve, despite women's increasing athletic competence. Women could play and succeed, but only up to the point where they challenged or threatened male masculinity and superiority. Hartley and Winifred's marriage represents this aspect of sports, particularly through Roller Derby. Once the newlyweds were in direct competition, Hartley's masculinity was threatened, just as women's equality in Roller Derby threatened the masculinity of the sports world. When that threat grew too great, social critics and the male-dominated American media questioned female athletes' femininity.

Even as sports became increasingly accessible to women, athleticism was still not considered a fundamental part of their identity. Sport was not viewed as a natural component of femininity in the way that it was of masculinity.[10] According to Susan Cahn, social commentators and journalists described women's athleticism as "by nature temporary" or as "a temporary transgression, rather than a constitutive feature, of true womanhood."[11] Women could "play" at being athletes, but athleticism could not be internalized in the way that it was for men. A woman could take on the persona of an athlete, but it would never be understood as her true self or her identifying feature. A woman's athletic ability was a fleeting façade that always gave way to a "truer, more rewarding feminine persona."[12] Roller Derby, however, openly contradicted this assertion by allowing women to play a rough co-ed contact sport on equal terms with men. But to stay afloat as a business venture, it simultaneously bowed to traditional gender roles by frequently reminding audiences that female skaters' femininity was not damaged by the sport and that male skaters' masculinity was not damaged by their association with the women athletes.

Robert Cromie, a respected longtime sports journalist for the *Chicago Tribune*, highlighted these issues facing female and male skaters. In a 1951 article, Cromie described the tough-tender duality of female skaters: "Nightly they [the Roller Derby Queens] survive assault and battery to the delight of thousands of adoring fans, but at home they're highly domesticated and gentle."[13] Cromie emphasized the drama and roughness of the game while also explaining that those aspects were due simply to the women's on-track behavior—at home they were like any other women. But in a 1952 article, Cromie described how the female skaters undercut the males: "Both men and women take part, altho [*sic*] not competing against each other, a fortunate thing for the pride of the masculine sex since the female skaters seem more ferocious than the male."[14] His articles showcase the double-edged sword facing both male and female Roller Derby athletes.

A 1970 *New Yorker* article provided a type of counterassertion for male skaters. The authors quoted a fan who explained why Roller Derby was the ideal sport for certain men, female competitors notwithstanding:

> This game is the perfect game for a guy who is the wrong size for any other major sport. . . . Firstly, the League's high scorer, Mike Gammon, . . . is five feet nine and a hundred and twenty-eight pounds. Secondly, Charlie O'Connell, Hall of Famer and eight times Most Valuable Player. He's six feet two, a hundred and ninety pounds. People his size are usually too slow for basketball, too clumsy for football, and too heavy for swimming, so if they can't hit a baseball, they're out of it. This is just the sport for the neighborhood bully, who is usually about his size.[15]

The fan stressed the male skaters' masculinity by highlighting how this rough-and-tumble sport was the ideal athletic opportunity for men who could not play other professional sports because of their size. There was no talk of female skaters undercutting the men's masculinity; instead, Roller Derby offered a uniquely exciting and tough opportunity for diversely sized men.

Masculinity and sport have long been tied, mutually reinforcing each other. This connection goes back at least to the Olympic festivals of ancient Greece, where each male competitor was "stripped of all excuses," and standing naked before the gods, he was to "demonstrate his ability to perform a well-defined task of his own choosing."[16] Sport and manliness or masculinity became further entwined in American society in the post–Civil War industrial era, when social commentators claimed that the middle and upper segments of society were becoming effeminate and sedentary. Large numbers of men worked at grueling manual-labor jobs on farms, in factories, and in mines, but for the first time, increasing numbers of men worked in offices. Furthermore, by the end of the nineteenth century, men could no longer rely on the frontier as space in which to prove their courage, grit, and superiority. Therefore, Progressive reformers of the early twentieth century insisted that athletics provided an avenue for men who no longer toiled with their hands to assert their masculinity, strength, and toughness.[17] Theodore Roosevelt, a proponent of strenuous exercise and rugged sports, helped promote athletics in the last decades of the nineteenth century.[18] He believed that many Americans undervalued "the need of the virile, masterful qualities of the heart and mind which have built up and alone can maintain and defend this very civilization."[19] He hoped to counteract that tendency: "Our object is to get as many of our people as possible to take part in manly, healthy, vigorous pastimes, which will benefit the whole nation."[20]

Throughout the late nineteenth century and the early decades of the twentieth, the sporting world served as an "important social phenomenon of man"[21] and developed as a space where men could prove their masculinity in the face of an increasingly urbanizing society. According to the highly esteemed physical educator Eleanor Metheny, sports also allowed an individual to compete under a specified rule set, "a rare opportunity to concentrate all the energies of his being in one meaningful effort to perform a task of his own choosing, no longer pushed and pulled in a dozen directions by the many imperatives he may recognize in his life."[22] In other words, sports allowed a man to "experience himself as a fully motivated, fully integrated, fully functioning human being."[23] Sports allowed performers to "restore their own sense of wholeness" and offered the "individual a chance for self-realization."[24] Sports, at least in theory, allowed competitors to demonstrate what they "can do and be at their utmost."[25]

If proving oneself at sports has long been a way to demonstrate masculinity and promote wholeness, female athletes have been placed in a no-win situation. Metheny claims that in general, sports serve as a "symbolic formulation of 'woman at her utmost.'"[26] But just as women have been denied full social, political, and economic equality throughout US history, their ability to experience wholeness through sport has been limited by norms imposed by the larger society. Patsy Neal, a sports philosopher and former athlete, explained that to experience self-revelation in sport, one must experience freedom of choice in sports: "Man reconfirms his own identity within the framework of the rules, and finds *his* own truth by his decisions. The more rules, and the more limited the framework of free choice, the less personal development and creativity one has the chance to achieve."[27] Women have long played sports that were modified for their sex, which has limited their freedom, personal development, and creativity in the realm of sports. As exemplified in the Hartley and Winifred story, women attempting to compete with their whole being or to achieve wholeness through sport threatened maleness or found their femininity under attack, or both.

Consequently, a major challenge for female athletes throughout the twentieth century was to reconcile feminine identity with athletic identity. Historically, women have been hesitant to identify themselves as athletes, despite their remarkable athletic accomplishments. Dr. Donna Lopiano, a former world-champion softball player, athletic director at the University of Texas, and president of the Women's Sports Foundation, has found that when women who grew up in the decades before the Title IX era are asked whether they consider themselves athletes, they generally reject the label: "[They] immediately say no even if they've run three marathons, because they think that being an athlete is being a high-level athlete, professional athlete, or scholarship athlete, you know, where every male who ever played intramural anything calls himself athlete, which is a huge difference."[28] For men, sports have historically been a prime signifier of masculinity; for women, they have been a marker of ambiguity that raises deeply ingrained questions about femininity. This difference harks back to the traditional link between sports and masculinity and the disconnection between femininity and athletics.

Roller Derby athletes provide interesting insight into the complicated negotiation between personal identity and social expectations in the twentieth century, particularly on a macro or national level versus a micro or local one. Roller Derby challenges the very framework laid out by sports historians because Roller Derby was a rough, full-contact, professional male-female sport that was not modified to suit societal expectations or the physical differences between men and women. In fact, Roller Derby openly confronted these expectations. Women participated alongside men as equal competitors, and the sport emerged as one of the most popular spectator activities of the mid-twentieth century. While both male and female Roller Derby skaters, with their unrestricted access to the track, came close to reaching the wholeness through sport that Metheny and Neal described, they still were constrained in many ways by entrenched gender roles and by rules that governed their lives off the track.

Roller Derby skaters found themselves negotiating their identities in ways that both mirrored and diverged from the experiences of other female and male athletes. For example, this negotiation was seen in Roller Derby skaters and other athletes in the business of "cheesecake." Roller Derby's management understood that sex sells (or at least pretty women do, and violent ones at that), but also understood the need to market female skaters as normal, everyday women who were unchanged by their athletic pursuits. Similar tactics were adopted by promoters of AAU basketball and the AAGPBL to draw in fans. Roller Derby diverged from other sports for women by celebrating its female skaters' marriages and motherhood while acknowledging their toughness and athletic identity. The derby promoted women as key figures in a sport that had not been changed or modified for them—they could be wives, mothers, and athletes on their own terms, not as ancillary or auxiliary figures, as women in other sports at the time were treated in regard to their male counterparts. This equality is what endeared Roller Derby as a sporting spectacle to its fans. It allowed Roller Derby, albeit imperfectly, to model how women could fuse their athletic and feminine identities into one cohesive being that was not forced to choose nor forced to play second fiddle to "true" athletes, namely, men.

IDENTITY ON AND OFF THE TRACK

Most women who later became professional Roller Derby skaters faced limited opportunities for organized sports during their youth. "At the time I was growing up," recalled Mary Lou Palermo, "girls didn't play too many sports. . . . I don't think there was anything then."[29] Often the women spent their childhoods playing games and sports with kids in their neighborhoods, in empty lots or in the streets.[30] Some of the female skaters had access to organized sports, but not on a level comparable to that enjoyed by their male peers. Gerry Murray, who grew up in Des Moines, Iowa, in the 1920s and 1930s, had a very active sports background. She played softball with the kids in her neighborhood, but in junior high and high school, she played many sports, including volleyball, track and field, and swimming. In her community, it was very common for young women to play sports, and she felt lucky to have a wide range of options.[31] Although presented with fewer opportunities than Murray, Loretta Behrens swam on a school swimming team and bowled in community leagues in the Bronx; Bobbie Mateer played sports in her gym classes and was a cheerleader at her high school in New Jersey.[32]

Perhaps unsurprisingly, the activity most Roller Derby skaters participated in during their youth was roller skating, regardless of their geographic location or social class. Roller skating was widely popular across the United States from the 1930s through the 1960s, and along with ice-skating, it earned a reputation as a feminine activity from its aesthetic associations with beauty and grace, although it was popular among both men and women, particularly speed skating.[33] Most cities in the country had at least one roller-skating rink, but it was also an activity kids could do on sidewalks and on the streets. After World War II, when ball bearings again became available, skates dropped in price.[34] In fact, as the skater Carol Roman Meyer stated, "That was about the cheapest thing you can do."[35] Mary Youpelle, who grew up on the South Side of Chicago, had access to two roller-skating rinks. "But," she explained, "I didn't skate in the rinks. I skated on the street. . . . My brother bought me my first pair of clamp-on skates when I was three years old."[36] Mary Lou Palermo recalled skating in both the local rinks and on the streets. She had clamp-on skates for street skating and shoe skates for rink skating. Gerry Murray also grew up skating, even with all the organized-sports opportunities that her school and community provided. Murray and her girlfriends often hitchhiked from Des Moines to nearby small towns to roller skate on the smooth sidewalks.[37] As Carol Meyer Roman recalled about her activities growing up in the projects of San Francisco, "[Roller skating] was our thing."[38]

Despite shared youths spent roller skating, most of the women never dreamed of becoming professional skaters, much less Roller Derby stars. Bobbie Mateer described skating at her local rink in New Jersey as "a nice social thing" that her family and friends did, adding, "There was never any idea of doing skating professionally."[39] Many of the female derby skaters, like other young girls across the country, grew up idolizing Sonja Henie, the famed ice-skating beauty, if for no other reason than she was one of the few female sports heroines in the public eye.[40] Mary Lou Palermo recalled how struck her parents were with Henie's skating ability, which encouraged Palermo to skate as much as she could. She stated, "I guess that's what pushed me forward was them being impressed by her talent."[41] Palermo skated on the streets but also tried to go to the roller rink three or four times a week. Henie's success encouraged other youngsters to ice-skate or roller skate, but few entertained any real notion of making a career out of it.

Although thousands of young girls admired Sonja Henie, she was not a particularly relatable sports heroine for many of the self-described "tomboys" who loved competitive sports. According to female athletes who grew up with the label, being a tomboy meant being a "girl who was more boyish than girlish, or a girl who was not feminine."[42] Girls who enjoyed sports, loved vigorous outdoor games, and liked playing with boys more than girls found themselves branded as tomboys, but Henie, the most visible female athlete of their time, was famous for her beauty, grace, and elegance. Not all girls had such qualities, or wanted them. "The only heroine I used to like because I wasn't very dainty was Sonja Heine," Loretta Behrens explained. "I used to love to watch ice-skating . . . [but] the feminine sports was not Loretta Behrens. Loretta Behrens had boxing gloves on."[43]

In many ways, the tomboy identity was a way for young girls to make a place for themselves in a family of brothers, or around neighborhood boys, or as an act of self-preservation. Behrens honed this identity as a way to deflect from her small stature and an unforgiving speech impediment: "I was kind of little and . . . when I went to school, you know, I had a lisp, and people used to make fun of you. And I became very, very bossy and very ornery and letting people know that they didn't scare me, and, you know, I kind of fought a lot of the kids, and I fought a lot with the boys."[44]

Still, many of the women were able to combine their tomboy identities with their feminine sensibilities. Mary Youpelle loved to play with dolls and doll carriages as a young girl, but also used her tomboy instincts for self-defense: "When I was about five, my parents gave me a doll carriage with a doll, and I took it out for walks on Christmas Day, and some little boy pushed me and made me mad. . . . My dad leaned out the window and says, 'Don't let him do that,' so I start fighting back. And from that time on, that was it. I swung back."[45] That confrontation gave her the confidence to do what she wanted and to stand up for herself. It also led her to pursue her athletic interests. "I roller skated, I ice-skated, and I played baseball, which was my favorite," Youpelle recalled.

Furthermore, the term "tomboy" could be either "an insult or a badge worn proudly."[46] Factors such as class, race, ethnicity, geographic region, and family expectations influenced the connotations attributed to tomboys.[47] As Babe Didrikson's biographer Susan Cayleff notes, age was also a determinant in the negative or positive associations of the label. Prepubescent girls were not held to the rigid social expectations imposed on young women and adults. After the age of twelve or thirteen, however, if girls did not break with their "boyish behavior" and "transition into adult femininity," they became at best a "curiosity" and at worst abnormal, mannish, or unfeminine, as poor Winifred discovered in the story at the beginning of the chapter.[48] Mariah Burton Nelson, a former college and professional women's basketball player, recalled adults constantly asking her at age twelve, "When are you going to outgrow this tomboy phase and become a lady?"[49]

Most physical educators and sports promoters tried to channel young women's tomboy pursuits and competitive spirit into appropriate venues and sports for respectable young women—particularly ones that limited direct contact with other participants (as in tennis and modified basketball), reduced their playing time, and relegated them to smaller playing areas (as in softball and basketball) than the ones men used. Yet Leo Seltzer, the founder of Roller Derby, denied the premise of modifying a sport to make it easier for women and instead provided them with a platform (or track) where they could compete as equals with men. He not only challenged the existing model of women's and men's sports but also revealed the conflicting strands of American sporting interests. On one hand, social commentators decried the masculinity of successful female athletes, but for decades the public flocked to see female Roller Derby skaters hold their own as equal competitors and teammates, and the matches sold out such venues as Madison Square Garden and consistently ranked on television among the nation's most popular sports.[50] As the journalist Alan Ebert explained, "You have to remember, they were huge at the time. Absolutely huge."[51]

The structure of Roller Derby provided the women with a sense of equality and importance that they may not have experienced in other aspects of their lives. By the time the game had evolved into a modern contact sport in the late 1930s, Leo Seltzer and his top management knew that the women were as important to Roller Derby's success as the male skaters, and maybe even more so. Seltzer knew that women made great athletes, but there were very few outlets for them.[52] This lack of sporting opportunities, combined with the entrenched social expectations for young women, made it difficult for Roller Derby to retain female skaters. Some women could not keep up with, or were not willing to dedicate themselves to, the rigorous training and travel schedule required by Roller Derby. The lifestyle was not necessarily conducive to settling down and raising a family, which was commonly expected of young women.[53] So if a man wanted to try out for Roller Derby, oftentimes he was required to bring along a female skater as well. When a boy named Kenny Randall asked Gerry Murray to try out for Roller Derby with him in Omaha, Nebraska, in 1938, she assumed he just wanted to date her. She later discovered that derby management would not let a boy on the track unless he had brought a girl skater along with him—thus, Randall's insistence that Murray join him.[54]

Roller Derby was the only sport in which men and women competed together on a team and contributed equally to victory or defeat. Each Roller Derby team consisted of five men and five women, with a couple of alternates. The women would skate a period against the opposing women, and then the men would skate a period against the opposing men, but the score was continuously tallied by team and not separated by sex. As Frank Deford observed, "The fact it was both men and women. I think that really is part of the charm of Roller Derby. It's one of the few sports where you have . . . the men and the women. . . . It's the total score that counts. So that makes the derby really unique."[55] On occasion, at least in the early decades of the sport, it was not uncommon for a woman to skate among the men if the men's lineup had been reduced by injuries.[56] Mary Lou Palermo insisted that "some of the girls were just as good as the boys." She recalled, "As a matter of fact, there were a lot of times when the boys would get hurt . . . , and [if] they didn't have an alternate, they'd put a girl in the field."[57]

This cross-gender teamwork made the women feel important and valued as equal contributors to the sport. "It was the only contact sport there was between men and women. I mean, you both skated by the same rules, skated together—it was unique because there wasn't too much for women to do [at the time]," explained Mary Lou Palermo.[58] Professional female athletes were somewhat uncommon on a national level; for them to be treated the same as the men was extraordinary. Yet as Gerry Murray asked rhetorically, since they were doing the same job, "how could they be treated any differently?"[59]

Women athletes *were* treated differently in most other sports in America. Their opportunities at all levels were limited, and in the few professional opportunities available, women were never paid the same as men. In part because of the relatively small number of female professional athletes, equal pay for men and women playing the same sport did not even become an issue until the tennis star Billie Jean King led the fight for equal prize money in the early 1970s.[60] Roller Derby skaters were professional athletes, and as such, they were paid for their athletic ability.

In Roller Derby, men and women generally earned the same pay and benefits. Sometimes female skaters were paid more than their male counterparts, in order to keep them with the derby.[61] "I got paid as much as my husband, or more," explained Gerry Murray, who was married to the popular skater Gene Gammon. "Usually, the girls got paid more, to keep them there."[62] Although pay was not based on gender, it was not equal across the board. Rather, pay reflected rank and talent, in what Jerry Seltzer described as a "star system," much like the kinds used by other professional sporting organizations and leagues.[63] The top skaters earned more, and women were always among the top skaters.[64] Mary Youpelle explained, "There were different levels. Like, the captains and the coaches would earn more money. . . . A top skater got a little more money than the guy that was just the sword-carrier, you know."[65] For instance, in the 1940s and 1950s, the biggest rivalry was between the two top stars, Gerry Murray and Toughie Brasuhn, and they were rewarded as such. Similarly, in the 1960s and 1970s, of the three biggest stars of the era, two were women.[66] Whether paid according to their official rankings or offered under-the-table benefits by management, the top skaters were compensated for their success.

Female Roller Derby skaters internalized the meaning of their participation in the sport in several ways. Besides being something they enjoyed doing, it was their career and livelihood. Many of the women either dropped out of high school to join Roller Derby or joined shortly after graduating but before gaining any other work experience. After years spent skating, it was the only job they knew or in which they had any real training. For some, it was a lucrative career that allowed them to stand on their own feet for the first time (or maybe again later in life). Mary Youpelle joined in 1937 in an effort to help provide for her parents, who had lost all their hard-earned money during the Depression. Enticed by a Roller Derby trainer who regaled her with stories of meeting interesting people and making lots of money, she thought, "Oh, goody. I can make money, and Daddy won't have to go to work anymore. He can stay home."[67]

Although Youpelle went on to become a big name in Roller Derby, she joined at a time when it was struggling to stay afloat. She described her early ideas of getting rich quick as "pretty naïve": "I just thought they made a lot of money because they were in the public eye. . . . Actually, we didn't. I think my mother and Dad would send me five dollars here and there while I was on the road before I ever earned a lot of money."[68] Gerry Murray was interested in nursing after graduating from high school in Des Moines, but did not have any real sense of her future when she tried out for the derby while visiting her mother in Omaha. Mary Lou Palermo had two young children to support after her marriage failed, and Roller Derby allowed her to support herself and her daughters. She recalled, "I made a good living, you know."[69]

Roller Derby not only provided a way for these young women to support themselves and their families but also became something they loved and with which they identified. As Palermo described the sport that was her career for decades, "I was passionate about it": "Well, it was something I loved to do, and it sure gave me a lot of experience. . . . It was just a very, very fulfilling experience, especially when you get to travel so much and go to Europe."[70] These same kinds of opportunities appealed to Loretta Behrens, who valued her independence. She relished the opportunity to "join a profession and go on the road." She reflected, "It gave me a new life. It gave me a life of growing up and getting out of New York. . . . It gave me an education, being that I was such a young age that I found out what the world is about."[71] Behrens learned more about life through her experiences in Roller Derby than she did in school: "People go to school and come out with reading and writing, but when they get out in the world, their reading and writing don't tell 'em how to live in the world. Roller Derby gave us all a lesson that we never would have gotten, you know, out of a school. We had the school of life."[72]

A worldly education and opportunities for travel appealed to these young middle- or working-class women. It provided them with a chance to do something exciting instead of working in traditional female jobs or taking the traditional route of getting married and having children at a young age. For Mary Youpelle and Mary Lou Palermo, the derby opened up avenues they would never have known otherwise. Youpelle assumed she would become a telephone operator, since she had a cousin who was one. Palermo rhetorically asked, "What else was there for a girl to do if you didn't want to be a nurse or an airline stewardess? . . . You work in Woolworth's or something."[73] Behrens believed Roller Derby gave her a chance for "an exciting life": "It took me away from . . . thinking like living like every other woman, getting married and having children"[74] From growing up in a big family, she knew that she wanted to work first before settling down: "I thought that I wanted to have a career, and later

LORETTA
BEHRENS

ROLLER
SERIES 104
DERBY

FIGURE 2.1. *Loretta Behrens on a Roller Derby postcard, 1952.*
Courtesy of Gary Powers and the National Roller Derby Hall
of Fame and Museum.

on, I would, you know, if I was ready to marry, then I would know the time that I wanted to do it, but Roller Derby gave me a chance to travel around the world and have an exciting life."[75] At the same time, Behrens viewed marriage and children as deterrents to her career. She envisioned doing one or the other but not both.[76]

The sport also tapped into these women's innate competitiveness and their drive to succeed. Mary Youpelle was attracted to the sport for the competition it provided: "Most of us were athletes at heart. We wanted to be what we were, you know?"[77] They viewed sport as Metheny described it: an avenue to reach wholeness and self-realization. These skaters had an athletic drive and enjoyed competition, yet had very few opportunities to participate in sports that allowed them to give full expression to those feelings. The excitement and roughness of Roller Derby drew in Loretta Behrens. What appealed to her most were the skaters "knocking the shit out of each other."[78] As a girl who had skated on the flat streets and rinks of the West Bronx, she liked watching the "fast-paced skating on the banked track" and experiencing "the excitement of listening to the crowd . . . when you hear somebody yelling and you see the excitement and then trying to understand what derby was about."[79] These women tapped into their natural athleticism and were thankful that Roller Derby offered them a venue in which to compete.

Their female fans were thankful as well. Many women were drawn to the game for the same reasons the skaters were—it provided an unparalleled sporting outlet for women. For instance, when interviewed by the *Chicago Tribune* in 1951, a couple named Herbert and Violet Conley had not missed a night of Roller Derby in Chicago in fifteen years. Herbert was drawn to the derby's thrilling nature, which combined elements from multiple sports, but his wife had her own reasons. Violet explained that she was drawn to Roller Derby "because the girls are so tough": "When they get fightin' one another I want to get in there and fight with them."[80] Charlie O'Connell reiterated this point twenty years later: "Mostly, tho [sic], the crowds are attracted by the women. Women in combat. The wives have had a tough day with the kids, and they come out and become a part of the skaters. I always watch the stands every night; during the action, the women bite their nails and whack their husbands."[81] A woman who could not join Roller Derby could nonetheless cheer on and live vicariously through the lucky women who did.

This outlet was critically important even in the 1960s and early 1970s. The women's movement was underway, but before Title IX (which was signed into law in June 1972), women did not have many athletic options. For instance, the skating superstar Joan Weston had been an outstanding softball player, but there were no scholarships available for her in the pre–Title IX era. As Frank Deford explained, "She didn't have any options but the Roller [Derby]. If Joanie Weston came along today, she would not be skating roller derby. . . . Joanie would've been a softball player or a basketball player or something, but there just simply weren't that many opportunities then for female athletes."[82]

Partly because of their unique status, Roller Derby skaters took pride in the difficulty of their sport and their identities as professional athletes. Behrens explained, "I considered myself an athlete. I'd always considered myself a professional roller skater."[83] "Not everybody could do it," Youpelle remarked. "We would go to towns and invite top speed skaters from local roller rinks to come . . . on our track. They couldn't make it around the track. And it was funny to watch, because these were 'top tens' in the local towns and are considered really good, and they get on our track and they're like real beginners."[84] Youpelle did not brag about her status as a professional athlete, but, she said, "If somebody brought it up, I'd be very proud and I would discuss it."[85]

Professional athletes in other sports frequently showed their respect for the athleticism of Roller Derby skaters. Gerry Murray met the track icon Jesse Owens in 1937 when the two appeared on a television show featuring a group of famous athletes. After the show ended, Owens sought out Murray and her husband to talk with them about roller skating and Roller Derby. Murray was so starstruck she could not find her voice and relied on her husband to do all the talking. Owens informed Murray that he enjoyed skating and admiringly stated, "I don't know how you skate every night and every night and every night without having a rest."[86] Many professional football players marveled at the roughness of Roller Derby and the skaters' lack of protective gear. According to the longtime skater Bert Wall, the Oakland Raiders and the San Francisco 49ers were among Roller Derby's biggest fans.[87]

While Leo Seltzer and, later, Jerry Seltzer valued the female skaters as much as the men, the fact that female skaters were professional athletes competing on the same level and even on the same teams as men threatened the masculine athletic identity on which the sports world was founded. Further, such gender equality challenged rigid definitions of team sports—which otherwise were single-sex—and this departure from the norm often led mainstream sports journalists to ignore Roller Derby or to condemn the sport as illegitimate.[88] Frank Deford wrote in his 1969 feature article in *Sports Illustrated*, "Women have always been included in the Roller Derby. . . . For that matter, it is the women who continue to give the game its tawdry, sideshow image."[89] Loretta Behrens believed that Roller Derby's inclusion of women threatened the order of mainstream sports as well as deeply entrenched social roles. "Unfortunately, sportswriters didn't accept it as a sport because they wouldn't accept women being in that kind of a sport," she explained. "And that was one of our biggest problems, because people that used to write about the women skating, they used to call us Amazons. . . . They would not accept that women belonged [in] a professional sport."[90] She further elaborated, "You gotta understand something. During the late '40s and the '50s, you were supposed to be home making babies." Behrens saw herself and her fellow female skaters as "doing things that were a [part of the] men's world": "Men feel that they belong in the sports world and . . . they resented the fact that women [were] now stepping into their business." Women in professional sports, as in many areas of patriarchal society, were viewed as incapable or problematic intruders into a masculine space.

This precarious balancing act of wanting to compete in a male-dominated sports world as legitimate athletes while still retaining their "normal" female identities—as opposed to a caricatured "Amazon" status—forced the women skaters to expand the boundaries of femininity to include their rough, contact sport, but doing so was harder in Roller Derby than in such modified sports as women's basketball. As Mary Lou Palermo explained, "You just wanted to be a woman in a sport that was competitive with men."[91] Despite the grueling training, hard hits, and almost guaranteed injuries, female skaters still wanted to be seen "just like any other woman." Even though the women were professional athletes, as Palermo stated, "You just wanted to look good. You just—you were—that was you." The skaters may have been tough competitors on the track, but their athletic identities did not, in their opinion, influence or contradict their identities as women. Palermo wanted to show the public that these two identities were not incongruous: "I . . . could play and then still be a lady." This assertion undercut the belief in the essential masculinity of sport.[92] Palermo and skaters like her were trying to reach individual wholeness through sport while simultaneously claiming sport as a normalized part of femininity.

The players may have felt no contradiction in combining participation in a contact sport with femininity, but the larger society did not necessarily agree—or at least felt that if women were going to partake in such masculine endeavors, they needed to prove their femininity in other ways.[93] Many of the skaters were aware of the stereotypes and the masculine associations that the public applied to them. Palermo believed that, in part, their larger-than-life images on the track as well as their competing alongside men led people to stereotype female skaters as masculine: "It was just that the idea that you were competing in a sport with equal rules with the men that, you know, they would expect—a lot of people expected you to be masculine . . . and it just wasn't so."[94]

Furthermore, she recounted, "They would be very surprised to see how petite you really were. . . . Because when you're on a track, you're on a 45-degree angle and you have skates on, you look like you're about ten feet tall. But, when you get off and you're only four or five feet, you know, it makes a difference and you do want to look feminine."

Some of the veteran skaters worked to instill in the female rookies the importance of maintaining a ladylike image for the fans, media, and larger public, which was critical for their acceptance. Behrens recalled that her captain on the Panthers team, Bobbie Johnstone, made sure that her girls were always "presented ladylike" when they were in the presence of fans.[95] Youpelle believed that a professional public appearance was important, too: "We looked like ladies and gentlemen. We weren't just tough sports people. So, we wanted to be talked about as ladies and gentlemen."[96]

For the women, this usually included showering after a game, doing their hair, and wearing dresses (or dress pants, when those became acceptable for women in the 1950s and 1960s). "When you went on the train or you went on a plane, you wore tailored slacks. You didn't wear dungarees, but you wore slacks. You wore sweaters. A lot of us had cashmere sweaters, cashmere skirts. When you came to the building [you were skating in], you were dressed in high heels," explained Loretta Behrens. "You were dressed like a professional. You weren't dressed like a bum."[97] Carol Meyer Roman, who abhorred wearing high heels, bemoaned the need for them: "I couldn't walk with the heels if my life depended on it, and I had to wear them. And it drove me crazy, because my feet hurt me so bad."[98] Bobbie Mateer further explained the expectations for their appearance: "You always looked nice, you know. It was part of being a skater."[99] In essence, it was part of the job to prove that athleticism and femininity were not at odds.

While some skaters worked actively to counter stereotypes about their femininity or lack thereof, the specifics of their efforts differed. "We all pretty much did our own thing," explained Mary Youpelle. "Like, I used to wear gloves. I used to wear a scarf all the time. Some of the girls did that. We always wanted to look our best when we went out there."[100] That was because, as she laughingly shared, they didn't always look great after a game: "But to go out there, we always dressed like women. Like, you know, you're flirting with everybody."[101] Yet the skaters were limited on how they could present a feminine appearance on the track, since they wore standard uniforms, which were not drastically different from the men's. This situation was not like the one in the

MARY YOUPELLE   ROLLER DERBY

FIGURE 2.2. *Mary Youpelle in a Roller Derby promotional picture, 1958. Courtesy of Gary Powers and the National Roller Derby Hall of Fame and Museum.*

All-American Girls Professional Baseball League, which forced female athletes to play baseball in short skirts. Both male and female skaters usually donned long-sleeved jerseys, tights with built-in kneepads, and shorts over the tights. At one point, Gerry Murray was able to advise the uniform makers on how to tailor them for a more feminine cut, but even so the male and female uniforms were not markedly different.[102]

Whereas some of the women made sure their hair and makeup were always properly done, others balked at that idea. They insisted that they

FIGURE 2.3. *The skaters Howard Raynes (left) and Midge Brasuhn (captain; right) talking with the reporter Gloria Gary at the Minneapolis Auditorium, June 28, 1947. Minneapolis Newspaper Photograph Collection, Hennepin County Library.*

did not go out of their way to heighten their femininity (at least not in such impractical ways), because they were skaters. Gerry Murray refused to engage in the whole makeup routine, since, in her opinion, it was completely useless while playing derby. "I never wore makeup. I couldn't wear [it] because you sweat so much," she exclaimed. "What's the use of wearing it when you sweat? You're sitting on the bench after you sweat. You've got a whole bunch of sweat down on the floor. You know, you really sweat. So why wear makeup and everything?"[103] Instead, Murray wore a scarf around her neck. It was fashionable and prevented the sweat from dripping. She also sported gloves to protect her hands when she fell, which was a trend among many of the women.[104] Mary Youpelle wore gloves to protect her long fingernails, for which she had a fondness: "You never knew what you were going to grab onto — the railing, or kick rail, or something — and break something, so I did as much to protect myself. . . . I wore gloves for that purpose."[105]

Sometimes the accoutrements that the skaters used to mark their femininity became weapons of choice on the track. Mary Lou Palermo's pigtails and hair ribbons became her signature look. They allowed fans to easily distinguish her from the other skaters on the track, especially when they watched the game on television. But the pigtails had a dual purpose. Palermo admitted that when she skated around the banked track, her long, heavy hair blew behind her "like when you're in a wind tunnel": "And when I would block somebody, my hair would whip around and it would hurt them!"[106] Ma Bogash likewise used her hair for strategic purposes, but perhaps in a more underhanded way than Palermo. Bogash would occasionally hide a large hatpin in her wavy coiffure, and when stuck in a particularly congested jam on the track and sure the referee's attention was elsewhere, she would pull out the hatpin and poke the other skaters to create room for her to maneuver around them.[107]

Despite the women's intentional or unintentional displays of femininity, Roller Derby continued to be viewed as a rough, masculine sport. As in other sports labeled masculine, the inevitable link with female homosexuality surfaced and lasted throughout the entirety of the sport's history. Deford outlined public beliefs about the sexuality of female skaters when he traveled with Roller Derby in the late 1960s: "The assumption was, of course, that the women, you know, to be this tough and everything, they had to be dykes, right?"[108] This stereotype had been around for two decades by the time Deford entered the scene. Much of the American public and sports media could not fully reconcile women's inherent toughness and athleticism with "true" femininity.[109] In Mary Youpelle's opinion, because female skaters were participating in "something that was rough and tough," the lesbian community assumed that lesbians played the sport and gravitated to it.[110] A 1971 *Chicago Tribune* article demonstrated the longevity of this stereotype: "Some of the women have also been wives and mothers, which might surprise those detractors who think they should all be skating in *Dyche* Stadium."[111]

Sexuality was not openly discussed during the early years of the sport. Youpelle knew of only one lesbian who played when she started skating with the derby, in the late 1930s, although more joined throughout the years. The realization dawned slowly: "We just kind of found it out because I think we were all pretty green on the subject at that point . . . because many, many years ago you never even mentioned a lesbian."[112] The reality was that over the five-decade span of the sport, lesbians did skate in Roller Derby, but it does not appear that they were ever the majority of female skaters, and they were indistinguishable from their straight teammates.[113] But the rough nature of the sport linked the female skaters with masculine behavior, which in turn linked the majority of the women with homosexuality, regardless of their actual sexual orientation or appearance.

Men in Roller Derby, it should be noted, did not have to counter the same stereotypes as female skaters. Throughout much of the twentieth century, stereotypes of gay men pegged them as weaker and effeminate, perhaps not even capable of succeeding in such a rough-and-tumble sport as Roller Derby. By participating in a contact sport, men did not have their sexual identity and masculinity questioned in quite the same way as the female skaters, and thus male skaters (of whichever sexual orientation) did not have to engage in apologetic behavior to counter stereotypes of their sexual identity.[114]

This association of roughness with female homosexuality did not dampen the enthusiasm for Roller Derby among its fans and supporters. In the late 1930s, 1940s, and 1950s, Roller Derby enjoyed great fan support and drew some of its most avid admirers from the ranks of Hollywood and New York stars, as mentioned in the previous chapter. Having famous actors, musicians, comedians, athletes, and radio and TV personalities attend their games gave the skaters a sense of being important and famous. Skaters made frequent appearances on popular radio and television programs and mingled with the stars off the set and when out on the town. Palermo recalled going out to the hot nightclubs in New York City, where other famous people gathered. She reminisced, "Then Jack Eigen—he was at the Copacabana. That's one thing about New York. . . . No matter where—you could go out. I mean, there was the Copa. There were so many places to go. There was the Blue Note. There were so many places."[115] Palermo was interviewed on the *Ed Sullivan Show* and the *Kate Smith Show* in the early 1950s and recalled a variety of stars attending their games in New York. Incidentally, both Smith and Cab Calloway informed Palermo that she was their mothers' favorite skater. "I was everybody's mother's favorite. . . . I think it's because of my pigtails. I think they knew how to pick me out," she said, laughing.

Earning the respect of America's most famous stars and other professional athletes provided Roller Derby skaters with a sense of their own importance and contribution to American sporting entertainment.

The respect and admiration of the rich and famous did not necessarily sustain them when they played in such locations as Louisville, Houston, Pittsburgh, and Omaha. The support of the average, everyday American family is what kept the sport going. These people attended Roller Derby in person, watched it on television, and followed it through newspaper coverage or by subscribing to the *Roller Derby News* or *RolleRage*. Palermo described Roller Derby fans as "great people," "all-American people," and "family people."[116] "We got some stars too," she recalled, but "it was a cross between everything." Mary Youpelle echoed this description: "We drew great crowds wherever we went. . . . People came out from all over the place to see Roller Derby because it was something to do, something different. . . . And inexpensive."[117]

In the early years of the sport, Roller Derby offered cheap entertainment, especially for families struggling to survive the Great Depression. Youpelle saw these fans as "everyday, normal people. We had from the rich to the poor—didn't make any difference."[118] In her opinion, it was the novelty of the sport that drew fans: "I think [it was] the boys against the girls. And occasionally we would have fights and something like that, which was exciting to people that didn't see stuff like that. . . . It's women out there doing the same as the men. . . . We opened the doors to a lot of things."[119] The biggest door these women opened was the possibility of female equality in the male-dominated sports world, and their fans loved them all the more for it.

Roller Derby fans showered the skaters with fan mail, gifts to show their love for them, and invitations to visit their homes. Youpelle received all sorts of heartwarming letters and presents from her admirers, although a few bizarre ones as well.[120] "We used to get letters from people that couldn't get out, and they'd watch it on TV and [tell us] how much they enjoyed it," she recalled. "And that was kind of rewarding too, that you had gotten into somebody's home like, you know, that they couldn't leave because they were sick or disabled somewhere."[121] The letters would say such things as how much the fans enjoyed the skating and how they hoped the skaters would return quickly. "And people used to give us gifts, wonderful gifts. It was just so wonderful that people were so kind, you know," recalled Youpelle, who received such items as homemade candy, cookies, and stuffed animals.[122] Skaters also frequently received invitations to join fans for lunch or dinner. Palermo described receiving all the fan mail and gifts as like having a birthday every day.[123] Several of the gifts, such as personal drawings and a hand-stitched evening bag, she has kept for decades.

REVISITING IDENTITY AND
"WHOLENESS THROUGH SPORT"

Female Roller Derby skaters were able to edge more closely to Eleanor Metheny's "wholeness through sport" concept than were most other female athletes of the same era. Female skaters were equal and integral members of their sex-integrated teams. Roller Derby was not modified to suit women's "needs," and the female skaters were largely responsible for drawing fans. Roller Derby became not only the passion of these female athletes but also their career.

Despite these factors, Metheny's "wholeness through sport" was still not quite within their grasp. The skaters continually had to counter the notion that such a rough sport was played only by "rough," masculine, or sexually suspect women, that is, lesbians. Many Roller Derbyists were aware of such stereotypes. Most female skaters actively worked to dispel such notions and thus engaged in apologetic behavior. Female Roller Derby skaters had a clear mission to prove their identities as women because of their identities as athletes. Roller Derby was popular nationally and thus had to directly confront national media sources and social critics that attempted to belittle skaters' femininity and, ultimately, their sport. This dynamic was in many ways emblematic of the female sporting experience overall. Although female Roller Derby skaters enjoyed more functional equality than other athletes, and wider boundaries within their sport, they still found themselves worrying about their identities in ways that other female athletes of the era had to do, because of their encroachment on the masculine-defined world of contact sports.

3 | "A Very Handsome King for a Very Beautiful Queen"

It seems the prettiest gals are also the ones with the most talent, as evidenced by last year's Queen Jean Porter. But here's where you elect the Roller Derby's beauty, and if she happens to be a top skater, so much the better.

ANGIE DOURIS, *ROLLER DERBY NEWS*

A Queen can't rule without a King. . . . Who shall it be? Red Smartt again, or some other handsome skating knight?

CHRISTY MARTIN, *ROLLER DERBY NEWS*

Two young, poised white women smile brightly for the camera in two pictures taken in the mid-1950s. Both women are beauty queens, and each embodies the standards of 1950s femininity, at least at first glance. One looks directly into the lens, showcasing her perfectly plucked eyebrows and full, rosy lips. Her tiara rests high atop her head amid a brunette coiffure. Dangly diamond earrings hang inches above her shoulders and sparkle where they catch the light. She proudly, but not conceitedly, holds her scepter in smooth, dainty hands, the same hands that helped her earn a medal for sharpshooting from the National Rifle Association.[1] A rich, dark fur-lined cape cascades over her shoulders.[2] She symbolizes the beginning of the Grace Kelly era, which promoted beauty, talent, grace, elegance, and a measure of intelligence. In fact, Kelly endorsed this pageant winner as the ultimate representation of these ideals.[3]

Another happy winner, even more slender and petite than the first—110 pounds spread thin on a five-four frame—sits on a bench, her legs bent at the knees and enclosed by her long, trim arms as she smiles over her shoulder, showing off her bright red lips and pearly white teeth. Something about her pose indicates an innocent, feminine flirtation. This "attractive" and "beautiful"[4] queen's "pleasing personality" and "winning smile" led a group of twenty-five US Navy servicemen to describe her as "one dish that has everything."[5] She is not wearing a crown on top of her honey-blond hair, but her svelte "all-American" beauty leaves no doubt that she is a beauty queen.

By all accounts, these two queens epitomized American beauty and femininity. Chosen by judges as symbols of the American woman, each beauty queen "has everything, and has it in all the right places."[6] Despite sharing the all-American characteristics of beauty, charm, and personality, these queens came from starkly different backgrounds. The first was Lee Meriwether, a twenty-year-old California college student who won the title Miss America 1955.[7] The second was Nellie Montague, a twenty-one-year-old native of New Jersey who was a three-year Roller Derby veteran and the newly crowned Miss Roller Derby Queen of 1956.[8] To the contemporary eye, the only discernible difference between them is their outfits. Meriwether sports a lacy sweetheart-necked white ball gown under her cape, while Montague is pictured in her polyester derby uniform, tights, and white midcalf skates.[9]

Although Jim Croce helped popularize the catchphrase "Roller Derby Queen" with his hit 1973 song of the same name, Roller Derby skaters, female or male, were not generally associated with beauty pageants or beauty contests. Indeed, Croce described his Roller Derby queen as "the meanest hunk o' woman that anybody ever seen."[10] She was a five-foot-six "bleached-blonde mama" weighing in at a hefty 215 pounds—not the elegant Miss America type. As Croce explained, his Roller Derby queen "knew how to scuffle and fight." No Miss America contestant ever listed playing Roller Derby as her talent. So why did roller derby skaters participate in beauty contests? The simple answer is that female Roller Derby skaters constantly had to prove their femininity to counter such descriptions as Croce's, even if they were made good-naturedly.

From the 1930s to the 1970s, social critics and the male-dominated national media considered female roller derbyists to be of a rougher nature than other women. Thus, Roller Derby promoters and managers emphasized their athletes' femininity and heterosexuality to offset concerns arising from their athletic ability. The sports sociologist Jan Felshin termed this phenomenon "apologetic behavior." Apologetic behavior included engaging in "behavior intended to reinforce the socially acceptable aspects of sports while minimizing the perceived violation of social norms."[11] Female skaters pushed the boundaries of acceptable behavior by playing a contact, mixed-sex sport, and this deviation from what was expected of "young ladies" often brought them into conflict with the cultural norms of their time. These female athletes engaged in "compensatory behavior," both consciously and unconsciously, when they participated in activities, actions, or deeds that emphasized their femininity.[12] Roller Derby's management and promoters both consciously and unconsciously extolled white middle-class ideals of femininity through Roller Derby's annual beauty contest. They intentionally worked to counter the stereotypes and negative press about the roughness and masculinity of their female athletes by adhering to a tradition that continually reproduced "the ideal American girl."[13] This apologetic behavior, among others, allowed the female skaters to transgress other social and sporting norms.

Two clear ironies emerge from the Seltzer Roller Derby's association with beauty contests. In the early years of beauty pageants, contestants faced the same criticism that female derbyists faced decades later: conservatives saw the pageants as risqué and therefore inappropriate for sensible, well-bred girls and women. Pageant contestants were considered to have loose morals and to belong to a lower class of women, much as female derby skaters were demeaned later.[14] Yet pageant contestants did little more than transform the everyday activity of male gawking at women into a sport, of sorts, one with the potential for rewards far in excess of what contestants' everyday lives could produce.[15] The second irony was that male roller derby skaters were not exempt from such ritual gawking, albeit in different ways and for different reasons. They too used a hybrid beauty-popularity contest, but in their case as a way to legitimate their masculinity, which was seriously undercut by participating alongside females in a professional contact sport.

"ONE LUCKY GIRL WINS THE CROWN"

The judging of female beauty has roots as far back as ancient Greek mythology.[16] Phineas T. Barnum, the great American showman and circus founder, initiated perhaps the first modern attempt at a beauty contest in 1854, but the contest did not really gain traction until the late nineteenth century.[17] Ultimately, the emergence of the women's suffrage movement, the professionalization of female models, the rise of the chorus girl, and the new acceptability of public bathing for women aided in establishing the legitimacy of beauty contests.[18] Beauty contests held at dime museums, carnivals, local festivals, and seaside resorts increased the popularity of pageants, even among the middle class, but "there was still difficulty when it came to a question of presumably refined women publicly displaying themselves before judges or the public."[19] Simultaneously, as women shed their strict association with morality and refinement, they became prey to the new commercial beauty culture. Women downplayed any professional skills they had, and instead used their looks and their physiques as selling points, and those attributes ultimately became their most valuable assets.[20] Women "became sex objects, competing in an arena where men were the judges and the promoters."[21]

In the post–World War I period, women gained the right to vote, threw off the restrictive clothing of the Victorian and Edwardian eras, danced to jazz music, displayed their athleticism, and adopted the newly fashionable bobbed haircut as active participants in expanding the commercialization of beauty. These upheavals of the gender status quo caused anxiety about women's new and much more public role in society. Within this context, and as a backlash against these social and political changes, the modern Miss America beauty pageant emerged.[22] In the fall of 1920, Atlantic City businessmen, hoping to prolong the summer tourist season after Labor Day, created the Fall Frolic, which included the beauty pageant that became the Miss America contest. Margaret Gorman, a sixteen-year-old from Washington, DC, won over the judges with her sweet nature and became the first Miss America, although the winner was not regularly referred to as such until the second year of the contest.[23]

The Miss America competition was heavily influenced by the popularity of the "athletic girl." The US public generally supported female athletes who competed in sports such as swimming and tennis. The famous Australian swimmer Annette Kellerman established and promoted the connection between athleticism and physical beauty in the 1910s, and the French and American tennis stars Suzanne Lenglen and Helen Wills built on her precedent in the following decade.[24] The weeklong festival surrounding the Miss America pageant featured such acceptable sporting events as a swimming exhibition by the Atlantic City women's swimming club. Pageant promoters, concerned with the contestants' reputations, made sure to consistently use language that emphasized their wholesome nature, virtuous qualities, and athleticism.[25] In fact, some contemporary social commentators speculated that Margaret Gorman won the competition due to her resemblance to "America's Sweetheart," the actress Mary Pickford. Pickford's image was carefully cultivated to portray innocence combined with youthful independence, and her press releases often referred to her sports skills. At least in the early years, Pickford was "neither a sex symbol nor a bathing beauty,"[26] so Gorman's resemblance to her added respectability to the Miss America pageant as well as indicated the type of American beauty that the judges wanted to promote.[27]

As beauty pageants increasingly gained popularity with the American public, critics maintained that they threatened the welfare of women and tainted their image of respectability. Conservatives continually claimed that the contests were salacious, drew in the wrong types of women, and offended middle-class sensibilities.[28] In fact, to avoid such criticism, organizers canceled the Miss America pageant in 1928, and it was not held again until the mid-1930s.[29]

Just as questions of class remained part of the criticism leveled at beauty pageants, so did race and ethnicity. The eugenics movement and physical "science" experts, such as the physician and psychologist Havelock Ellis, promoted the notion that, in the words of the writer Candace Savage, "there was, in nature, an absolute, objective scale of beauty along which the races were ranked, with Negroes at the bottom and Europeans at the top," which meant "when it came right down to it, white was beautiful."[30] Armed with these theories, beauty contest organizers often floundered when Black or Jewish contestants fit their general criteria of idealized womanhood and received popular community support. The ladies of the Green Twigs social group in Flushing, New York, found themselves in quite a conundrum in 1924 when they held a popular-ballot beauty contest to select the queen of a local community festival. First a young Black woman pulled ahead, only to be bested by a young Jewish woman. The women's social group suspended the contest rather than be represented by such supposedly unfit women.[31]

During World War II, the Miss America pageant gained the general public acceptance that eventually led to public idolization of the ideal American woman, an ideal that came to influence even Roller Derby skaters. A woman by the name of Leonora Slaughter took over as the pageant's director in the years immediately before the war. According to Frank Deford, "She salvaged an expensive gimmick that was altogether frivolous and usually discredited and turned it into a responsible institution that came to possess respectability and a wide base of popularity."[32] As American women were called to "man" the home front, they took on traditionally unfeminine jobs. Concern arose over workingwomen's new masculinity (women were wearing pants, for crying out loud!) during a time when American men were fighting, in part, to defend American women's wholesomeness and femininity. Thus, outward demonstrations of femininity became increasingly important. Under Slaughter's revamped pageant, Miss America represented everything for which US soldiers were fighting.[33]

As the Miss America pageant came to represent the ideal American woman throughout the next few decades, local and national beauty pageants helped establish and redefine her characteristics through the community values and norms the winners supposedly represented. Indeed, they "offer a glimpse at the constantly changing and always complicated stories about the nation itself."[34] The feminist scholar Beverly Stoeltje saw modern beauty pageants not just as a reflection of society and its ideals but also as a response to changes in gender relations that challenged the patriarchal status quo. Pageants established an ideal woman who held no real power or authority and was simultaneously relegated to the social sphere. This powerless woman, judged mainly on her beauty, reflected the modern social system, which still subordinates women even as they make social, economic, and political advances in the larger, mainly patriarchal society.[35]

As with any other ideal, the archetypal American woman changed throughout the twentieth century. Focusing attention on female athletes helps refine our understanding of this evolving ideal and the context in which it belongs.[36] Within the first couple decades of the new century, the "athletic girl" emerged as "a striking symbol of modern womanhood," and descriptions of the New Woman often included her athleticism.[37] The weak, passionless, and restrained prototypical Victorian woman gave way to a new energetic, spirited, healthy, and independent woman who represented a new model of beauty. As with any cultural transition, the newer athletic standard "led observers alternately to praise and damn the 'athletic girl.'"[38] Unsurprisingly, because Roller Derby pushed the boundaries of acceptable female behavior and activities, beauty contests were used to demonstrate that the sport's participants still fell within the realm of the ideal woman and that they were still subordinate to men, or, at the very least, different from them. Female skaters walked a thin line between demonstrating an acceptable level of female athleticism and overreaching for "masculine privilege and pleasure."[39]

The femininity of derby skaters was often challenged in the press, and their appearance was often described unflatteringly. For instance, a traveling female skating troupe called the Skating Vanities made it exceptionally clear they did not want to be mistaken for roller derby women. Robert Cromie with the *Chicago Daily Tribune* wrote in the fall of 1949, "The Vanities, as thousands of fans thruout [*sic*] the world . . . can tell you, is a roller skating spectacle which should NOT repeat NOT be confused in any degree with the Roller Derby. There's a Big difference! 'The Derby,' says Mrs. Drummond with an almost imperceptible shudder, 'is a rowdy thing. The Vanities are in good taste.'"[40] Sports promoters did not want their skaters described as reckless Amazons "even meaner than the men"[41] who engaged in a "good, old-fashioned hair-pulling between fishwives,"[42] despite the not-uncommon occurrence of such behavior. Nor did they embrace such descriptions as Croce's when he sang about his Roller Derby Queen being "built like a 'fridgerator with a head." Disparaging coverage prompted rebuttals highlighting the benefits of sportsmanship, poise, confidence, and personal grooming. To battle rumors that female skaters were aggressive and lacked appeal, *RolleRage*, a roller skating and Roller Derby publication, published a self-described "cheesecake" photograph of three of the most attractive skaters in the August 1945 issue, along with a robust defense of the skaters' charms:

> Unkind rumor has it that there are a few fans who consider the feminine half of the Roller Derby somewhat lacking in that important ingredient called "glamour" . . . According to them, our whirling lassies should be described only by some such word as "pugnacious." If there be any who agree with that train of thought, we offer the above in direct rebuttal—note, if you please the pretty smiling faces of Tillie Mudri, Mary Gardner and Annis Jensen, not to mention the—ahem!—shapely "limbs" so fetchingly posed. We admit that these girls CAN be pugnacious on occasion . . . but we will always maintain they've got plenty of glamour too![43]

Participating in beauty contests and the like allowed these female athletes to push social boundaries while simultaneously adhering to and even propagating the kind of "mainstream" values inculcated by such social institutions as Miss America. After all, as *Roller Derby News* pointed out in 1958, "a woman wants to be a woman regardless of her profession. . . . Roller Derby or otherwise, women the world over want to be feminine."[44]

"Prettiest Girl on Skates"

Beginning in 1938, a mere three years after the first Roller Derby game, and continuing almost uninterrupted until the early 1970s, Roller Derby held an annual Roller Derby Queen contest. Thousands of Roller Derby fans voted for who they believed should be crowned that year's queen. It is unclear who initiated the contest, but it was probably Leo Seltzer, who often held contests and gimmicks alongside his walkathons in the early 1930s. At first, voters chose the most popular skater as queen, with beauty only a secondary factor. Mary Youpelle won the first Roller Derby Queen title, in 1938. She described the contest as one in which fans chose their favorite skater, a selection likely based on a combination of skating ability and looks. She humbly recalled, "I was a good skater. I was a beauty queen, or whatever—I don't know, but it's a favorite skater, whatever people chose, you know. When you go to anything, you pick . . . someone you like and that's evidently what happened."[45] In 1941, Peggy O'Neal, described as "a 'baby-faced' nineteen-year-old youngster whose exploits on skates have made her a national favorite," won the title of queen.[46] When a Chicago fan wrote *RolleRage* to ask who the editors believed to be the prettiest female skater, the staff responded, "We are afraid that if we attempted to answer your question it would start a 'battle royal' among fans and skaters alike, since a question such as this is purely a matter of personal opinion."[47]

The publication's response in 1941, when Roller Derby was still working hard to build a fan base and establish itself as a respectable sport, is not surprising, given the history of beauty pageants. They did not gain widespread popularity until the postwar era, so the Derby may have wanted to avoid association with supposedly disreputable events and unrefined women. Proving that female Roller Derby skaters were beautiful, feminine, and athletic was critical. Holding a beauty contest, however, was perhaps a riskier move than the management was ready to engage in as it tried to make the derby acceptable to the mainstream sports world.

Despite not having a formal beauty competition in the late 1930s and 1940s, the Roller Derby league and skaters worked hard to cultivate an image that appealed to mainstream Americans. As the skater Bert Wall explained, "Leo [Seltzer] wanted girls to be girls and to look nice."[48] An important aspect of promoting that image was to highlight the femininity and good looks of its female skaters. For instance, the cover of the February 1941 issue of *RolleRage* magazine featured a professional portrait photograph of a female skater in a black sweater. The caption read, " 'Gorgeous' is the only word that can adequately describe this photographic study of Roller Derby skater Kitty Nehls."[49] Later in the same issue, a small full-length picture of Nehls appeared with the following caption: "Kitty is one of the most attractive of all feminine Roller Derby stars — in or out of skating attire."[50] Comments like this highlight the organization's insistence that the female skaters were indeed feminine, on and off the track, and even if they were Roller Derby skaters, they were still ladies at their core. The skaters time and again insisted their athleticism did not undercut their feminine identity. The derby had to insist on this to survive as both a sport and business. It was easier to highlight the female skaters' femininity than make the case that toughness, aggressiveness, and athleticism were not simply masculine attributes.

Skaters such as Bobbie Mateer and Mary Youpelle understood the importance of this image to the organization. Mateer made sure to look her best when skating, in part to appeal to the fans: "I made sure my uniform fit me very, very well, and I had, when I skated, a long ponytail, and I used to flip that around — prance around a little here and there. It was good for business."[51] Along the same line, Youpelle explained, "I think we were all very conscious of how we dressed and how we acted because we were invited out to people's houses. We met governors and mayors and what have you, and you have to be a lady to do that. . . . We looked like ladies and gentlemen. We weren't just tough sports people."[52] The skaters were clearly conscious of stereotypes portraying female Roller Derby athletes as rough, tough, or unfeminine — which were both class and gender issues. Despite their participation in a physically demanding sport, they did not see themselves in these stereotypes, and they actively worked to counter them, as well as to promote the idea that the sport was appropriate for women.

According to the skater Gloria Mack, Youpelle tried to instill this idea in rookie female skaters over the years. Mack skated with the Westerners team under the tutelage of Youpelle. She credited Youpelle with showing her how easy it was to remain feminine and how important it was for their image as female athletes. Youpelle served as a surrogate mother for young skaters, making sure they looked well kempt, remained polite to their fans, and refrained from using profanity. Mack stated, "As an athlete and a woman, I like to think of myself as a lady. . . . Despite the fact that derby is a tough sport, there isn't any reason why a girl can't remember her femininity. Off the track, I try to be neat and presentable. The same applies for when I'm in competition."[53] Taking Youpelle's advice to heart, Mack successfully won over fans and reporters alike, who described her as a "lovely honey-voiced gal who exudes charm and politeness."[54]

By the 1950s, the Roller Derby Queen contest had shifted its focus, probably in response to the growing acceptance of beauty contests and their new role in identifying the ideal American woman. It was, in fact, during the 1955 live-television coronation of Lee Meriwether as Miss America that the master of ceremonies first sang the lyrics now synonymous with the pageant: "There she is, Miss America. There she is, your ideal."[55] In 1956, *Roller Derby News* proclaimed that its beauty contest was "one contest where skating ability is *not* the prime requisite"[56]— stark evidence of a revived emphasis on beauty over skill, which had been reversed during the Rosie the Riveter era of World War II, when the government depended on women's abilities in the home and workforce to keep the country afloat.

After the war, the media lauded a distinctly "American look" as a direct link with the economic and psychological superiority of the United States. The look was considered "an authentic national characteristic, a creation of the American way of life . . . [one] that has become as much a part of the national scene as the corner drugstore or the Mississippi River."[57] The look supported the postwar reordering of gender with its emphasis on beauty as a defining characteristic of the American woman as she turned in her rivet gun, though not her skates, and headed back into the home. This distinctive American look entailed a "natural manner, freshness and enthusiasm, a friendly smile, an easy, confident stride with head held high, an unaffected elegance in make-up and dress."[58] It also included good grooming, which consisted of personal cleanliness and well-brushed hair; nice shoes were a plus, as were long legs, confidence, agelessness, domesticity, and, simultaneously, glamour—surely an easy combination for the average woman to pull off.[59]

The look acknowledged important benefits of American womanhood that had been unavailable to previous generations. According to a *Life* magazine article analyzing the look, the modern American woman had been raised in "a land where schoolgirls are encouraged to participate in competitive sports and where free medical clinics and physi-

Figure 3.1. *Gloria Clairbeaut, winner of the 1951 Roller Derby Queen contest, receiving her award. Courtesy of Gary Powers and the National Roller Derby Hall of Fame and Museum.*

cal examinations are familiar features of academic routine. From these things have evolved the straight limbs and glow of health that distinguish the American girl."[60] The modern American woman gained her confidence from these competitive physical activities: "She walks erect, holds her head high, and she is not nonplussed by the admiring glances or whistles that follow her. Whether short or tall she does not mince as she walks but steps forward with graceful athletic stride she acquired as a roller-skating, ball-chasing tomboy."[61]

While the mainstream media acknowledged girls' and women's right to athletics at least on some level, they simultaneously reduced her to how she looked while doing it. By 1957, the skater "most deserving of the title, Roller Derby Queen" had become simply "the prettiest girl in Roller Derby."[62] The best or the most popular skaters could win separate competitions that declared them the most valuable skaters or fan favorites, but the queen was the prettiest of them all. Similarly, Miss America crowned the "queen of femininity," with her "All-American face and form."[63] This separation of contests within Roller Derby revealed the shift in American culture to an emphasis on women's beauty as their most valuable and defining characteristic. Ultimately, the practice of beauty "was the feminine road to fulfillment."[64] According to C. C. Crawford, a professor of education, in the foreword to a beauty course book in its twelfth printing in 1953, "Whether in the office or in the drawing-room, or even across the breakfast table, appearance and behavior make the difference between success and failure."[65]

The voting for the new beauty contest was simple: *Roller Derby News* printed ballots for fans to fill out and mail in, designating the one derby girl they believed should be crowned queen, based on her looks alone.[66] Fans were clearly instructed to allow "beauty, not skill, to decide."[67] After receiving ballots for two or three months, the staff tallied the votes, and a winner would be announced and honored during a game. The contest winner was usually presented with a trophy from a sponsoring business, along with roses, but sometimes she also received a crown, sash, or cape, just like winners of other beauty contests around America.[68] Unlike Miss America contestants, female skaters were not paraded in front of a panel of judges in bathing suits and evening gowns on one glamorous yet nerve-racking night while judges ranked them based on their poise, all-American beauty, and voluptuousness. Ultimately, the skaters were judged by these criteria every time they rolled onto the green Masonite track. The fans, who simultaneously doubled as judges in the Roller Derby beauty contests, had the opportunity to pass judgment every time they attended a game or flipped on the television from the comfort of their La-Z-Boys. Harking back to the advice of Mary Youpelle and Gloria Mack, it was continually important in this era for a girl to "remember her femininity," because female skaters were constantly on display whether they wanted to be or not.[69]

Roller Derby News diligently reported on the leaders of the contest in the months leading up to the announcement of that year's queen, informing readers which "skating beauties" were in the top rankings.[70] Once the winner was announced, the magazine published a front-page write-up on the contest and the queen. In the 1950s, tens of thousands of dedicated fans mailed in their ballots in an effort to reward who they believed was the most attractive skater. For instance, in 1958, the year when Joan Weston won the crown, she received 9,142 votes. The top ten

FIGURE 3.2. *Gerry Murray, winner of the 1959 Roller Derby Queen contest. Courtesy of Gary Powers and the National Roller Derby Hall of Fame and Museum.*

contenders that year collectively drew in 58,487 votes.[71] Two years previous, over 65,000 fans voted in the contest.[72]

A "HANDSOME SKATING KNIGHT"

Roller Derby held a beauty contest to highlight female skaters' glamour, downplay their roughness, and appeal to fans, but as a proponent of gender equality, the organization did not exempt its male skaters from this ritual of legitimation. Regarding the annual Roller Derby King contest, Jerry Seltzer stated, "We were equal. . . . That was it."[73] As in the early queen contests, the king was elected based on popularity. By the 1950s, however, the king contest had likewise shifted its focus to appearance, although apparently not to the same extent as the women's contest. This shift may have been due in part to "uncertain and changing concepts of masculinity"[74] as well as to a larger change in the representations of masculinity in the postwar period. As the historian Kenneth Krauss explains, cultural representations of American manhood in the postwar era emphasized younger, "more aesthetically attractive and sexually ambiguous" men.[75] Krauss shows how "there came a tacit, often wary, realization that men were and could be beautiful."[76] Whereas American society had formerly judged men on such personal qualities as wisdom, loyalty, and strength, "beauty was always regarded, especially from a male point of view, as dubious"; but "the postwar shift in masculinity changed that."[77] By examining cultural artifacts such as movies, plays, and physique magazines, Krauss demonstrates how social ideas and attitudes changed, albeit "often confusingly," toward a new representation of masculinity that acknowledged male beauty.[78]

Mirroring the evolution of male beauty tracked by Krauss, the Roller Derby King was noted for his good looks, but his general popularity, skating ability, and personality were more integral to his election. Part of his purpose, it seemed, was to serve as an accessory to the queen in a way that legitimated her femininity and his masculinity: "We must keep the women happy, and the woman we mean is our new Roller Derby News Queen. . . . A queen can't rule without a King. . . . Who shall it be? Red Smartt again, or some other handsome skating knight? . . . We will crown our 'King' in March, so he shall reign with our attractive Queen."[79] For the king contest, fans were instructed to mail in their ballots for their "favorite male skater," as opposed to merely the best-looking one, as was touted for the women's contest.[80]

Unlike women, men have rarely been defined primarily by their physical beauty, so it was not the foremost concern of the Roller Derby King contest. When fans voted Russ Massro the Roller Derby King in 1956, they cited a plethora of reasons for their choice. Most who wrote in supporting Massro's election commented on his good looks but also highlighted other important aspects of his character and skating ability. One reader wrote, "My vote goes to Russ Massro because I feel he is just about the greatest male personality on skates. . . . Being handsome doesn't hurt him one bit either and I feel he would make a very handsome King for a very beautiful Queen—Nellie Montague."[81] Another woman stated, "He is such a neat and nice-looking guy. He also seems to love to skate and has a lot of charm. I think he's the greatest." Yet another fan effused, "He is one of the cleanest skaters in Roller Derby.

He is also a one-man team, and should be elected King, Coach, and anything else that requires a top skater." In other words, he had every masculine quality that a male skater ought to have, on top of being attractive. His association with female skaters, particularly the "very beautiful Queen," did not make him less of a man—indeed, it made him more of one.

This assertion of enhanced masculinity was important, given the prominent 1950s cultural critique of a feminized mass culture and an insistence by some that masculinity had to be reshaped around otherness. The historian James Gilbert argues, "Concepts of masculinity were sometimes rebuilt around ideals of difference (a racially, gendered, or sexually oriented other), and in ways that, if only vicarious as in the emulation of celebrities or sports and war heroes, still reasserted some sort of male social dominance."[82] This implicitly required superiority was problematic in Roller Derby, a sport built on gender equality. How then could it highlight or reinforce masculinity? Roller Derby explicitly challenged the rise in what Gilbert dubbed "spectatorship masculinity—in which identity was formed (or imagined at least) around observation and emulation of masculine heroes in sport and public life, within the literary imagination, or through mass culture."[83] Indeed, many cultural critics insisted that "overbearing and overpowerful women" were ruining the identity of men.[84] This trend was evident in Roller Derby coverage of the time, with journalists claiming that the women made the men look weak and the female skaters were more prone to violence and held grudges longer than their male teammates. As Robert Cromie wrote in the *Chicago Daily Tribune* in 1949, "The best way to tell male from female during the evening, at least at a distance, is to know that the girls are even meaner than the men and add hair pulling to their assault."[85]

The *Roller Derby News* king contest may have been a gesture toward equal treatment of the sexes, but the queen contest received more hype and coverage. In fact, the magazine used the queen contest to play up female rivalries and highlight the importance of the queen title as well as skaters' femininity. This emphasis was critical to downplaying the idea of the "overbearing and overpowering" female skater. In June 1956, months before voting for the Roller Derby Queen contest began, a small article among the box scores aimed to drum up interest and show how intensely female skaters vied for the queen title. The article stated, "SERVES NOTICE—Attractive Barbara Mateer of the N.Y. Chiefs has served notice to one and all that she is ready to fight to the hilt to win this year's Queen of the Roller Derby title. The attractive New Jersey

BOBBIE"Queenie"MATEER   ROLLER DERBY

FIGURE 3.3. *Bobbie "Queenie" Mateer on a Roller Derby postcard, 1958. Courtesy of Gary Powers and the National Roller Derby Hall of Fame and Museum.*

miss has been close several times but just missed reaching the top of the ladder. Barbara is one of the most attractive girls in Roller Derby play."[86]

In the late 1950s, *Roller Derby News* provided monthly updates on voting for the queen and let the fans know which skating beauty had pulled ahead.[87] The king contest did not rate the same type of hype and updates. *Roller Derby News* gave considerably more coverage to the men's All-Star and Rookie of the Year contests or to the male Hall of

Fame elections.[88] This imbalance in coverage suggests that the queen contest was very important for the female skaters. Contests highlighting the men's skating skills were more integral for them. These differences repositioned the femininity and masculinity of the skaters in ways that reflected the values of mainstream society.

Like other aspects of Roller Derby, the queen and king contests simultaneously challenged and reproduced mainstream popular culture. By hosting beauty contests for women, Roller Derby attempted to showcase the female skaters' normality, physical attractiveness, and femininity and to highlight their adherence to mainstream beauty culture: "She is no different than any other girl," Roller Derby publications adamantly declared.[89] Yet Roller Derby pushed boundaries by hosting a male contest too, run in the same manner as the female one.

Since, for many Americans, sport is the "leading definer of masculinity in mass culture,"[90] as the sociologist R. W. Connell notes, Roller Derby's gender equality made many people in the mainstream sports establishment question the legitimacy of the male athletes and the nature of the sport itself. Furthermore, male Roller Derby skaters' masculinity was compared unfavorably to that of other male professional athletes, because of the former's association with female skaters.[91] As the skater Billy Bogash remarked, "A lot of people in the newspaper and radio business looked down on us because there had never been a sport where women and men were side by side."[92] Indeed, as a newspaper article in 1949 stated, "If you still think women are the weaker sex, ponder a moment or two on the body checks, battles and black eyes of the roller derby girls. . . . The men who alternate with the girls . . . seem almost gentlemanly and courteous in comparison."[93] The writer noted that even though the women do not skate quite as fast as their male counterparts, they "more than make up for it in roughness." Competing in a rough contact sport hindered the "true" femininity of the female skaters, a deficit that was countered by the beauty contests, while the male skaters' connection with the female skaters hindered their "true" masculinity. Masculinity as an ideology or practice is often defined in opposition to femininity or in response to changes in femininity.[94] This essential contrast has particularly been true in the sporting realm. The equality on the Roller Derby track complicated traditional ideas of both masculinity and femininity.

Roller Derby and its queen and king contests provide a pre-women's-movement example of what the sports sociologist Michael Messner dubs the "contested terrain," where women seek equality within sport but challenge male superiority and dominance as they do so.[95] Thus, the Roller Derby King contest perhaps unintentionally served a twofold purpose: it was used to reposition the male skaters' masculinity in relation to that of other male athletes (from a marginalized position to a dominant one) and to reassert the male skaters' "hegemonic masculinity." Connell coined this term to denote "the configuration of gender practice which embodies the currently accepted answer to the problem of the legitimacy of patriarchy, which guarantees (or is taken to guarantee) the dominant position of men and the subordination of women."[96] Within Connell's and Messner's framework, Roller Derby provided a unique space where both sexes challenged, contested, reproduced, and negotiated traditional ideas about femininity and masculinity.[97]

On the surface, the queen and king contests seemed to indicate that Roller Derby reinforced mainstream notions of normative femininity and masculinity, but this was not always the case. Jerry Seltzer claimed he did not view the later beauty contests in these terms, even though the fans may have. By the time he took over as commissioner of the league, in the late 1950s, fans were again voting for skaters they really loved, in his opinion, as opposed to voting on looks alone; as evidence, he pointed out that some of the queens were not necessarily "raving beaut[ies]" (although some certainly were).[98] While fans still voted on the queens and kings, the league management also had a say in the outcomes of the contests during his tenure, and the management was privy to information that was not always public.[99] Although the fans never really knew it, gay and lesbian skaters won queen and king contests, proving that a skater who looked the part of a heterosexual man or woman would be rewarded by the fan base.[100]

Much like gender, sexuality was another contested social issue on which Roller Derby was seemingly more open and accepting than other sports of the era. Still, it could not fully escape the conflicts over sexuality that plagued American society, particularly the stereotype of the "mannish lesbian athlete." Lesbians tended to find a relatively safe space in the world of women's sports as long as they were quiet about their sexuality.[101] Often, lesbians who were outed, or women who were suspected of being lesbians, faced real consequences. For instance, a player was released from the AAGPBL's South Bend Blue Sox simply for getting a "butchy" haircut.[102] Roller Derby, however, did not discriminate against skaters based on their sexual orientation, even in the pre-Stonewall era. While some skaters were openly gay, what happened in their personal lives remained there for the most part.[103]

By and large, homosexuality was not a concern for the owners, management, or skaters. Leo Seltzer "just looked at people [as] good athletes,"[104] and when his son Jerry took over, he upheld his father's sense of equality. Jerry stated, "We had quite a number of gay skaters, and we knew it, but it didn't mean anything. And I'm talking both men and women."[105] Frank Deford witnessed this acceptance when he traveled with the derby in the late 1960s: "It was a very, very fair culture that was sort of ahead of the time. . . . All I know is that Roller Derby was [a] pretty free society, and everybody was pretty much allowed to be who they wanted to be and you never heard people saying things like 'faggot' and stuff. . . . I never heard any of that stuff at all. And I sure heard it in a lot of other places."[106] Because the sport pushed boundaries by including women, because the skaters viewed one another as family members (and you take care of your family), and because the Seltzers refused to tolerate discrimination within their organization, Roller Derby cultivated a welcoming space for gays and lesbians, in stark contrast to nearly all other sports in the twentieth century.

It is important to note, however, that these accounts of Roller Derby's sexual inclusivity and acceptance came, by and large, from people who identified as straight. Heterosexual athletes and observers provided an outsider's perspective regarding queerness. That is not to say that their interpretations are incorrect, but rather to acknowledge the limits of the heteronormative lens through which they viewed their experiences and to highlight the need for more queer voices.[107] Conflicts over sexuality sometimes occurred in the first two decades of the sport, in part because of personal bias and in part because of a lack of education on the subject. Homosexuality was not commonly addressed in society during the early decades of Roller Derby, and the gay rights movement was still in its infancy by the time the Seltzer Roller Derby folded.[108] But even in the early years of the sport, no discrimination occurred publicly, according to management and a number of skaters.

Mary Youpelle recalled that the lesbian community assumed the female skaters were all lesbians because they "were doing something that was rough and tough" and thereby challenging traditional ideas of femininity.[109] Yet she remembered only one lesbian skater in the late 1930s and early 1940s. According to Youpelle, the rest of the skaters were heterosexual and "very feminine and acted that way."[110] This caused some tension among the skaters and the lone lesbian because she, apparently, was actively searching for a girlfriend, which made the other female skaters uncomfortable. Youpelle stated, "She didn't get along too well because she was kind of—she was a nice person, but I think the rest of us kind of didn't enfold her as much as we did each other." Over seventy years later, Youpelle struggled to articulate the conflict with the lesbian skater: "She didn't fit in with the rest of the girls. We were—the rest of the girls were that: girls. They weren't, uh, I don't know. They weren't that lesbian type . . . [and] she was looking for a mate." Youpelle's trouble with candidly discussing the tension between the gay and straight skaters highlights the commonly applied stigma of homosexuals as the Other—lesbians were not seen as real women or "normal" women throughout much of the twentieth century.

The presence of gay skaters was not something Roller Derby openly promoted to the public or its fans, and it did not intentionally recruit gay skaters. "When skaters were picked up, they weren't picked up because you were gay or you were straight or you were black or green or yellow," explained Loretta Behrens. "You picked up talent."[111] At the same time, Roller Derby did not tolerate open discrimination or conflict between skaters based on things like race and sexuality.[112] It was not a topic the heterosexual skaters openly talked about, and as Youpelle remembered it in the early years of the sport, "We just kind of found it out because I think we were all pretty green on the subject at that point . . . because many, many years ago you never mentioned a lesbian. Nobody did, you know? So, it was just an unspoken thing. You didn't talk about it."[113] This hands-off attitude toward sexuality suggests that homosexuals in the derby perhaps did not fear for their skating jobs, but nonetheless knew that they were members of a community not willing to address or discuss homosexuality openly, a midcentury version of "Don't Ask, Don't Tell" instituted to protect the organization's reputation.

As time went on, a more tolerant atmosphere emerged for homosexual skaters, although sexuality still was not openly discussed.[114] Countering Youpelle's earlier statement, the former skater Mary Lou Palermo explained, "It was never brought up. . . . There was no need for it because . . . they never did anything to cause any alarm, or—they were just girls. It was just 'people are people.' . . . I can't explain it. It's just that it was never, never even thought of, you know?"[115] Bobbie Mateer further emphasized this point: "I know we had lesbian skaters, but skaters were skaters. I never personally felt any different. It's part of life. . . . It didn't interfere with the game or anything that we did. It didn't bother me one way or the other."[116]

Loretta Behrens noted that in general, the gay skaters "weren't selling their sexual orientation."[117] She recalled one skater who was "very butchy" in appearance—"You didn't know whether she was male or female."[118] Although this skater's sexuality was not in question, Behrens described her as having "never flaunted her gayness."[119] And according to her, that was the general rule: "Whatever she did on her time off, nobody questioned. . . . You skated, you played your game. After the game, whatever lifestyle you had, you went your own way. There were people you knew were gay [and others] you didn't—they're all our family. They never presented themselves in any wrong way of doing things."

It seems that Roller Derby fostered a generally accepting community for gay and lesbian skaters, free of any personal and institutional discrimination, as long as their sexuality did not affect the game, fan attendance, or the organization. Gay skaters did not have to fear being outed to management or to worry that their sexuality could cost them their jobs. Essentially, whatever the skaters wanted to do on their own time was their own business. According to Behrens, "Nobody bothered [them], that's your lifestyle. . . . It wasn't condemned."[120] Gerry Murray confirmed this semiaccepting, semiclosed atmosphere: "They never talked about it. Nobody talked about it. It was just something that everybody kept to themselves."[121]

Not every skater was tolerant. Jerry Seltzer recalled, "Some . . . you know, made fun of them . . . just like real life. But they all had to live together, and get along together."[122] The management could not monitor or control every skater interaction, but Seltzer insisted that skaters tolerate one another and one another's differences. The Seltzer Roller Derby had a clear "no discrimination" policy, so regardless of personal beliefs, skaters had to get along. In the 1960s and early 1970s, gays and lesbians on occasion even formed the majority of skaters on a few teams. Seltzer stated, "In a lot of cases there was more gays than, you know, straights. . . . It never crossed my mind. Nobody ever came up and said, 'You know we have too many gays on this team.'"[123]

Roller Derby proved to be more inclusive than most traditional sports on the issue of race, too, in the mid-twentieth century. The derby historian Keith Coppage noted, "Roller Derby was free of the kind of institutional racism that dominated other sports. . . . African American skaters were easily accepted into the game by management and fans alike."[124] This acceptance was particularly notable given the fraught history of segregated roller rinks across America in the twentieth century. As the historian Victoria Wolcott explained, the nonviolent struggle to integrate amusement and leisure spaces such as roller rinks in cities like Chicago, Cleveland, and Flint, Michigan, in the 1940s and 1950s often led to violence toward recreational activists and "reflected segregation's persistence."[125] Within this context, Maurice Plummer integrated Roller Derby when he became the first Black skater with the New York Chiefs in 1953. Management predicted that the very athletic Plummer, who had played baseball in the Negro leagues with the Indianapolis Clowns, would "be a hit."[126] That hope, however, proved unfounded. Plummer's tenure in Roller Derby did not last long, and in fact, he is often left out of historical memory because he failed to develop into a star skater.[127]

Darlene Anderson became the first Black woman to skate with the Roller Derby, in 1957, and won Rookie of the Year honors in 1958 at age nineteen. George Copeland, the second Black man to join the derby and the first Black male star, joined about the same time as Anderson.[128] Roller Derby did not hype these monumental occasions of integration. To the management and the skaters, it was not a "big deal."[129] But it was a big deal to the Black skaters and the Black community. As the *New York Amsterdam News* reported in April 1960, "Quietly but steadily the number of Negroes participating in the increasingly popular Roller Derby has climbed from one in 1958 to eleven in April of 1960."[130] Darlene Anderson did not view herself as the "chosen one"—the person hand-picked by God or the white community to break down barriers—but she did see her skating career as integral to the process: "Just as other blacks were removing bricks one by one. . . . I too was just another person, I believe, given talent—God-given talent—to make some type of a history mark on America."[131] She felt the eyes of her fellow Americans, both Black and white, on her: "I was black and the only black female on that banked oval."

Races and ethnicities besides Black and white were represented in the Roller Derby, too. Skaters with Mexican, Spanish, Samoan, German, Italian, and Asian backgrounds played, such as Gil Orozco and Sam Tiapula.[132] Frank Deford attributed this inclusiveness to the accepting culture created by Leo and Jerry Seltzer: "There was equality in the roller derby. That's the simple thing. It was absolute equality in the roller derby. He was ahead of his time. He walked the walk."[133] Jerry Seltzer, a little more modestly, stated, "I'm not saying, you know, that I'm the most tolerant or whatever person, but we just thought, who would help the team? Who would help the gate?"[134]

Seltzer made sure to give everyone the same kind of opportunities, regardless of race, sexuality, or gender.[135] Several Black skaters rose to star prominence during their skating careers, and were beloved by fans of all races: George Copeland, Darlene Anderson, Ronnie Robinson,

Cliff Butler, Bob Woodberry, and Ruberta Mitchell were among the top skaters and fan favorites. Like their white counterparts, these skaters were either heartily cheered or booed, depending on whether they skated for the home team or were "red shirts," but not because of their skin color. Ronnie Robinson, the fourth Black person to join Roller Derby and the son of legendary boxer Sugar Ray Robinson, acknowledged this colorblindness in fans: "Fans in general are just about the same all over the world. If you are on the home team, they love you regardless of what color you are or national origin or what have you. If you are on the visiting team, they are going to dislike you regardless of what you do."[136] Despite tense racial relations in the South, Robinson found that fans acted much the same regardless of their geographic location. He stated in 1971, "Now I'm primarily on the visiting team even in the South. And I don't think this encourages any more problems than you would find up here in the North. There are always going to be a few bigots that are going to call you names, no matter where you are. Derby fans are really the same everywhere."[137] Robinson's comment implies that Roller Derby fans, at least while attending games, were more concerned with cheering on their home team, regardless of the skaters' race.[138]

Darlene Anderson wholeheartedly believed that she was treated well by the other skaters. She said years later in a newspaper interview:

> Myself being black, I don't think ever mattered to anyone as I was respected, treated by all skaters on an equal level, and I don't ever remember once that black was an issue. In fact, I think if you ask anyone of our age group, or of our skating group, we saw no color. No, black wasn't an issue or, if it was, the person was kind enough to respect me and keep it to themselves. We were family. We were not color. I truly believe this.[139]

Other Black skaters corroborated this idea. John Hall, a skater for Roller Derby in the late 1950s and early 1960s, stated, "I've known, both being a Negro myself, and knowing how George Copeland, Ruberta Mitchell, Darlene Anderson, Janice Williams, and all the others were treated—there was definite equality."[140]

This is not to say that Roller Derby was exempt from racial tensions or that no skater ever expressed racial animosity. Roller Derby increased in popularity in tandem with the civil rights movement. For instance, in 1969, two Roller Derby games were canceled by local police because of racial tension erupting in the area around Richmond, California, after a surge in civil rights activity.[141] After several Black skaters joined the Roller Derby ranks, they refused to travel to the South if that meant skating in segregated venues "where blacks were relegated to the 'nosebleed' section of the arena."[142] Seltzer encouraged the skaters to give the South another try and to trust him and his planning. He agreed they would not skate in any segregated venues, and they did not, which earned him the respect of many skaters.[143]

Despite avoiding segregated venues, Black skaters had trouble finding accommodations in the South in the 1960s, since they were denied access to certain restaurants, Laundromats, and motels. Carol Meyer, a skater of Spanish and German descent who grew up in the projects of San Francisco, revealed that she never knew what discrimination was until she traveled through the South with her Black teammates. She recalled a time when a group of white waitresses refused to serve their mixed table of skaters until the manager forced them to do so.[144] Mike Gammon, a white skater, recalled Black skaters sometimes having to meet up with the team after staying in a different town. He shuddered when recalling the following:

> When you go into a town and they've got these signs that say "Home of the Ku Klux Klan," and you walk down the street and the black people get off the sidewalks so you can walk by. . . . Coming from the East, it was like they were twenty years behind the times. A hundred years of progress just doesn't happen overnight. You know, I never saw that because I grew up in the Derby, where there was no black and white.[145]

Racial tensions were not limited to the South, and indeed occurred in northern urban areas and in the West, particularly in leisure and amusement spaces. Recreational facilities were staunchly segregated in northern cities like Chicago and Cincinnati and as far west as Pasadena, California. Bert Wall witnessed blatant racial discrimination against his teammates while skating in Las Vegas, Nevada: "The Black skaters couldn't stay at the same hotel. They couldn't swim in the swimming pool."[146] An even more disturbing example of racism occurred in Kansas. Wall stated, "We stopped at a bowling alley and dance place. . . . This is after the race. . . . We'd dance with the girls, the Black girls, and think nothing about it. And what happened is they served us, the white people, and wouldn't serve the colored ones, and we just about tore the place up."

Despite both Black and white skaters' insistence that there was a lack of discrimination in the derby, an occasional snide racial comment could be heard in their ranks. Sometimes the skaters' actions could be attributed to the politically incorrect language of the times, postgame tension between skaters, or personal bias. Policy does not always govern individual behavior, and thus racism sometimes reared its ugly head.[147] Frank Deford caught such an exchange between the San Francisco Bomber star Charlie O'Connell, known for his lack of couth as well as his cockiness, and Bob Woodberry, when Deford traveled with Roller Derby in 1969. O'Connell, angry over a botched call at the end of a game, turned his anger on Woodberry, a rival, in the men's locker room:

> Naturally disposed to get mad at Woodberry under any circumstances, Charlie seizes on that mild utterance as an opportunity to turn on him. He whirls in his chair and points menacingly at Woodberry. "Listen," he says, "you stay out of this. And also, if you don't mind, don't bleed on my uniform." O'Connell holds up his bloodstained shirt, and adds more sarcasm to his voice. "It's such dark blood anyway."
>
> "Oooo," [Ronnie] Robinson cries in mock anger. Besides Woodberry, he is the only black on the All-Stars. "Bitter, bitter, bitter. You see, Thumper [Woodberry]: bad losers."[148]

After this give-and-take between O'Connell, Woodberry, and Robinson, the male skaters turned their attention to a more pressing issue: beer. Nothing further was said about the game as the skaters knocked back beers while getting dressed. O'Connell's racist remarks about Woodberry demonstrated that racial issues were never far from the surface, even in this seemingly harmonious community. At the same time, Robinson's retort and his insult of O'Connell suggest that he did not feel physically threatened by O'Connell despite the blatant (and very real) racism.

Regardless of the official Roller Derby stance on racial and gender equality, the derby's promotion of an "ideal" version of beauty, femininity, and masculinity in their skaters reflected the ideals of mainstream society.[149] Although the general inclusivity of Roller Derby sets it apart from many other sports of its era, Roller Derby was also a producer of culture. By not fully and openly rejecting the larger social restrictions placed on women, Blacks, and homosexuals, it propagated these inequalities. The idealizations thus promoted objectified white women while excluding women of color and nonheterosexual skaters.

Roller Derby, its beauty contests, and its emphasis on the femininity of female skaters reflected larger social and cultural trends even while complicating them. In the same vein, the historians Elwood Watson and Darcy Martin found something similar about the country's most iconic beauty contest: "The microcosm of the Miss America Pageant provides invaluable insight into broader changes and trends in American culture for most of the twentieth century and into the present one. For better or worse, the pageant reflects commonly held values, beliefs, and attitudes that Americans share about women."[150] Roller Derby furthered stereotypes that emphasized women's physical beauty as a primary measure of their worth, while also providing women a forum to showcase their physical strength and endurance through a rough competitive sport— a place where beauty could not stop an opponent from sending a skater flying over a banked railing and crumpling in a heap on the ground after a fifteen-foot fall, most likely with their hair and makeup in shambles.

The femininity and ladylike attributes of the white female skaters that were highlighted in the pages of Roller Derby magazines, in newspapers, and in cheesecake photo-ops, particularly in the 1940s, '50s, and early '60s, reinforced the social and cultural hierarchies that promoted Eurocentric standards of beauty and excluded Black women from the status of "ladies."[151] Black and white women historically have been defined by different public meanings of womanhood, which "were partly grounded in divergent experiences of work and in the disproportionately black experience of poverty."[152] Black women were most often defined by their ability to perform manual labor or by their allegedly hypersexualized and immoral nature, which put them at fundamental odds with being recognized as ladies.[153] While white female skaters worked hard to prove they could simultaneously be skaters and ladies, that dual status was one that Black skaters never could achieve.[154]

In addition, Black women were denied access to ideal beauty standards, based on their race. The psychologist Rita Freedman found that in American culture, the idealized image of beauty "is built on a Caucasian model," and culture reinforced this image: "Fairy-tale princesses and Miss Americas have traditionally been white. This fair image weighs most heavily on the brown shoulders of minority women who bear a special beauty burden."[155] Though both Black and white women were taught from a young age that beauty was imperative for success, the former discovered that the ideal standards of American beauty did not entail traditional Black features.[156]

The Miss America pageant, reflective of the larger society, historically "rewarded the beauty of white bodies and disregarded the beauty of black bodies."[157] In fact, rule 7 of the Miss America bylaws prevented women of color from participating in the pageant.[158] No Black contestants were allowed to compete until 1970, and a Black winner was not crowned until 1984.[159] While Roller Derby did not have such overtly racist policies, no Black woman skater ever won the title Roller Derby Queen. This snub reflected voters', that is, fans', conscious and unconscious prejudices regarding beauty standards. When Joan Weston won the contest in February 1958, one fan summarized why she was elected queen: "Joanie personifies the lean, scrubbed look of the All-American beauty. She is tall and stately, and has the sense of humor the American male goes for."[160] Weston, a "big, beautiful blonde," personified the ideal, all-American woman with her white middle-class femininity, according to Roller Derby fans. A good portion of American women could never live up to these standards because of their skin color, hair texture, and physical features. The *Roller Derby News* staff writer Pat Farley determined that whether in "Roller Derby or otherwise, women the world over want to be feminine," but what went unacknowledged was that femininity was a privilege and "achievement only afforded to white women."[161] Even such inclusive sports such as Roller Derby were not free of the racism entrenched in American society.

While Black women were denied access to femininity and the status of lady, white women often "played" unaccustomed but assumed roles. Some white skaters engaged in what can be described as "parody[ing] a social reality" or "play[ing] at what they are not," in this case, middle-class ladies.[162] While the Roller Derby management worked hard to create an image of pretty, feminine women who simply happened to participate in a rough sport, in reality a majority of the skaters came from working-class families.[163] Many had quit high school and left home to skate. Like beauty contestants who "play into gender or play out race or play around with social class . . . [to participate] in [their] own construction as a hyperfeminine creation,"[164] these women were not necessarily the ladies that they or the management pretended they were. Some skaters were considered rough women who used language that "would make a longshoreman blush," but they were not the face of Roller Derby.[165] While their behavior on the track might be seen as entertaining or as part of the sport, it was downplayed when they were off the track, countered with images of them as faithful wives, dutiful mothers, or American beauties. Alan Ebert, a former journalist for *Roller Derby News* and a lifelong derby fan, stated, "You know there weren't too many women in Roller Derby that I would use the word 'lady.' A lot of them were very rough. They quit school at sixteen. They had foul mouths. . . . They were rough people, some of them, and others were not."[166] To counteract skaters' unladylike behavior on the track, it was important to maintain a façade of white middle-class womanhood. Thus, Ebert's interview with Gloria Mack, "(a Lady)," ends with the following: "As to Gloria's eventual goals: 'I don't mean to sound corny, or pull the All-American girl bit, but I want what I think every girl wants—my husband to be happy in his work, own my own home, raise a family and live a normal, everyday life. When you come right down to it, there really isn't much else that matters, is there?'"[167]

The last three decades of the twentieth century showed a slow but gradual expansion of beauty standards that included more women of color as the civil rights, Black Power, and women's movements fought against racial and gender discrimination. The "Black is Beautiful" campaign aided in public awareness of the exclusion of women of color and demonstrated the agency of Black women to embrace their own beauty versus the standards set by a white patriarchal system. Beauty contests from the 1930s through the 1960s, as represented by the Miss America pageants and the Roller Derby Queen contests, reflected and promoted the deeply entrenched ideals of a white heterosexual middle-class image of the American woman. Furthermore, a specific type of masculinity was put forth through the Roller Derby King contest, to counter male skaters' athletic association with female skaters, reassert their "hegemonic masculinity,"[168] and put them on par with other male athletes. The contests also indicated that even though women's roles were expanding, a woman's beauty was still the most important aspect of her femininity, and a crucial way to attract attention to her accomplishments. By highlighting the female skaters' beauty and the traditional masculine qualities of the male skaters, the "hegemonic masculinity" of the male skaters was restored.

4 | DIAPER DERBIES

I went to have [my son] Ricky, and it was like, okay, now we delivered, let's go home. So, I think the skating made me a stronger person.

MARY YOUPELLE MASSRO, MOTHER AND ROLLER DERBY SKATER

[My daughter] came first. . . . The advance man would make arrangements to have, you know, cribs in the room, and we took a babysitter with us that was one of the trainees.

BERT WALL, FATHER AND ROLLER DERBY SKATER

I was fortunate enough to always have my kids with me. And my wife [Dru Scott] worked her ass off to maintain the house, maintain those children, and maintain our marriage. And still perform every night.

BUDDY ATKINSON JR., FATHER AND ROLLER DERBY SKATER

Roller Derby provided an alternative sporting model for the athlete-mother, challenging dominant social norms that restricted women's attempts to combine their roles as wife, mother, and athlete. In many ways, it did the same for its men. Roller Derby not only accepted and supported athlete-mothers but also embraced families as a whole. A caption from a photograph in the 1952 Roller Derby yearbook illustrated this dual acceptance: "Three generations of Bogashes smile happily as Ma Bogash is awarded a cup symbolic of her election to the Roller Derby Hall of Fame. That's son Billy on the far left and Bill Bogash, Jr., standing in between mother and son."[1] Unlike most other sports for men, Roller Derby challenged dominant social norms for male athletes. Generally, male sports focused only on players' roles as athletes, while fatherhood was viewed as a separate event that occurred outside, and secondarily to, their professional athletic careers. Whereas the governing bodies of traditional female sports attempted to force mothers out, Roller Derby's management and publications highlighted the mothers in the sport's ranks as a way to soften the image of the stereotypical rough female derbyist. The same 1952 yearbook published an article and picture featuring the "children of the wheelers." "On the far left, taking a seat is young Buddy Atkinson," proclaimed the author, "and sitting on his lap is the very cute Pamela Reynolds who looks like she will be as good looking as her mother Mary Gardner."[2] While certainly not perfect, and undoubtedly influenced by heteronormative cultural expectations prevalent in the larger society, the Seltzers' Roller Derby managed over time to create a sport that embraced, valued, and promoted mother-athletes while highlighting the important parental role played by their male athletes. The athletes were not forced to choose between the competing identities of parent and athlete, and children of the skaters were included as part of the Roller Derby family.

A FAMILY AFFAIR

From the outset, Roller Derby was a family affair. Members of the Seltzer clan were involved in Roller Derby management positions and officiating capacities, and were employed by the Roller Derby Skate Company. Created by Leo Seltzer and run by his brother Oscar, the skate company sold rink and outdoor skates and advertised its products in all the Roller Derby publications.[3] Leo's daughter Gloria was managing Roller Derby's front offices by the late 1940s, and her husband, Ken Gurian, worked for his father-in-law as a referee and in other management capacities.[4] In the mid-1950s, Leo's son Jerry worked as a salesman for the skate company before taking a management position in Roller Derby. When Leo retired, in 1959, after decades of weathering the ups and downs of the sport he created and loved, his son decided to take over the enterprise.

As discussed in chapter 1, Roller Derby's first real superstars and gate attractions were a family affair. A mother-son skating duo was largely responsible for attracting women's interest in the sport, particularly housewives and middle-aged to elderly women. These women were

FIGURE 4.1. *Three generations of the Bogashes: Billy Jr., Bill, and Ma Bogash, 1950. Courtesy of Gary Powers and the National Roller Derby Hall of Fame and Museum.*

drawn to the sport through the efforts of the fortysomething diabetic housewife determined to excel at Roller Derby. Josephine "Ma" Bogash became a huge hit with audiences and a mother hen to younger female skaters. As Mary Youpelle recalled, "She kind of looked out for the girls."[5] Women made up at least half the fan base throughout the history of the sport. This was due to the pioneering efforts of such unique, driven, and competitive women as Ma Bogash, who demonstrated that women, even aging mothers, could succeed at the sport.[6]

Many siblings joined Roller Derby together or followed in the footsteps of siblings who skated. Pairs of skating brothers included the talented Buddy Atkinson Sr. and Tommy Atkinson, Johnny and Paul Milane, Ken and Doug Monte, and Bob and Don Lewis. Roller Derby's sister duos counted such skaters as Annis "Big Red" and Sheila Jensen among its ranks. Some families had more than two siblings skating in the derby—for instance, Monta Jean, Georgeanna, and Buddy Kemp. The Gardner family had four sibling skaters: Lewis ("Punky"), Billy, Helen, and Mary.

The unique nature of the co-ed sport meant that two sorts of relationships generally developed between male and female skaters who were not biologically related. Because so much time was spent living in close quarters and traveling long distances, skaters often viewed one another as devoted family members. One might take on the traditional responsibilities of a protective big brother or a spunky little sister, at least off the track. Mary Lou Palermo recalled having this sort of relationship with the men: "The boys that we skated with, they were like big brothers."[7] Russ "Rosie" Baker explained how the men looked after the female skaters as if they were their sisters: "A girl couldn't take a breath without our asking, 'Where are you going?'"[8] During her first year of skating, Gerry Murray observed one form of this protective behavior when a male skater physically abused his wife, who was also a skater: "He used to beat her up all the time, and then the guys would take him and beat him up to try to keep him away from his wife."[9] This example highlights the more traditional male-protector role within the Roller Derby family.

Most skaters underscored this idea of Roller Derby as one big family, for better or worse. Rosie Baker explained, "We lived together, slept together, ate together, skated together, fought together."[10] Loretta Behrens described the men and women as helpmates and siblings: "The guys were always there to help the girls, you know. We always called each other brothers and sisters. We were family."[11] Mary Youpelle corroborated this experience: "Everybody knew everybody and were friendly and it was just, when you put that uniform on, you were on another team and you were out there to do your best and to have your team win."[12]

Yet with male and female skaters spending so much time together, it was only natural that romantic feelings often surfaced. Bobbie Johnstone equated dating someone outside Roller Derby for two years to dating someone for just a few months inside the derby: "In those days in Roller Derby, you got to know someone. . . . You saw each other at breakfast, trained with each other all day, you know."[13] Plus, because of their grueling schedules, the skaters "didn't really have time to go out and get acquainted with strangers," as Mary Youpelle noted.[14] Still, during the early years of the sport, Leo Seltzer attempted to discourage skaters from becoming romantically involved with each other. It was made very clear that dating within their ranks was forbidden—absolutely no "hanky-panky."[15] "When I first started," Gerry Murray recalled, "a boy and a girl weren't even allowed to talk because they did not want, they called it fraternization then, and they didn't want anybody to get serious and then get married, and the woman would have a baby and they'd lose a woman. . . . They kept a good eye on you too."[16] If skaters were caught, as Murray further explained, "why, they would just not stand for that. Anything at all, there was no second chance—you went home right away."[17]

Gene Vizena and Joe Nygra were prevented by Roller Derby's management from cohabitating for the first ten days of their marriage because of Seltzer's strict rules. While it seems ridiculous that married couples were not allowed to sleep together, from Seltzer's perspective, it was a rational business decision. As Vizena and Nygra showed, when married couples were allowed to live together, particularly in the era before birth control pills, it was highly likely the woman would become pregnant, and then the derby would lose an athlete, at least temporarily. Vizena laughingly recalled, "It's a good thing we were separated for the first ten days because . . . we didn't get started until the next month. We were married . . . ten months and three days and I had my first child."[18] Some skaters went so far as to marry on the sly and told others about it only later, in an attempt to hide their relationship from the management, for the fear that they would be separated and sent to different teams, which occasionally happened.[19] Once management heard that Rosie Baker and Annis Jensen had developed romantic feelings for each other, it transferred them to different skating units to keep them apart. According to Frank Deford, "Once, moving from unit to unit, Annis had to skate ninety straight days" to prevent her from coming in contact with Baker.[20]

The Roller Derby management's attitude toward skaters' romantic lives may have seemed paternalistic or worse, but such relationships posed unique problems. The difficulty of the derby way of life made it challenging to retain talented skaters, and Leo Seltzer could not risk civilians attempting to convince skaters to settle down to a more conventional and stable routine. As Bobbie Mateer explained, "You travel a lot . . . and you know, it's pretty hard to have a boyfriend in New York and you're all over the country."[21] Skaters were discouraged from dating nonskaters, so they had little choice but to either date internally or uphold a celibate (and wholly unrealistic) lifestyle. Young men and women traveling together across the country, partaking in exciting new adventures, were unlikely to remain chaste. Seltzer ultimately realized that intra-derby relationships were the lesser of two evils, later admitting that "he actually encouraged Derby marriages as a way of discouraging 'civilian' dating and marriage."[22] A clip of Roller Derby footage from the late 1940s or early 1950s encouraging women to join the sport indicates Seltzer's change of heart: the announcer proclaimed, "If there's a wedding ring on your mind, there's a men's team. With the Roller Derby, a girl has a good chance of meeting the right guy."[23]

Relationships between skaters—heterosexual ones at least—were a unique feature of the co-ed sport. Once intra-derby relationships were more accepted, it became quite common for skaters to date other members of their team or members of opposing teams. These relationships raised all sorts of questions and many potential problems never experienced in other sports. For instance, what if a man and a woman on different teams began dating and wanted to be transferred to the same team? What if they then broke up? How would management handle skaters' requests based on their love lives? Most professional sports organizations never had to deal with these types of issues. As Jerry Seltzer lamented, "How many other general managers in athletics have to worry about breaking up families when you trade someone?"[24]

In the approximately forty-year history of Roller Derby, nearly every relationship dynamic and scenario undoubtedly played out, and some were more complicated than others. Ultimately, though, all the intra-derby dating and intermarriage between skaters tied them together in even more intimate ways than merely as teammates. They understood being dog-tired and sore after a rough game. They understood the physical rigors of skating for hours on end during daily training sessions, and they understood the lure of an arena full of fans cheering them on, which spurred them to travel to yet another city under the cover of night. The famous skater Ann Calvello explained, "If two people are going together in Derby, marriage would be very good. It would be, because they know what the job is, how it is with traveling. They understand what they have to do and everything."[25] Bobbie Mateer concurred: "Somebody's in your corner. You travel a lot and, you know, have the same interests, the same hours."[26]

The Roller Derby schedule was grueling, and became complicated as it evolved over the course of the sport. It undoubtedly affected Roller

Derby relationships as well as the families of skaters. The schedule went through three phases in Roller Derby's history. The barnstorming years lasted from the founding of the sport until the postwar period, wherein Roller Derby traveled across the country and put down temporary roots in one location for three to six weeks at a time. Management operated out of the Chicago area and northern Indiana. In the second phase, starting in the late 1940s, Roller Derby's base of operations shifted to New York City, where Seltzer had secured a television contract to broadcast approximately twelve hours of Roller Derby a week, every week, with no off-season. Teams were established in cities across the country; they played against visiting opponents and also traveled to games in other cities. Teams were on the road frequently, and as one season came to a close, the next one started up: there was no down time.

The last phase began when Seltzer relocated the base of operations to the West Coast and his son took over in the late 1950s. Jerry Seltzer established a home season that was played up and down the Bay Area of California from April to September.[27] The off-season tour began in January, and skaters would crisscross the country seemingly haphazardly, covering, at times, fifty-five cities in sixty-two days.[28] The scheduling during any phase was unconducive to dating, marriage, or family life in a traditional sense.

Although having both male and female teammates provided a ready dating pool for those seeking a significant other, derby politics and logistics could complicate relationships. One of the longest-lasting couples in Roller Derby, Bert Wall and Bobbie Mateer, who were married for over sixty years, had to request transfers in order to be together in the beginning. Mateer met Wall when her team, the New York Chiefs, traveled to Chicago to play Wall's team, the Chicago Westerners, in early April 1950.[29] The two developed an interest in each other right away, but they did not begin dating until the Westerners traveled to New York City in June of that same year for the playoff series. The couple went to a matinee movie, and according to Mateer, "We went out and that was it."[30] After the playoffs drew to a close, the couple faced the difficulties of maintaining a long-distance relationship. "Upon occasion, we'd skate opposite one another and we'd see each other and we'd write letters and phone calls and so forth," explained Mateer. She finally requested a transfer to the Westerners. To be transferred, however, spots on the team had to be open. Wall's team was skating in California and Mateer was skating in Asbury Park, New Jersey, when she got word of the transfer. A couple of female members of the Westerners had gotten injured, so Mateer and another skater, Loretta Behrens, were transferred to the Westerners.[31]

Many skaters married other skaters and settled down into monogamous relationships, but this lifestyle proved exceptionally difficult to maintain in the 1930s and 1940s. Logistics prevented newly married skaters from living together: all skaters lived at the venue where they skated, and co-ed quarters were nonexistent.[32] Gerry Murray recalled sharing a room with her married teammate Monta Jean Kemp while their husbands, Gene Gammon and Carl Payne, respectively, were required to stay in the men's quarters.[33] Once Roller Derby teams began staying in hotels rather than in the arenas where they played, cohabitation became easier, and couples were afforded a measure of privacy.

Personal problems between skating spouses sometimes caused tensions during a game. Carol Meyer recalled her husband, Tony Roman, getting on her when other skaters were pushing her around on the track. "Well, sometimes we'd get into little tiffs about certain things. You know, he'd say, 'Don't let her do that to you.'"[34] Occasionally, Roman could not help getting involved in matters pertaining to Meyer. A week before their wedding, in 1965, Meyer got into a fight with another skater during a game and received twenty stitches as an engagement present. Roman was unhappy with how the referee had handled his fiancée's situation. Meyer recalled, "Tony had the biggest fight with the referee. . . . He didn't like the way he talked to me," adding, "One thing you don't do is get a short little Italian man mad." While Meyer ended up with stitches and Roman got a black eye, the referee caught the brunt of it, as Meyer noted: Tony "apologized for it, but I don't think anybody saw the little madman and what he did to [the referee.]"[35] Both men later apologized for letting their tempers get the best of them, but the tussle showed that personal feelings often spilled onto the track.

Reflecting postwar marital trends, many skaters married young, but in a divergence from those trends, they divorced and remarried within the ranks of their derby peers.[36] Less restrictive working-class mores, the carefree life of young skaters out from under the watchful eyes of their parents, and the rise of the sexual revolution of the 1960s influenced skaters' personal lives.[37] Many Roller Derby skaters were described as maintaining a "very sexual life."[38] Alan Ebert, a *Roller Derby News* journalist and Roller Derby publicity director, explained, "I mean, there was a lot of bed-hopping. I'm sure the younger people [today] would be very surprised to learn there was sex in the fifties and sixties. And a lot of it!"[39] It became a sort of joke among the Roller Derby crowd that when a new young male skater joined, an "older woman would grab him."[40] Ken Monte, who joined Roller Derby at age eighteen, admitted to having an affair with the star skater Midge "Toughie" Brasuhn, who was already in her mid-twenties and married to the referee Bill Golba.[41] Monte recalled, "Actually, I broke up her marriage. I was the third party." After Brasuhn and Golba divorced, Monte and Brasuhn married, and Monte helped raise her and Golba's one-year-old son.[42]

It was not uncommon for there to be a significant age difference between derby spouses, often with the female being older. For instance, Mary Youpelle was ten years older than her second husband, Russ Massro; Toughie Brasuhn was five years older than Ken Monte; Bert Wall was ten years older than Bobbie Mateer; and Ann Calvello was fifteen years older than her on-again, off-again boyfriend, the skater Eddie Krebs.[43] When Bert first met Bobbie, she was a seventeen-year-old still wearing her "high school pleated skirt and angora sweater and saddle shoes."[44] He was immediately interested in Bobbie, but because of their age difference, he gave her a nickel and told her that when she was "old enough to date boys, to give him a call."[45] According to Bobbie, his wife of the past six decades, "He never got his nickel back."[46]

Once the Roller Derby management accepted intra-derby marriages, in the 1950s, it made a concerted effort not to separate spouses. Jerry Seltzer stated, "Now one thing we never did, is put a husband and wife on a different team. It was just kind of a rule they had to be on the same team."[47] But sometimes couples had such bad breakups that management had to accommodate skaters' requests for transfers in order to keep the peace and avoid internal conflicts. This was a risk that skaters took when dating other skaters. If a couple broke up, it was very difficult not to run into an ex.[48] Charlie O'Connell and Ann Calvello, two top stars, had a "stormy romance" and an even stormier breakup, which resulted in "some bitter memories."[49] Jerry Seltzer recalled, "Charlie and Ann were very uncomfortable with each other after—afterwards, you know. . . . They rarely skated on the same team afterwards because of that. And so that's something we had to pay attention to, the personality clash."[50]

DERBY PREGNANCIES

Pregnancy disrupted the athletic careers of mothers in ways that it did not fathers. Some skaters did not dwell on how pregnancy might influence their careers. "I don't know if I even thought about whether I wanted to come back skating," Bobbie Mateer explained. "It wasn't an issue at the time. I didn't give it a whole lot of thought."[51] Loretta Behrens, conversely, was fully aware of the disruption that children would cause to her skating career: "Well, being in the exposure of other skaters and couples that were married and watching them raise their children on the road, that was not something I was looking forward to doing."[52] Skaters who were parents "lived a different kind of life."[53] Behrens was not ready to embark on a lifestyle that included skating late at night, traveling from city to city while worrying about the comfort of your children, hunting down babysitters while you skated, and forgoing personal time, as she made clear: "That's one of the reasons that until I really had settled in my mind that I was ready to settle down, I wasn't even interested."[54] After she married, Behrens insisted that the only thing that would tie her down was pregnancy. Four months later, she found out she was pregnant, and only six weeks after giving birth to her first child, she became pregnant again. It was two years before Behrens was able to return to the skating world.[55]

For obvious reasons, pregnancy and motherhood had dramatic effects on female athletes' lives because of the physical nature of their athletic pursuits. At the same time, many of the issues facing female athletes who became pregnant or mothers can be situated in the larger history of women's labor throughout US history, particularly in the mid-twentieth century. During this time, motherhood and homemaking served "as expressions of U.S. values of home, family, and freedom," and women were expected to quit their jobs, or were fired, when they became pregnant.[56] Women were inundated with idealized images of the happy housewife and doting mother who cleaned, cooked, and cared for her family with a smile plastered on her face. Women in the 1950s and 1960s, as Susan J. Douglas and Meredith Michaels explain, were "supposed to internalize this ideal, to live it and believe it."[57] This ideal was just that, however—an ideal.[58] What made this paragon and its celebration dangerous was that it hid the "reality that more and more women worked outside of the home for wages. In no other era were women's roles in the wage economy so hidden by the image of a stay-at-home mom and primary consumer of the family's food, clothes, and other domestic necessities."[59]

Critical statistics about women in the workforce in the 1950s undercut this image of domesticity that was bombarding women. As Douglas and Michaels highlight, "By 1955, there were more women with jobs than at any point in the nation's previous history and an increasing number of these were women with young children. By 1960, 40 percent of women were in the workforce. Many of these were white middle-class women, and almost half were mothers of school-age children."[60] Twenty percent of these workingwomen had children under the age of six. These figures were the result of steady growth over the previous decade: "The ranks of professional women grew by more than 40 percent during the 1950s, faster than any other category except clerical work. The figures were even higher for African American women."[61] Approximately 6.6 million mothers were in the workforce by 1960, an increase of 400 percent from 1954.[62] Despite the stereotypes portrayed on television or in newspapers and magazines, women of all sorts were leaving the home to work.

Female Roller Derby skaters grappled with the near impossibility of trying to reflect some version of ideal womanhood, and thus be accepted by the same media that promoted it, even as their reality mirrored workingwomen's lives and struggles. The idealized image of the happy housewife and mother further harmed female athletes by allowing American society to devalue their labor and underpay them as they attempted to balance a host of roles. Shona M. Thompson posits that in the twentieth century, "women's responsibility for domestic labor and child care constrains their full participation in sport, while at the same time the labor they do in these realms facilitates the participation of others."[63] Looking across women's sports in this era, the statement is by and large true women gave up any hope of athletic dreams when they married and had children, while the labor they did by caring for their children, husbands, and homes allowed men to pursue sports as professionals or amateurs. Roller Derby, by contrast, at least allowed women the space to combine their roles and not have to give up the sport entirely because of motherhood. That did not mean, though, that they did not have to consider how the media would judge them for pushing against the ideal or how adverse coverage would affect their personal lives. Thus, pregnancy and motherhood, while not necessarily career killers, were something to take seriously for Roller Derby skaters and management.

For mid-twentieth-century Roller Derby skaters, birth control was not readily accessible. "Birth control was not [around] in those days!" Bobbie Mateer explained.[64] To Gerry Murray, however, it seemed as if most couples had kids at times when they were not skating or waited to have children until they were older, since "you wouldn't keep skating if you were pregnant."[65] Realizing that there were many married skating couples, she explained, "For all I know, maybe they used some kind of protection."[66] This was a possibility, since the federal government over-turned the Comstock Law in 1936, but the possibility was slim.[67] The Comstock Law, passed by Congress in 1873, had prohibited the sending of any materials deemed obscene through the US mail. Birth control products as well as all advertising related to them were considered obscene, and violation of the Comstock Law was a federal crime. Even after the law's repeal, over half of the states continued to ban the advertisement of contraception, along with contraception itself. The birth control pill was approved by the FDA in 1960, but even then access was often limited to married couples.[68]

An abortion was even more difficult to obtain than birth control. In fact, it was illegal. If a married female skater became pregnant, she could at least rely on her husband for moral and financial support. This was a luxury single women did not have. Apparently, none of the single women who skated with Roller Derby ever had a child out of wedlock, yet many engaged in sexual relationships, which suggests that they were using some sort of birth control. More likely, as historical tradition suggests, these skaters tapped into informal networks of knowledgeable and trusted women to help them deal with sexual and reproductive problems.[69] According to Alan Ebert, a skater protocol was established to help any single woman who accidentally got pregnant: "If a girl got pregnant and wanted to have an abortion, which was illegal then, the other girls would conspire to do a pileup."[70] A pileup occurred when all the female skaters on the track crashed into one another and ended up in a large heap, which, as Ebert noted, "looks extremely dangerous."[71] Ebert explained why they resorted to such drastic measures: "It was the only way they could fool management when a girl had to take some time off to get an abortion. They would say that she hurt her leg or she did this in the pileup or her spleen was hurt—wasn't the case at all! She was flying off to Puerto Rico or wherever they went, and to have the abortion."[72]

Most skaters continued skating until about their third month of pregnancy before taking a leave of absence or quitting the sport altogether. Pregnant skaters were in such good physical shape that "they could skate a lot longer than other people might have thought they could."[73] Mary Youpelle did not have her first child until she was in her late thirties, but had very easy pregnancies, which she attributed to her skating career. "I skated—I was three and a half months pregnant with both boys and I felt absolutely wonderful," she recalled. She had a little trouble delivering her firstborn, but the delivery of her second child went very smoothly: "When it came time for delivery, I went to the hospital and—Rusty was a little—he was my oldest. He was a little difficult because by now I'm thirty-seven years old. . . . But when it came time for Ricky. . . . It was like, okay, now we delivered, let's go home. So, I think the skating made me a stronger person. Physically."[74] Youpelle stated that most skaters had very healthy pregnancies and relatively easy deliveries, which was a source of pride among the Roller Derby personnel.[75] She recalled, "I don't know of any of our girls that had any problems with their pregnancies. I think they were all healthy right up until they delivered their children."[76] Ann Calvello bragged that she was in the delivery room at seven forty-five and out by eight.[77]

Many of the women insisted that skating and playing Roller Derby eased the labor process, but childbirth also provided a "corollary advantage" to skaters.[78] Throughout their derby careers, many female skaters damaged their coccyxes (tailbones) through repeated falls on their backsides. The frequent impact essentially pushed the coccyx inward, which could be immensely painful. According to interviews with skaters conducted by Frank Deford, "This is where the childbirth comes in. The story is that when a Roller Derby skater has a baby, the process of delivering somehow straightens the coccyx back out again."[79] While no scientific studies have been conducted to show that Roller Derby made pregnancies or labor easier, it undoubtedly improved the physical shape and overall health of the women, which was systemically beneficial.

RAISING CHILDREN AROUND THE DERBY

Marriage and children were a common facet of derby life, whether skaters were married to other skaters or "civilians." "Everybody had children once they got married," explained Mary Youpelle. "That was kind of expected."[80] The question of how to raise children around Roller Derby affected everyone associated with the Seltzer organization. The Seltzer family was based in Portland, Oregon, where Leo's first wife, Rose, and their two children, Gloria and Gerald (Jerry), lived. Jerry loved his father and enjoyed spending time with him, but because the derby traveled nonstop in its early years, Jerry generally saw his father only during the holidays or on special occasions like birthdays. But in the summer, when Roller Derby was booked on the West Coast, he had more access to his dad. Jerry explained, "At that time, it was like a twenty-eight-day thing. I think it was twenty-eight days in Los Angeles and maybe three weeks in San Francisco. And there'd be five games a week. . . . We'd go down and live in Santa Monica . . . and go to the Pan-Pacific Auditorium at night . . . and all the Hollywood stars would come out."[81] Once the summer series were over, the Seltzer clan, minus Leo and his brother Oscar, would head back to Portland. Rose relied on their larger family network, which included both sets of parents and other relatives, for support while her husband was gone.[82]

When Jerry was about ten years old, his mother passed away from cancer. As the sole parent responsible for Jerry and Gloria, Leo relocated the family to Chicago, where Roller Derby was headquartered. Jerry grew up idolizing famous Roller Derby skaters and was embraced by the larger Roller Derby family: "These were my childhood heroes, my DiMaggios, Red Granges, Hank Luisettis. And many were the great women athletes. Of course they mothered me, and I will never forget their affection towards me."[83]

Skaters had three realistic options for raising children. The first was to bring them up around Roller Derby and take them on the road when the team traveled. The second was to quit the derby, at least the traveling portion of it, and settle down in one place. With this option, skaters could occasionally skate on home teams that did not travel or could skate when Roller Derby played in their city. The third was to let the children be raised by a spouse or by close relatives, at least while the team was out on the road. Some skaters combined these options or used them at different points in their careers.

Gerry Murray and Bobbie Mateer opted to take their children with them on the road.[84] Murray and her first husband, Paul Milane, had their son, Michael, in early November 1942 in a hospital in Milwaukee.[85] At the time of Mike's birth, neither Milane nor Murray was skating with the Roller Derby, both having fallen out with management. The couple's marriage ended shortly thereafter, and Murray decided to return to the derby, taking her thirteen-month-old son with her.[86] Murray remarried a few years later, to the skater Gene Gammon, who had previously been married to the derby skater Tillie Mudri. Murray and Mudri had a young child but divorced shortly after the birth. Gammon returned to Roller Derby, where he met and then married Murray in 1948.[87] Gammon helped raise Mike, who eventually adopted his stepfather's last name, becoming Mike Gammon.

As a young boy, Mike was always with Murray, even while she was practicing. She recalled, "I took care of him all the time. He was never out of my sight!"[88] The large banked Masonite oval track served as a

FIGURE 4.2. *The Gammons: Gene, Gerry (Murray), and Mike, 1949. Courtesy of Gary Powers and the National Roller Derby Hall of Fame and Museum.*

playground for Mike, who had his own uniform, sewn by his mother, and a pair of customized skates when he was just a year old. Murray recalled the details: "Jack Wilson made him some skates. . . . I got pictures with him on [them,] trying to stand up and everything. Jack Wilson is kind of holdin' him, and then we got pictures of him by himself. He's thirteen months old when we put the skates on him!"[89]

For skaters like Murray, Roller Derby provided the benefit of a built-in network for child care during a game. Skaters in training often got paid to watch the children of veteran skaters. Murray recalled, "The

only time somebody took care of him was when we had new kids training . . . and they would take care of the kids, like Monta Jean [Kemp's]
son, mine, and they would take care of them. At nine o'clock, they'd put
them in bed."[90] When Bobbie Mateer was a new skater, she babysat for
Helen Gardner and Billy Bogash's oldest daughter, Pam.[91] A few years
later, after she and her husband, Bert Wall, had their daughter Debra,
they used the same skater-babysitting arrangement by having Margie
Laszlo, a trainee, babysit for them.[92] If new skaters were not available or
were not on the road with the team, Roller Derby advance men would
arrange for a local agency to provide babysitters for derby parents when
they were in a new town. "A babysitter would be all set up when we got
into town, and so forth," Mateer explained.[93] The parents could then
focus on the upcoming game or series instead of having to worry about
finding child care.

Mateer and Wall decided they would continue skating until their
daughter entered school, so she went on the road with them as a baby
and toddler. This was not always an easy arrangement, even with babysitters available. Roller Derby used to travel from city to city by bus,
but Mateer recalled that "the bus could get pretty rowdy sometimes,"
so they would on occasion rent a car.[94] "We tried to make it as normal
a life as could be [while] traveling on the road," explained Mateer. To
that end, Roller Derby provided children with their own rooms while
on tour. Skaters generally shared a room, but that was not feasible if they
had little kids, since no one wanted to wake up the children when return-
ing to the hotel late at night after a match.[95] And as every parent knows,
traveling with children means traveling with a lot of child-related stuff.
Mateer's husband Bert was responsible for making sure their hotel room
was always equipped with a stroller and a crib.[96]

Mary Lou Palermo left Roller Derby in 1953 when she married a
nonskater. The couple had two daughters, a mere sixteen months apart,
but Palermo's marriage did not last. She had earned a good living with
the derby and knew she could support her girls as a single mother if she
returned to skating.[97] She would take her daughters with her on the road
from June through September and then would return to Chicago, their
permanent residence, once the school year began again.

Palermo considered the time spent skating and traveling with her
daughters "really special."[98] She has a lot of fond and funny memories
of taking them on the road as little girls, since whether growing up in
a Chicago suburb or on the road with Roller Derby, kids will be kids.
Once when Palermo was skating in Hawaii, she rented an apartment

on the same street as the arena and hired a babysitter to watch the girls while she skated. While she was at the arena, she laughingly explained, "[The girls] came in, and I said, 'What are you doing here?' Allison said, 'Stacy fired the babysitter.' Stacy was younger than Allison! . . . They fired the babysitter. I said, 'Oh why—these kids!'"[99] When Palermo traveled on short weekend trips for Roller Derby, she took her daughters with her on the team bus: "After the race—they had pillows and that in the glove compartment in the bus, and that's where them and their dog, they'd sleep up there until we'd, you know, pull up to a truck stop or someplace to get something to eat, and here's these two little kids with all these grownups, you know."[100]

Like Palermo, Cliff Butler married a nonskater and had to juggle his career with marriage and child rearing. Married at just eighteen, Butler found himself handling adult responsibilities while still a teenager. He admitted that it was a lot to deal with: "I got married too young, but I got married. . . . Now here I am out there skating and doing this man's job, and I thought I was one, but [I] was still a kid."[101] He met his wife, Evelyn, early in his time with Roller Derby: he was fifteen years old when he started skating and when they met. Evelyn had been the friend of a female skater, and she started training, although she did not end up joining the derby. The couple had their oldest son, Vincent, in 1968, followed by a second son, Justin, in 1971. When Butler skated locally in California, his wife and his mother would bring the children to every game, but he also skated on the road from four to six months a year. Butler believed that Jerry Seltzer was very accommodating to the needs of his skaters' families: "What Seltzer used to do was if you were married, he would fly your wife out to you once a month and she would travel around with you . . . and then they would send her back home, so that made it kind of neat." Sometimes his oldest son would make the trip, too. Butler recalled a fond memory of a winter trip to the Midwest: "I remember almost losing Vincent in the snow in Ohio. He'd never seen snow, and he was crawling through a little hole up underneath the snowbank [near] the hotel . . . and he got in there somehow, and I had to find him."[102]

Mary Youpelle and her husband, Russ Massro, took their children with them on the road when the kids were young, and then were able to arrange their schedules to avoid conflict with the school calendar when the kids grew up. She recalled, "We took them everywhere we went."[103] But the couple did not travel regularly when the boys were in school. Instead, they skated for five years straight in Los Angeles. "So that worked out great for us, because the boys went to school and we could skate at night," Youpelle explained. Massro also owned several liquor stores and car lots, and he would oversee these businesses during the day while Youpelle was home with their children. She had her children fed, bathed, and ready for bed by the time a babysitter arrived on the evenings when she and Russ had a game to skate.

Some skaters traveled with their children while they were young, as Youpelle and Massro did, but then quit Roller Derby once they entered school.[104] This was the case with Mary Lou Palermo, who gave up the sport for her girls. She explained, "Well, I think the girls got too old. They wanted to stay home to be with their friends, too. So I said, 'Okay—we will stop.'"[105] Palermo skated her last game in 1967 in Houston—coincidentally, the same city where she skated her first game.[106]

Neither quitting the sport nor taking their children on the road was a viable option for some of the women and their families. Sometimes they chose to leave their children with close family members—and sometimes circumstances forced their hand. Carol Meyer and her husband did not give up skating after they had their first child, but they also did not want to subject their infant to the rigors of life on the road. So when their daughter, Dina, was a baby and then a toddler, Meyer and Roman left her at home with Roman's mother from September until around Thanksgiving. Once she was potty trained, they took her on road trips with them. "She was traveling with us until she was about four years old," recalled Meyer. When Dina started school, they again quit taking her on the road, but they also curtailed their travel when possible. They remained at home with her in the summertime.[107]

A more permanent version of this route was taken by Ann Calvello, one of the most famous skaters in Roller Derby. Calvello joined the derby in August 1949 as a young woman just a couple years out of high school. Although she later became famous for her role as a notorious red-shirt skater with wild hair and even wilder antics, the first few years of her seven-decade career were spent skating with home teams.[108] Soon after joining Roller Derby, she fell madly in love with a derby referee named Roy Langley. The two married in 1952, and their daughter, Teri Ann, was born the following year. Calvello wanted to spend the rest of her life with her husband, but their relationship turned abusive.[109]

Calvello had witnessed her parents' abusive relationship as a young girl, which undoubtedly affected her childhood. Although aware of the dangers of this type of relationship, she didn't see them at first, as she later stated: "When anyone gets married and [is] in love and everything,

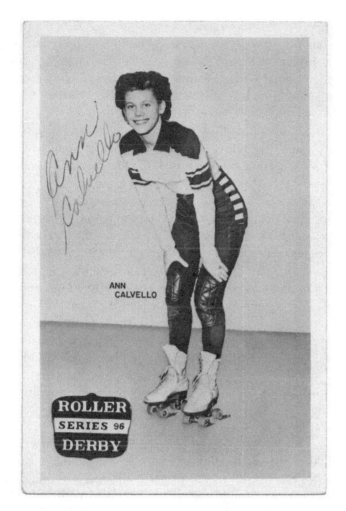

FIGURE 4.3. *Ann Calvello on a Roller Derby postcard, 1952. Courtesy of Gary Powers and the National Roller Derby Hall of Fame and Museum.*

you don't know you're going to be in an abusive relationship."[110] According to Gloria "Miffy" Mifsud, a former skater, neighbor, and friend of Calvello's, Calvello was "simply crazy" about her husband, but he had a drinking problem. He became physical after drinking to excess. Despite her love for her husband and their having a daughter together, Calvello found it increasingly difficult to live in that explosive environment.[111]

The breaking point occurred when Teri was two years old. On a road trip, Calvello was chatting with two gay male friends who were her pregame hairdressers. Calvello's husband got so jealous that he attempted to go after the men, but then turned his fury on his wife. Langley allegedly punched Calvello in the stomach and "was just out of control."[112] Calvello realized she could not stay with him: "I'm not going to do it. I'm not going to be beat up," she told herself.[113] Fearing for her life, she made an immediate decision about what to do next: she grabbed her daughter, the ironing board, and the crib, and left. She stated, "He would've killed me."[114] Even decades after the crumbling of her marriage, she cried as she lamented the loss of the life she could have had and what she and her husband could have been together.[115]

Going it alone forced her to make some hard decisions. One of those included giving up her daughter. When Teri was young, Calvello believed that she could not raise Teri on her Roller Derby salary.[116] Her limited finances allowed her to support herself, but not a family. Calvello had been skating since she was nineteen and had no other real job skills.[117] Her parents would not take her in, so she turned to Langley's family: she left Teri to be raised by her husband's mother and grandmother. Calvello felt as if she was abandoning Teri, but also believed it was something she had to do, for both of their sakes.[118] While she did not vilify her mother for leaving her, Teri questioned her mother's motives: "My personal feeling is that she just wanted to skate and that's what she did."[119] She believed that was simply the choice her mother made.[120]

Around the time Teri was fifteen, she began spending more time with her mother, and by the age of seventeen, she lived with her in an apartment in San Francisco. Despite not raising her daughter as a young child, Calvello considered herself to be motherly: "I remember as a kid going [to Golden Gate Park] to the playground and everything, and all of a sudden I have my daughter and I can take her to the same playground, and I got like eleven nieces and nephews and, believe it or not, I'm very domestic. I don't want to ruin my image, you know, with the fans."[121] She believed in what she called "old-fashioned" manners and bringing her daughter up "right," which perhaps helps explain why she gave her daughter up; she may have thought she could not provide her with that type of upbringing. When she did have her daughter with her as a teen, she tried to instill these important values. "I still say please and thank you, and respect the elders," she explained in the early 1970s. "In fact, my daughter has her boyfriends, and when they call I won't let them talk to her until they say can I please talk to her, and thank you, cause that's the way I was brought up and still do."[122]

Like any concerned parent, Calvello wanted the best for her daughter. "Really, the only reason I go on the road now is to make sure my daughter gets her education," she explained around 1970. "She's a senior in high school now, and I'd like to put her through college. I'd like her to do whatever she thinks she's gonna do the best at . . . I'm not bragging or anything, but she's a beautiful girl, got a beautiful figure, a wonderful personality."[123] Calvello was even open to her daughter becoming a skater, but she wanted to make sure she did it on her own terms. "She gets a kick out of skating now and then. . . . But she's not going to do anything till she graduates from high school. Then it's up to her. She likes skating, but she's very independent, like I am. She's a Leo, too, and she says, 'Mom, I don't wanna live on your name. I wanna go out on my own.' Some skaters' kids, they want their parents' names and everything. And some don't."[124] She explained, "If she wants to she can go in it. But if she does, she'll go in as Teri Langley. She comes right out and tells me, and I admire her for it."[125]

Despite Calvello's Roller Derby fame, her career both helped and hurt her relationship with her daughter. Whether Calvello was unable to financially provide for her daughter by herself or whether she was forced to make a choice between her career and her family is still uncertain. Her situation exemplifies the difficult choices that athlete-mothers faced. Athlete-parents often had to choose between being present parents or zealously pursuing their athletic careers. Those who attempted to combine both faced the difficult reality of raising a family on the road.

DIAPER DERBIES

The children who grew up in the Roller Derby family tended to have unconventional childhoods. They could wake up in Los Angeles and go to sleep in Texas. Many of the parents tried to provide as stable and normal a childhood as possible, but since their children traveled with them across the country and spent their youths growing up around skating arenas, that goal was not always attainable. Many of the parents tried to incorporate normal activities for their children wherever they were skating. "We'd go to parks, you know, in cities. We'd go visit whatever attractions were in [the towns] . . . the zoo or the circuses, or whatever you take kids to do," explained Bobbi Mateer.[126]

Like Mary Youpelle and Mary Lou Palermo, some skaters did not travel from September to May so that their children could attend school uninterrupted.[127] Others completed their schooling on the road with tutors or attended private schools paid for by Roller Derby to accommodate the parents' hectic schedules. Bobbie Mateer was a sixteen-year-old junior in high school when she joined Roller Derby, with her parents' permission. The derby paid for a tutor to help Mateer keep up with her studies and finish high school. She worked with the tutor twice a week and graduated on time with her class a year after joining the derby.[128]

Mike Gammon's entire childhood was spent around Roller Derby. He began skating at age three and turned professional at fifteen. He was the son of the star skaters Gerry Murray and Gene Gammon, and Roller Derby paid for him to attend a private school in Westchester County, New York, when his parents were with the New York Chiefs.[129] And when Murray was transferred to the San Diego team, the derby paid for Mike to attend a private school there.[130] Later in life, his mother asked him, "Did you miss having a normal life as a kid, even going to school?" Mike replied, "No, Ma. It was all right. I enjoyed it."[131] Mike later stated, "I think I had everything that a kid growing up needs, and then some. I mean it was different, but I don't think it was bad. And for me, it was a good life."[132] Even so, Murray admitted, "he never really had a normal life."[133]

Watching thousands of fans either cheering or jeering your parents every night, combined with the lively atmosphere of a Roller Derby game, must have been an exciting environment to experience as a child. Gerry Murray recalled dressing her son up in a cuffed navy shirt with a tie and little dress shoes and taking him with her on interviews when he was very little. She would introduce her son to the reporter, and "Mike'd stick his hand out and say, 'Glad to know ya!'" At the age of three and a half, Mike was already skating by himself around the track, in full uniform, at night. If a skater threw his or her helmet, he would skate to pick it up and then place it on the side of the track so that the offending player could skate around and retrieve it.[134] Skaters' children were very much a part of the derby atmosphere.

Buddy Atkinson Jr., son of the famous skaters Buddy Atkinson Sr. and Bobbie Johnstone, shared many experiences with Mike Gammon. In fact, the two were best friends as children. Like Gammon, Atkinson Jr. enjoyed growing up around Roller Derby, particularly the built-in family network. "Honestly, it was fantastic," he reminisced. "It was like having a lot of aunts and uncles around."[135] Atkinson Jr. loved having other children to play with, and he loved staying in the venues with the skaters and eating in the Roller Derby kitchen. He traveled with his parents until he was school age; after that, he traveled with them only

FIGURE 4.4. *The Roller Derby skaters Gerry Murray (left)*
and Midge Brasuhn, with their children Mike and Billy, at the
Minneapolis Auditorium, July 1, 1947. Minneapolis Newspaper
Photograph Collection, Hennepin County Library.

during the summers, and his mother would try to visit at Christmas. He
lived with his grandmother, with cousins in Utah, or, for at least one
year, with a couple in California who were fans of his parents. Although
he liked the relatives and family friends he stayed with, he sometimes
resented being away from his parents and Roller Derby:

> I didn't really understand it. I was upset at times, being away from
> them, there's no doubt about that. . . . I would be annoyed at moments.
> But I got along with everybody pretty good. I always have been some-
> body who could fit in just about anywhere. And learn very quickly how
> to get along, what to do, what not to do, you know. It was unusual, let's
> put it that way.[136]

Around 1953 or 1954, his mother, after a series of back injuries, broke her back and could no longer skate. At about the same time, Roller Derby left New York for the West Coast, and it was not going to relocate an injured skater who might not recover.[137] The Atkinsons remained in New York, and Buddy's father started working in the linoleum business. The couple, no longer traveling with the Roller Derby, and with Bobbie bedridden for some time, sent for Buddy Jr. to live with them. He was ecstatic to reunite—permanently, he hoped—with his parents and his younger sister, Julie, who was five and a half years his junior. Yet he remained fearful that they would one day return to Roller Derby and he would be sent away again. He stated, "It was always kind of in my mind."[138]

Since Buddy Sr. was no longer skating, he handed his skates to his son. Buddy Jr. used them in the same way that other neighborhood children used their own, much less famous skates. "I skated in them in the streets and played hockey . . . It was nothing that I followed day in and day out."[139] Essentially, whenever the other neighborhood kids said they wanted to skate, Buddy would join in, and occasionally they would go to a rink. Much as he enjoyed being around Roller Derby, Buddy Jr. wasn't particularly passionate about skating: "I never really followed and pushed skating that much."

This nonchalance toward skating drastically changed when he was fifteen or sixteen. In 1957, his parents learned that Seltzer's Roller Derby was heading back to New York. Buddy's parents, particularly his mother, were enthused about its return. He stated, "My mother was extremely excited. I started seeing her get up out of bed more, started . . . doing more, and they would talk about it a lot."[140] Although Buddy Jr. loved Roller Derby and the people in it, this triggered his longtime fear of being sent away from his parents: "At that point, I started to worry. . . . I thought they might leave me again." His fears increased when his parents began going down to the armory where Roller Derby had set up shop: "I wouldn't see them when I came home from school. So, the worry got in there. So it ended up, I started going with them." The deep-seated fear of being separated from his parents led him to join Roller Derby. He explained, "That was my motivation. I wanted to be around them." Buddy Jr. began skating at the training school with other people wanting to join, including his best friend, Mike Gammon, who was fourteen at the time. The pair trained hard together while biding their time until they were old enough to be officially picked up by the derby.

Children who grew up around the banked track had a distinct advantage. This was exemplified by such skaters as Mike Gammon, Buddy Atkinson Jr., and Barbara Baker, who were raised in or around Roller Derby and then joined themselves later in life. As an article in a 1953 Roller Derby program explained, "The youngsters of today are the stars of tomorrow. . . . The children of wheelers have a head start on all competition in the race for berths on Roller Derby teams. Most of the junior editions of today's stars have already received their banked track baptism and several have shown tremendous potential for the future."[141] In fact, the article predicted the star power of eleven-year-old Gammon: "Young Mike Gammon is perhaps the most outstanding of all the young skaters whizzing around the Masonite at speeds that would do justice to many present day rookies."

Roller Derby often featured "Diaper Derbies," races between the skaters' children that took place at halftime. The winner of the mini-derbies usually received a silver dollar. Mike Gammon won his fair share of races before officially joining the derby. His proud mother claimed, "He won all of them!"[142] These races went along with the popular match races in which two adult skaters challenged each other during halftime in timed trials with contact to order to win extra prize money—and provide the audience with some extra entertainment. The same could be said for the diaper derbies. Mike Gammon recalled, "I did halftime attractions when I was about four, I was out in the infield when I was ten. The last match race I did when I was fourteen or fifteen, against Buddy [Atkinson], Jr."[143] Even in his seventies, Atkinson Jr. corroborated the claims about Gammon's stellar skating ability from a young age: "Mike Gammon, he was ready to rock and roll at a young age, but couldn't skate because he was too young to be put on the team and all that."[144] When the two young friends began training as teens for Roller Derby, Atkinson was motivated by Gammon's talent: "I was very fortunate that he was so good, because it was another thing that drove me." During the first six months or so of their training, they would compete in five-lap races. Gammon had the distinct upper hand at first, but after Atkinson had trained regularly with Gammon and other trainees such as Frank Macedo, Dave Battersby, and Nick Scopas, whom he described as "pretty damn good," he began to win some of the races.

As the audience became more familiar with their favorite skaters' offspring, fans founded family fan clubs. By the early 1950s, over 150,000 Roller Derby fans belonged to 310 thriving fan clubs. Gerry Murray and Toughie Brasuhn were the focus of over thirty fan clubs between them. There were plenty of "Mr. and Mrs." fan clubs for married couples in the derby, and family fan clubs sprang up to support the kids of popular skaters. According to an official Roller Derby program of 1951, "the Gammon and Monte Family Fan Clubs give presents to the children of both families, and if this sort of thing keeps up unto the third and fourth generations, the Gammons and Montes won't ever have to worry about where their next mouthful is coming from."[145]

Children proved to be avid fans of the sport and also formed an integral part of the fan base. Junior fan clubs were available for kids ages ten and eleven who, apparently, "name themselves after their favorite team and challenge all comers to a playground battle."[146] As a young girl in the mid-1950s, Carol Meyer Roman remembers watching Roller Derby on television with her grandmother, who was Spanish. She recalled, "All I know is my grandmother would watch it, and I would like it. And my grandmother didn't speak English, so I hear her in her language."[147] Similarly, Lenny Berkman first started watching Roller Derby on television with his father, and later he watched it live at the 14th Street Armory in Brooklyn. When he was in the sixth grade, Berkman took it upon himself to cover the Roller Derby for his class newspaper:

> We had a school—class, rather—blackboard newspaper, and we had to each of us basically write a report that could fit within the chalk boxes we were allotted, and then the class would vote on the best story to go into sports, the best story to go into news, so forth. And there was one other Roller Derby fan with me in the sixth grade, and he and I traded putting up the Roller Derby news that week.[148]

Roller Derby appealed to younger fans throughout its tenure. As a kid growing up in western Massachusetts, David Ketchum was not really interested in mainstream sports and did not play any himself. He "kind of like[d] the off-the wall things," so when he stumbled on Roller Derby on television in 1968 at age thirteen, he was hooked. He became a fanatic fan: "The moment I saw it, I was addicted to it. I . . . couldn't wait until the next week to watch it again."[149] He watched it every week and attended live games whenever he could. Ketchum had a longtime obsession with villain skaters—the red shirts—and thus always pitted himself against America's favorite Roller Derby team, the San Francisco Bay Bombers. His favorite team was the New England Braves, and his second was whoever was playing against the Bombers. He followed the games so closely that he often imagined himself in the shoes of Jerry

FIGURE 4.5. *Two* Minneapolis Tribune *carriers cheering on their favorite Roller Derby skaters at the municipal auditorium, August 6, 1937. Minneapolis Newspaper Photograph Collection, Hennepin County Library.*

Seltzer: "I would create ten regional teams, and I would decide what cities they should be in, and what skaters should be on every team. And it was kind of, in a fun way, consuming to me. I just loved it." Ketchum was not alone as a young fan or, later, as an adult fan. He was plugged into nationwide pen pal and fan club networks centered on Roller Derby.

A FAMILY ATMOSPHERE

After initially trying to prevent derby marriages, Roller Derby's management worked hard to cultivate a family atmosphere that appealed to their fans, countered the image of rough female skaters, and provided a sustainable lifestyle for skaters with children. *Roller Derby News* and *RolleRage* often highlighted the mothers and fathers in the skating ranks. For instance, they published birth announcements like the following one, which appeared in the May 1956 edition of *Roller Derby News*: "Former Roller Derby referee and public relations man Fred Carpenter is passing out cigars today. His wife, Mickey, presented him with a baby girl. The Carpenters have a 2-year old son."[150]

The publications made sure to emphasize how important marriage and family were to both skating sexes. Feature stories or columns on specific skaters introduced readers to their backgrounds and lives off the track. In a feature on the skater Gerri Abbatello, Sandy Lepelstat stated, "While it may be true that there's nothing Gerri would rather do than skate, she still wants very much to be a good wife and mother, and to own her own home someday."[151] Lepelstat highlighted Abbatello's dedication to skating but made sure readers knew that desire did not detract from conventional feminine wants and needs. To enhance an image of traditional femininity, Lepelstat added, "Spaghetti and southern fried chicken are her favorite dishes, and she likes to wear dressy clothes and her blue and white pumps. Gerri has no favorite colors in clothes, just 'anything that goes with my brown eyes,' she stated."

Similarly, when Mary Youpelle announced her retirement because she was pregnant, the paper lamented skating's loss but lauded her decision to have children. A *Roller Derby News* editorial in March 1957 stated, "Mary 'Pocahontas' Youpelle sounded the death toll of an era of Roller Derby. With these simple words: 'I'm retiring from Roller Derby,' Pokey filled us with a great sadness."[152] But the editorial took an uplifting turn: "Pokey must have realized that we wouldn't let her go easily, so she eased the blow, and filled us with joy, by saying these beautiful, simple words: 'I'm going to become a mother.'" The author continued, embracing Roller Derby's family atmosphere:

> Pokey, who has given us so much, is now giving us even more. She is letting us share in this wonderful experience that is happening to her and Russ. Pokey said, "Maybe someday Russ and I will have a little one of our own skating around the track." When we heard this, we knew Pokey was not deserting us—instead, she is giving us a great treasure—for someday there will be a young girl or boy skating in Roller Derby. . . . Yes, our Lady has retired, but she will always be in our hearts. God Bless Pokey, Russ, and their baby-to-be.

Roller Derby men were not exempt from this type of coverage. In a feature on the skater Edward "Chick" Chokota, Lepelstat provided the regular background information on how Chick had joined the Roller Derby and who had helped him improve as a skater. Then she added, "In the vital statistics department, girls, Chick is 5′11″, 155 pounds, has brown hair and eyes, is single, and said his ambition is to get married."[153] In the same article that discussed Mary Youpelle's retirement, it was announced that Russ Massro, her husband, had been voted the 1956 Roller Derby King. Massro was to be "King and Papa the same year."[154]

Roller Derby publications often featured pictures of both male and female skaters with their children. The November 1939 issue of *Roller Derby News* included a large picture of Johnny Rosasco and his son, Johnny Jr., who sported a pair of miniature roller skates. The caption read, "Looks as though the youngest Johnny is preparing to follow in his daddy's footsteps . . . and if he turns out anything like his 'old man,' a very welcome addition to the Roller Derby he'll be in about fifteen years! The Rosascos were recently blessed with another child, a girl."[155] When Toughie Brasuhn and Gerry Murray were elected to the Hall of Fame, *Roller Derby News* featured front-page pictures of each skater with their sons. The caption below the picture of Brasuhn stated, "Handsome Billy, willowy son of Roller Derby star Midge (Toughie) Brasuhn[,] is all smiles and presents his mom with new official Roller Derby skates after the good news was released that she was voted by the nations' sports writers in the 'Hall of Fame.'"[156] The picture of Murray and her son Mike Gammon featured the two reading about her election together.

Roller Derby provides a unique case study on motherhood and female athletes, but also on parenthood and professional sports in general. Roller Derby's management adopted many of the traditional family values of the era, particularly by acknowledging the importance of motherhood and women's roles as mothers, and used these values to the sport's advantage. Unlike mainstream sports, Roller Derby did not treat being a parent and playing professional sports as mutually exclusive endeavors. In many ways, Roller Derby was a progressive sport that included and lauded mothers in its ranks. Family was very much a part of the sport, and was publicized as such. Roller Derby's management tried to accommodate parents' needs while traveling so that they could be athletes as well as mothers and fathers. It should be noted that in keeping with social norms of the time, general parenting duties fell heavily on mothers' shoulders, although both parents were available to do them.

But Roller Derby's liberal ideology and behavior went only so far. The derby did not deviate from many conventional mid-twentieth-century practices. No maternity pay was available for pregnant skaters when they took time off, unless they continued working as coaches. The emphasis on heteronormative family dynamics continued to obscure queer voices and space, thus limiting Roller Derby's inclusivity. But the critical point remains that having children did not weaken the value of female skaters or automatically force them into retirement, as it did for female athletes in most sports. Roller Derby needed female skaters, and so motherhood came to be an accepted and expected part of their lives. Instead of pushing athlete-mothers out of their sport, Mary Lou Palermo explained, Roller Derby "always worked it out."[157]

5 | CALIFORNIA OR BUST

The show is the show is the show. Everybody wants to see the home run.

BUDDY ATKINSON JR., ROLLER DERBY AND ROLLER GAMES SKATER

*The games, as far as I know, even before I became involved, had
always been a measure of sports entertainment. Every skater relied
on his reputation, his image as a skater. But they also realized that
this was a business and that the income they made depended upon
the income of the operation they were skating in.*

JOHN HALL, ROLLER DERBY SKATER AND ROLLER GAMES SKATER,
MANAGER, AND PART OWNER

New York City can be a fickle place. You can make it big, or your
dreams might die there. Roller Derby experienced both in the Big
Apple. By 1936, Damon Runyon had put Leo Seltzer in contact with
Mike Jacobs, a major boxing promoter in New York City who partnered
with Runyon to form the Twentieth Century Sporting Club, in order to
get Roller Derby in New York. According to Jerry Seltzer, "[Jacobs] was
the Don King of his day, and he did all of Joe Louis's bouts."[1] Runyon
was certain Roller Derby would be a success in the New York Hippodrome, a giant, majestic theater located on Sixth Avenue between West
Forty-Third and Forty-Fourth Streets, where Jacobs promoted fights.
Runyon, however, was badly mistaken.[2] The Roller Derby bombed, and
"nobody showed up."[3]

For quite a while, Leo Seltzer did not think Roller Derby could succeed in New York and did not go back until the late 1940s. When the
derby returned, the city helped propel it into its golden era and into
the homes of Americans across the country via the increasingly popu-

lar medium of television. But television, too, can be a fickle beast. The tension between business, sport, and new technology caused dramatic highs and lows for Roller Derby in New York and then later in California. It forced the Seltzers to adopt a level of unsustainable spectacle that played well on TV—spectacle that continued to highlight the gender and sexual tensions of the sport—and allowed them to keep up with increasingly stiff competition. This cycle of innovation and evolution caused the Seltzer organization's downfall in the mid-1970s.

In late 1948, Leo Seltzer decided to give New York another chance. He scheduled a seventeen-game series to be played at the Sixty-Ninth Regiment Armory on Lexington Avenue between East Twenty-Fifth and Twenty-Sixth Streets. He planned to take advantage of the growing popularity of television as a way to boost publicity for the sport. He had previously, without success, pitched the networks to broadcast his games, but this time he enticed CBS to buy the rights to a thirteen-week series in November 1948 at the armory. On Sunday, November 28, CBS featured a half hour of interviews with skaters, but did not broadcast a game until the following night, even though the series had already begun. The New York Chiefs and the Brooklyn Red Devils debuted during prime time at eight thirty on November 29.[4] Roller Derby had handed out a significant number of free tickets and strategically placed the spectators at key spots around the track to make the armory appear jam-packed on the small screen.[5] This staging, in combination with the exciting narration of Ken Nydell, Roller Derby's broadcast announcer, and the game itself, made the derby a hit, a decade after its birth.

Almost immediately after the televised game, the Seltzers were inundated with requests to buy tickets. In fact, Leo Seltzer and his wife, Belle, fielded calls from their apartment into the wee hours of the morning when the office phone lines became overloaded. In the following days, lines formed around the block as fans vied to get in to see the action. By December 3, Roller Derby had sold out the Sixty-Ninth Regiment Armory, with 5,300 spectators paying $3.30 for full-price tickets.[6] Roller Derby had made it big in New York.

Indeed, after the televised CBS series, the other networks sought to add Roller Derby to their programming. As the sportswriter Frank Deford rightly surmised, this popularity "was really not as much a Derby success story as it was a tale of TV."[7] Leo Seltzer, though, did not understand this at the time. Fans were ecstatic about Roller Derby and loved to see it on television, and as box-office sales showed, they increasingly wanted to watch it in person. Yet it was this relationship with television that made Roller Derby a success in New York in the late 1940s and early 1950s. Television desperately needed Roller Derby, and Roller Derby needed television. As Roller Derby came to find out, "television is like fire—it's a good servant but a very difficult master."[8]

Leo Seltzer signed a long-term TV contract with ABC that based Roller Derby in New York. He established the National Roller Derby League and restructured his organization into six teams: the New York Chiefs, Brooklyn Red Devils, Jersey Jolters, Philadelphia Panthers, Washington Jets, and Chicago Westerners. Each team played games in their home cities (with the exception of the Red Devils, who served as a travel team without a real base) and on the road.[9] Roller Derby continued to thrive. In June 1949, it sold fifty-five thousand tickets to its five-day World Series played at Madison Square Garden. On top of that income, ABC paid Roller Derby $5,000 a week to broadcast as much as twelve hours of derby a week. ABC, which was struggling at the time, found success with its derby programming and began showing three full Roller Derby games a week as well as the second half of a game for an hour on Saturday afternoons.[10]

Seltzer, extremely pleased with the TV money and the box-office sales, wanted to end the 1949 Roller Derby season with the World Series and then, like most other sports of the era, give the athletes an off-season. ABC, however, would have none of that. Because of its financial struggles and its reliance on revenue from Roller Derby programming, the network insisted that Roller Derby not take a break but instead continue broadcasting, like any other prime-time television show. According to Keith Coppage, "ABC executives told Leo that if Roller Derby took a break, it would *stay* off the air."[11] Bound by his contract with the network, Seltzer kept Roller Derby going year-round. When one season finished, a new one began the next day. ABC broadcast Roller Derby live every week for three years.[12] Roller Derby's consistent airtime helped deepen its association with entertainment. Roller Derby became part of regular television programming, as opposed to a seasonally featured sport, and most often appeared in newspapers as such.[13]

Buoyed by his success at ABC and a reported $2.5 million in earnings, Seltzer decided to negotiate a new contract elsewhere, one that would allow his teams to take an off-season break, so he parted ways with ABC in 1951. While Roller Derby had gained unprecedented popularity, it had simultaneously oversaturated the market. After exposure of up to twelve hours of Roller Derby every week for three years, fans grew weary of the sport and began to question its legitimacy as well as its respectability. Leo met with rejection when he approached the other major networks, and just like that, Roller Derby was no longer regularly on television. The sport continued without a stable TV contract for a little while, drawing 82,000 fans over the course of its five-day World Series at Madison Square Garden in 1951. Still, Leo understood that regular television appearances were going to be necessary for future success, particularly since Roller Derby had morphed into a television-like program. Seltzer still viewed Roller Derby as a sport, but viewers treated it primarily as entertainment. Roller Derby as television show had essentially come to sponsor or subsidize the live game, and since Roller Derby relied on gate receipts, without that subsidy it would be lost.[14]

In January 1952, Roller Derby was in dire financial straits. The situation was so bad, in fact, that Seltzer was temporarily unable to pay his skaters, although he still provided funds for room and board. Live attendance in the New York area began dwindling, which further diminished his ability to negotiate a new TV contract. When people's dreams die in New York, they often head to California. Emulating the television industry's migration from the East Coast to the West, Roller Derby took off: California or bust.[15]

FROM FATHER TO SON

Roller Derby packed its wagon so to speak, believing in its version of manifest destiny. The derby played games at a few locations such as Chicago and Kansas City on its westward trek before settling down in Southern California.[16] Unfortunately, California was not the land of milk and honey that Leo Seltzer had hoped it would be. Roller Derby limped along for another year or so, trying to drum up fans in California and scheduling derbies in other potentially lucrative areas—Texas, Hawaii, Chicago—but mostly to no avail. Increasingly frustrated, Seltzer considered shutting down Roller Derby operations to pursue real estate opportunities. Then the TV fires kindled just enough to keep Roller Derby alive for a bit longer. Seltzer secured a deal with KTLA, an independent Los Angeles–based television station that featured lower-grade programming such as wrestling, boxing, and old-timey westerns. It was enough to keep Roller Derby going but not enough to put it back in the limelight. Seltzer made one last attempt to revive his New York dreams in 1958, but despite recruiting some excellent skaters out of the training school established for the New York series, the brief stint was a flop.[17]

Seltzer realized that KTLA was using Roller Derby for its meager survival, and he was determined not to be burned twice by overexposure on television. His beloved sport was not taking hold in Los Angeles the way he had hoped it would, and support in other areas of California did not seem strong enough to sustain the constantly struggling organization. Although ready to exit the stage, Seltzer did not want to betray the trust, loyalty, and constant hard work of his skaters by shutting down the business.[18] After all, Roller Derby had always been a family affair, and you do not turn your back on family. This was instead the moment when family stepped in. Entering from stage right on the Roller Derby drama: Jerry Seltzer.

Jerry had graduated from high school in 1949 and, like Roller Derby, headed west. He studied at Stanford University for two years before transferring to Northwestern University in 1951. In 1954, just a few credits short of graduating, Jerry left school for the army. He served in the Counter Intelligence Corps and was stationed mainly in Austria. After completing his military service in early 1956, he finished his degree at Northwestern. He married his sweetheart, Marjorie, in May 1956, and their first two children, Steven and Ellen, were born by the end of the decade; their youngest, Richard, joined the family in 1963. In the meantime, Jerry had begun working for his uncle's Roller Derby Skate Company. He helped open a warehouse in Redwood City, California, and was earning about $125 a week by selling roller skates. Leo knew Jerry was not earning a lot of money, so he offered him the opportunity to make some extra income by doing trackside announcing when Roller Derby came to the San Mateo area. According to Jerry, "Well, I was very introverted, and it just scared me to death. . . . And he said, 'You'll find it's fine.' So I did it, and I guess I did OK at it."[19] Jerry earned $125 for the five-game series, effectively doubling his weekly salary. From there, Jerry took on a management position. Several other employees were called elsewhere within the organization, and as Jerry recalled, "In essence I became the unit manager. This was in 1958."[20] It was not long until Jerry found himself in charge of the entire operation.

About the time Jerry's management involvement increased, Leo realized that he wanted out. Roller Derby was more or less dead on the East Coast, and he was reliving the television battle that had forced the move to California in the first place. Roller Derby had been on air with KTLA for five years, but Leo was still pushing for an off-season with a TV hiatus; the station would not agree to that.[21] Leo was tired of the television battles and of constantly scraping by in order to keep the Roller Derby afloat. He decided to relocate Roller Derby from the Los Angeles area to the Bay Area, but he had also begun pursuing other interests, such as creating a television series for children and developing real estate in Antelope Valley in Southern California.[22] According to his son, "He wanted out of the area. He wanted to do other things. . . . So he just called me and said, 'I'm going to shut down Roller Derby.' I said, 'Well, what if I wanted to continue operating it?'"[23] Leo had no money to give his son to invest in the sport, but he was willing to give him the banked track and said that if Jerry could work out a deal with the skaters, then by all means, go for it. At age twenty-six, Jerry Seltzer was now at the helm of the longtime family enterprise.[24]

Jerry's vision and management style differed drastically from his father's, and it was these two qualities that both reignited the popularity of Roller Derby and in part tarnished the image of it as a legitimate sport. As his father had discovered over the years, it was very difficult to achieve both popularity and legitimacy, so the son stopped trying. Jerry had more of an "it is what it is" kind of attitude, and his motivation was to simply keep Roller Derby going and to make it profitable.[25] Jerry understood that television was critical to the success of Roller Derby, but he approached the medium from a different angle than had his father. Fortuitously, Jerry took over at a time when the use of videotape by media outlets was becoming widespread, and that development would shape the operational patterns of Roller Derby.

Soon into his tenure, Jerry struck a deal with a local independent television station, KTVU Channel Two, in the San Francisco Bay Area, in what he described as a "joint venture" to televise Roller Derby. KTVU was trying to establish itself as a station and therefore needed programming, and Jerry was trying to establish himself as the new owner of Roller Derby and needed airtime for his games. KTVU televised Roller Derby live on Saturday nights and split the sponsorship revenue with Jerry. The early broadcasts were staged promotional setups. Jerry explained how contrived the matches were:

> We went on the air in '59 from a former garage that repaired cars in Oakland. It was a big clear space, building. We put some bleachers in there and set up a platform. . . . We couldn't have paid spectators in there, but we had the trainees and their families come in, which was a terrible audience, because they didn't like the fact that these other people were skating and they weren't, you know. The whole thing was just kind of bizarre.[26]

Yet it worked, and it marked the beginning of the Jerry Seltzer era of Roller Derby, one that was innovative in concept, savvy in business, and pliable in seeking legitimacy as a sport. Seltzer quickly initiated four critical changes affecting how Roller Derby operated: he booked "one-nighters," reduced the track to a more portable size, used a "bicycle network" for taped games, and critically analyzed market data derived from television ratings, mail response, and live attendance. Seltzer approached Roller Derby as a business venture and understood the fundamental need to build a fan base via television while retaining control. Despite his father's love-hate relationship with the medium, Seltzer's instincts told him television was still the key: "TV is the answer; we have to build viewership. As long as the program gets good ratings, it's going to stay on. How can we help it in the market?"[27] Although Leo had engaged in similar tactics, Jerry used the skaters to drum up publicity. He would send an advance man, usually a derby referee, and two top skaters, such as Ann Calvello and Joan Weston, and the group would travel ahead of the other skaters to give local interviews about themselves and the upcoming game. Seltzer was occasionally exasperated at the topics covered in the interviews. He laughingly explained, "Because sometimes people get on the interviews and they're, you know, 'Yes, I have a dog, and I have this,' and I'd be screaming at the TV screen, 'Goddammit, Joanie, mention where you're going to be playing!'"[28]

The first major critical change was Seltzer's adoption of the one-nighter, which was directly tied to the need for a more portable track. For the majority of the sport's history, Roller Derby would hunker down in one location for approximately a month at a time, but television made that model ineffective. When Roller Derby was in a location for several weeks in a row, only the locals would read about it in the papers and watch it on television. According to Seltzer, "Now it was that television was everywhere, so it didn't make any difference [where you were playing]. There were no more boundaries."[29] He came up with the idea to play for one night in cities in California from April through September of each year, and this served as the main team's—the San Francisco Bay Bombers—home schedule.[30] On Sundays, the Seltzer Roller Derby would play at Kezar Pavilion at the edge of Golden Gate Park in San Francisco, and on Mondays would skate in San Jose. Teams would play another night at either the Cow Palace or the Civic Auditorium in San Francisco during the week, and then play weekend games in Oakland. The derby would rotate smaller towns such as Santa Rosa, Sacramento, and Stockton that could not support weekly derby games

FIGURE 5.1. *San Francisco Bay Bombers pennant with an image of Joan Weston. Gift to the author from Mark Roman.*

onto the schedule. Once the home schedule was finished, Roller Derby held league playoffs. Following the playoffs, the derby would lay off the skaters who would not be on the travel teams for the winter tour. The tour locations and venues were scheduled for places where Roller Derby tapes had been regularly televised and received good ratings. The travel tour began after the holidays, in early January.[31]

This mobility was possible because of the newly downsized, portable Masonite banked track. The track was reconfigured to be no wider than a basketball court, which was 54 feet wide. The Masonite pieces of the track came in 12-foot segments, so the track could be one of three lengths: 96 feet, 108 feet, or, if playing outside, 120 feet. The length of the track affected game play. The shorter the track, the faster the game, and, ultimately, more excitement for both live and television fans.[32]

The portable track led to the third key component of Roller Derby's success under Jerry Seltzer: the bicycle network. In essence, Seltzer began a syndication network for Roller Derby. It worked like this: he would have the last hour of the Sunday-night game, which was played at Kezar Pavilion, videotaped. He described Kezar as an ideal facility for recording the game because the derby's management could organize and influence the production: "We'd be at one end—and it's all bleacher seating—and as people would come in, and we'd try to estimate the crowd, we'd have them fill this side and this side and then the end, so it always looked packed. Then eventually we could open the balcony, and they could sit up there if we needed [them] to. . . . [The fans] paid very little to get in on Sunday night. I think two dollars, and it was more of a studio kind of thing, and we could really control it."[33] The last hour of the game typically covered the fifth through the eighth periods and also featured an interview with a skater. Copies of the tape of the last hour would be sent out to television stations across the country. The stations could show the tape whenever they wanted, even multiple times.[34] Since the games were not being broadcast live and rankings did not really exist in Roller Derby, the order in which the games were shown was irrelevant to viewers. It was simply the action they were looking for. Once the tape had been shown, the television station was responsible for sending it on to other stations, thus forming the "bicycle": each station was dependent on the previous one, like the wheels of a bike. If a station forgot, the chain was broken, which apparently happened often. According to Coppage, "Jerry learned to anticipate their ineptitude by making sure all stations always had a back-up tape on hand for emergency use."[35] At the peak of this bicycle network, tapes were being circulated to 120 stations across America.[36]

While Seltzer leveraged this idea to promote Roller Derby, it did not originate with him. Gateway Chevrolet in San Francisco had long been a TV sponsor of Roller Derby, particularly under the supervision of Jim Wessman. Wessman, ever anxious to sell cars, called Seltzer to inform him that Gateway had recently opened a dealership in Portland, Oregon. Wessman wanted to show Roller Derby in that area and have Gateway sponsor it, since, as Seltzer acknowledged, "Roller Derby sold a lot of cars for him."[37] Seltzer, who knew that videotape was now available, told Wessman, " 'Well, we could tape the last hour, and if you'll pay for that, and then if we decide to play Portland, you know, [we'll] give you a couple spots."[38] Seltzer sent some tapes of Roller Derby games to Portland station KPTV, which aired them. Wessman had also begun saying that Roller Derby should travel to Portland to play a live game. Seltzer was hesitant to travel that far from his California base, so he wanted confirmation that the derby would be well received. He told Wessman that fans should write him if they were interested in seeing Roller Derby live. Shortly thereafter, Seltzer received a giant bag of mail indicating Portland's enthusiasm for the derby. He decided to give it a shot.

The track was sent north on a truck, and the skaters were sent on an old DC-3 airplane. The track had a fine trip, but not so the skaters. The flight was terrible, and the plane had to attempt to land twice while facing 80 mph headwinds.[39] "The game is supposed to start at eight o'clock. They get into Portland Airport about ten to eight. These skaters—there's no pressurized cabin. They're cold, they're miserable, they're all tight. We had a police escort arranged, brought them to the building, and they went out and they probably skated the worst game I've ever seen," Seltzer recalled. "But," as he noted, "the people loved it, because they'd [been] preconditioned from television."[40] Seltzer understood that this could be a workable model for the sport. He remembered thinking, "Gee, if it could work in Portland, why can't it work everywhere else?" It turned out that it could, and thus began Roller Derby's syndication network to support the live games, effectively flipping the television model that had bedeviled his father.

The final critical change made by Jerry had to do with how he leveraged data gleaned from the bicycle network. He required Roller Derby to be broadcast locally for a minimum of thirteen weeks before teams would skate live in a location. Seltzer believed it took at least three months to build a solid fan base and generate interest in attending a live game. While Roller Derby tapes were being shown on a local station, Seltzer would check both the television ratings and the mail response from that area. In each telecast, Roller Derby dropped in two pieces of information. The first was an offer to send a free copy of the official rules to any fan who wrote in requesting it, and the second was to encourage fans to join a mailing list to learn when Roller Derby would be coming to cities near them. The idea was that anyone willing to take the time to write in for the rules or to get on the list would be willing to purchase tickets to a game in their general vicinity. A location had to have both high television ratings and a large mail response for Seltzer to consider booking a game there: "If the two things didn't add up, we wouldn't play it."[41]

During telecasts, Roller Derby's management ran frequent advertisements to promote upcoming live appearances. Seltzer explained, "We did that for every station, every place we were."[42] The television stations paid $25 or $35 for a tape and gave Roller Derby two promotional spots during the game and two outside it, which could be accumulated. Seltzer described the process: "We started using those spots for when our live appearances were. The ratings would go up in the market for the TV show, you know, so it was kind of a whole synergy going on."

As Jerry Seltzer worked out the logistics of how to manage, promote, and televise Roller Derby, he and the skaters were figuring out the type of game that they would be playing and selling. Leo Seltzer had always pushed legitimate skating, but with a degree of showmanship. According to Jerry, Leo "didn't like the garbage," but the fans did.[43] In addition, Jerry admitted the staginess of some of the action: "A lot of times the unit managers would kind of encourage it because they felt it brought more people back. . . . And they'd say to the skaters, you know 'We need a fight now,' you know, or something like that." This was the inherent difficulty constantly facing the Seltzers: Roller Derby depended on money from the gate, which required ticket-buying fans, and if fans liked spectacle, did it make sense not to give them what they wanted, even at the expense of the game? Leo tried to treat the derby as a true sport while still allowing for some color. By the beginning of Jerry's tenure, that formula was not necessarily working.

The prime example of this occurred in the 1959–1960 season in what was called the "Open Game," wherein all restrictions were lifted from the skaters, that is, they weren't told to fight or not to fight, or to win by five points rather than twenty.[44] In essence, Jerry Seltzer mandated a season of straightforward skating in order to gain the kind of respectability on the West Coast that Roller Derby had garnered on the East Coast. It was, in part, an effort to recruit the media to cover Roller Derby as they did other sports, at least according to several skaters. John Hall noted, "It was my best period ever in Roller Derby, and not only for me, but for many other skaters, because it gave us a chance to truly show what we had—what we could do. . . . It gave every skater a chance to show his true ability."[45]

But the fans did not like it, and cried foul. Games expected to be pretty close in score were outrageously lopsided. Home teams got drummed repeatedly in front of their fans. The point was to gain legitimacy for West Coast teams such as the Los Angeles Braves and the San Francisco Bay Bombers, to prove that they were talented, but what happened instead was that New York fans lost interest and claimed that the games were rigged. Hall explained, "The New York Chief team would go against . . . the team I was on then, the Brooklyn Red Devils, which they fully outclassed us with youth, experience, and talent. Every fan in New York was ecstatic. They were happy; they were pleased." When the Braves came to town and dominated the Chiefs, "that was a different story." The Chiefs lost to the West Coast team and then lost to the Bombers at the end of the season. As Buddy Atkinson Jr., a skater on the Chiefs at the time, recalled, "And when that happened, when we would get beat, the fans would say we were fixing the game. It was unbelievable."[46] Hall corroborated this account: "[The Bombers] came in, and they gave the Chiefs a lesson in how to skate. The rumors started: 'It's fixed, it's fixed.' They tried to develop promise for the West Coast at the expense of the New York Chiefs."[47] In fact, everyone was simply skating

FIGURE 5.2. *Darlene Anderson and Joan Weston skating at the Cow Palace in San Francisco, 1960. Photography by Dick Clark. Courtesy of Gary Powers and the National Roller Derby Hall of Fame and Museum.*

straight, letting the chips falls where they may. The rumors continued and attendance dropped, but Jerry Seltzer recalled the upside: "It sure was exciting, though."[48]

Purely legitimate Roller Derby was not working, but Seltzer's new management style and the syndication network were. He continued to embrace a hands-off management style that allowed the skaters to control the game and respond to the fans, as he acknowledged, "I left the skating up to the skaters. You know, it was up to Charlie [O'Connell] and Joanie [Weston] and Ann [Calvello], you know, to kind of decide who they would be using at all. I never came out and said, 'All right, we're going to do this tonight.'"[49] The skaters and unit managers knew what pleased the crowd. They witnessed it every time they skated. Seltzer explained, "You know, we had to play what the fans wanted, what they saw on television."[50] Color, probably more so than at any other point in Roller Derby's history, was expected and proffered. Excellent skating and athleticism were still on display, but the derby became "a controlled game."[51] This is not to say that outcomes were fixed—they did not need to be. Under Seltzer's model, as he admitted, the final score was irrelevant: "Whatever seemed to be happening, happened. Because nobody paid attention to whatever the score [was] the next day. It was the game they would want them to see. . . . There was no reason to [fix a game]." Buddy Atkinson confirmed this, "The real truth is, only to a few people did any of that matter. To me, it didn't really matter. I don't remember scores of final games."[52]

Outcomes became relevant only in the yearly playoffs, where legitimate skating was important. Sometimes, though, players had to be re-

FIGURE 5.3. *Roller Derby Official Program number 6.*
International League, 1965 Season. Gift to the author from
Mark Roman.

FIGURE 5.4. *Roller Derby Official Program number 7. International League, 1965 Season. Gift to the author from Mark Roman.*

minded of what was at stake. Seltzer recalled having to remind Ann Calvello to take it down a notch: "I'd have to go at halftime and say 'Annie, stop that shit.' You know these games are way too important . . . and you're sitting in the penalty box; you're not helping anybody."[53] It was occasionally hard to determine what was most important in Roller Derby, since the ultimate goal was always to entertain.

Like other team sports, Roller Derby had set plays, as well as a clear understanding of each team member's role. According to Seltzer, during his tenure at least, skaters skated what was dubbed "ad lib" during the first couple of periods of play, meaning that "nothing was set or planned in terms of plays."[54] Skaters were getting a feel for the opposing players and the flow of the game. By the third period, skaters began orchestrating particular plays to run: "They'd go out, and they'd say, 'OK, let's try this. . . . All right let's try for a double whip.' . . . And they'd see if they work, and then they'd do it throughout the game. . . . There were plays, as there are in basketball and everything, but they went back virtually forty or fifty years," Seltzer stated. Perhaps the best explanation of the combination of athleticism, strategy, and showmanship in Roller Derby comes from Buddy Atkinson Jr.:

> Roller Derby was a lot of showmanship. I mean, it was a great deal of showmanship, but the part that was so unique and so special, and the chip that we all had on our shoulder, was [that] we were so good at what we did, that whether it was showmanship or not, we could really do that stuff. I mean, we could do it as real as real could possibly be. And the part that was so amazing, that people couldn't get through their heads, . . . is that most of the things they saw happened. There wasn't like, "Stop the cameras. Let's do that again." It's just, we did it. We did all this stuff. We did these blocks, we did these falls, we did these jumps, we did these spins. We did stuff off the top of our heads. We were there to please an audience, and we all knew it.[55]

It was this tension between pure sport and pleasing the fans that had both fans and critics loving and criticizing the games, often at the same time.

As previously mentioned, everyone had a specific role to play. Some skaters had particular moves they were known for, such as Cliff Butler and his jump block or Tommy Atkinson's hip block.[56] There were pack skaters, who helped move the game along but blended in with the rest of the pack, and at the top there were star skaters, who ran the show. During Seltzer's tenure, the skater Charlie O'Connell called the shots, along with Joan Weston and Ann Calvello—they were the top three draws. As Buddy Atkinson Jr. explained, "Charlie O'Connell ran the game. . . . He was the guy that would make sure it always looked good. And he was good. I mean, he was top-notch. No two ways about it. But nobody's ever as good as they may think they are, without help."[57] Ultimately, skaters had to figure out what their roles were within the organization and then fulfill those roles in order to keep things operating smoothly.

CHARLIE O'CONNELL
ROLLER DERBY

FIGURE 5.5. *Charlie O'Connell in a Roller Derby promotional picture, 1958. Courtesy of Gary Powers and the National Roller Derby Hall of Fame and Museum.*

As Atkinson reflected, "You had to be humble enough to understand what your position is, and what you have to give to keep it going." He added that many of the top skaters were not famous for their skating ability, even if they were nonetheless talented. Rather, they were tremendous organizers of skaters and did whatever they had to do to keep the game going.

THE LASTING RIVALS

Under Jerry Seltzer's "synergy," Roller Derby came back in a big way, but it also faced a formidable opponent that appeared on the scene shortly after he took over from his father. In 1960, a group of skaters left the Seltzer Roller Derby to start a new organization. Relatively often in the sport's history, skaters would organize their own roller derbies, which often were temporary, and then would come back to skate for the Seltzers. However, the unit that became the National Skating Derby, aka Roller Games, had staying power.[58]

This group of breakaway skaters, which included Ralphie Valladares, Honey Sanchez, Julie Patrick, Shirley Hardman, and John Hall, decided to do an eight-week European and North African tour. After the two months abroad, they returned stateside and took a monthlong hiatus. Following their break and after rounding up more skaters, they held roller derbies in Philadelphia, Washington, DC, and Johnstown, Pennsylvania, for about six weeks. That East Coast tour was a box-office failure. According to John Hall, "Then we all just figured we'd just go back and be retired skaters until the main hierarchy of the group, the girls mostly, got in touch with Dick Lane in Los Angeles of KTLA TV station, and the fellow that ran the parking lot at the Olympic Auditorium, Herb Roberts."[59] Roberts had been interested in organizing a roller-skating event of some sort for a while, but the Seltzers, with their trademark on the Roller Derby name, had effectively cornered the market in Southern California. This changed when Roller Derby left the LA area in 1958 for San Francisco. Southern California became wide open, and Roberts and the renegade skaters took advantage of the opportunity.[60]

Roberts founded the Roller Skating Championship in March 1961. He organized about four teams of outstanding skaters based in El Monte, east of Los Angeles. The skaters were, by and large, former Roller Derby skaters who had been unhappy with the Seltzer organization over pay or could no longer travel outside the Los Angeles area.[61] As John Hall put it, "They had lives here, families here, jobs here. So when a local operation started up, [and] they could skate either on the home team, or skate every six or nine weeks on a visiting team and make good per-game money skating fifteen games, they said, 'We're going to have the best of both worlds.'"[62] Roberts and his Roller Skating Championship started strong, with their abundance of talent and solid box-office draws, but Roberts struggled to manage the finances of the new organization. As Hall recalled, "[Roberts] didn't have a good business mind for this roller derby thing, and the person he had responsible for his business affairs was not too good either." Roberts ran into trouble with the IRS over a question of payroll taxes.[63]

In the meantime, Jerry Hill and Bill Griffiths, who were responsible for advertising the Roller Skating Championship on KTLA, liked what they saw of Roberts's organization, and they were very familiar with the skaters. Hill and Griffiths offered to buy out Roberts and take over the Roller Skating Championship. At that point, the skaters met among themselves to discuss their options. According to Hall, "We felt it would be in the best interest of us and everybody if we had new owners, as well as, Herb was taken care of. They gave Herb a lifetime job at a certain salary as long as he could do the in-house announcing and other duties for them, and [Hill and Griffiths] took over the operation."[64] They renamed the business the National Skating Derby, Incorporated, and it became known as Roller Games. Immediate conflict ensued with the Seltzer Roller Derby over the name, but litigation failed, since Hill and Griffiths were not using the name "Roller Derby."[65]

Jerry Seltzer's Roller Derby and Hill and Griffith's Roller Games developed in tandem and at odds with each other over the next decade, in what could best be described as a mutually beneficial and mutually destructive relationship. The leagues occasionally helped each other through publicity campaigns, in making connections for booking stadiums, and in interleague play. Yet skaters often played one organization against the other for pay raises, and as Roller Games became more theatrical, Roller Derby had to keep up, which in turn partly diminished its reputation. The futures of the organizations were intricately entwined, whether they liked it or not.

Roller Games gained popularity with its main team, the Los Angeles Thunderbirds, or T-birds, and big-name stars such as Terri Lynch, Ralphie Valladares, John Hall, and Shirley Hardman, who came to rival the standouts of Roller Derby.[66] Roller Games relocated to LA, and the franchise expanded rapidly across the country from there. The organization had good skaters, good managers, and knowledgeable owners who were skillful at advertising and promotions. Like the Seltzer Roller Derby, Roller Games changed its style of play throughout its (nearly fifteen-year) existence. Early on, the Roller Games version was hardly distinguishable from Roller Derby. Hill and Griffiths gave players and coaches the freedom "to handle the game and keep it entertaining and professional."[67] Roller Games skaters emphasized offense over defense and encouraged "entertaining showmanship" as long as it was professional. Individual skaters riled up the crowd in different ways, and perhaps more so than in Roller Derby, but it worked.[68] "There was a beautiful relationship for many years, and Roller Games—National Skating Derby—became established so well that we finally had over 120 stations syndicated. . . . At the peak of this popularity, each station was paying rights fees of $5,000 to the National Skating Derby," recalled Hall. Financially, the organization was doing well, and the profits were trickling down to the players, who had guaranteed yearly salaries.[69]

But according to skaters who skated with both Roller Derby and Roller Games, as Roller Games units expanded across the country and internationally to Australia, Canada, and Japan in the late 1960s, managerial competence declined and so did the quality of play. Promotional aspects such as skater conflicts, deliberate fan engagement, and match races were emphasized over the game itself. Hall believed that this "was the beginning of the decline" for Roller Games.[70] Buddy Atkinson Jr. moved over to Roller Games in 1967 and first worked directly under Jerry Hill in Philadelphia before taking over the Philadelphia Warriors unit. Atkinson explained that he changed his skating style a bit to accommodate the National Skating Derby's methods, but, he said, he found it difficult to stray too far from the roller derby game as he knew it: "[My game] wasn't National Skating Derby, and it was part of the thing that would drive Bill Griffiths crazy. He wanted all the games to be the same."[71] Atkinson worked to keep the Philadelphia teams skating closer to the Seltzer Roller Derby style, but that conflicted with the type of Roller Games derby played on the West Coast. The contrast worked for a while, but Atkinson admitted, "At the very end of it, of Philadelphia, we got where it was heavy-duty production." Roller Games became known as a "cartoon show" akin to wrestling because of its over-the-top antics such as featuring a little person with a megaphone, "mock fighting [and] spanking."[72]

The evolution of Roller Games had to do, in part, with the owners. Jerry Hill has been described being like Leo Seltzer. Hall recalled, "You listened to Jerry [Hill] with respect and admiration, and you believed him."[73] In the owner-skater relationship, he was the good cop. Atkinson described Hill as having a big heart and being a good guy to work for, "but [Hill and Griffiths] both knew their position, they both knew what they were doing and they played their parts extremely well."[74] Griffiths provided the color, the show, and the ego. Known for wearing a fedora and a shirt and tie, he looked like the quintessential promoter and often was in the midst of the spectacle himself.[75] Hall explained, "Griffiths you listened to because he was very knowledgeable, but you also knew that he was a promoter first."[76] Skaters perceived Griffiths's main interest in Roller Games to be money, and they often struggled to cope with his ego.[77]

Griffiths's ego led to the downfall of his partnership with Jerry Hill and ultimately of Roller Games' popularity in the 1960s and early 1970s. In September 1972, Jerry Seltzer, Jerry Hill, and Bill Griffiths joined forces to host an interleague Roller Derby–Roller Games competition at Comiskey Park in Chicago. The game between the LA Thunderbirds and the Chicago Pioneers was a huge success, and fifty thousand fans packed the sold-out stadium.[78] Hall reminisced, "The T-birds lost the game, but they lost in a way that neither team was discredited. It was a professional performance by both teams. The media accepted it. Everybody accepted it."[79] After the game, the three owners spoke at the media conference together, and "Bill Griffiths boldly stated that, 'I'm happy that everyone is pleased with what I accomplished.'"[80] Seltzer apparently ignored the barb, but it did not sit well with Hill. A few days later, Hill told Griffiths that he did not seem to need him anymore, and he wanted to dissolve the partnership. Griffiths stated that he would have lawyers draw up the payout schedule, but Hill wanted an immediate partnership dissolution for cash. Hill supposedly received over $2.5 million, but that loss of funds hurt the viability of National Skating Derby, which was spread thin across the globe and skaters were paid on contract.

Several other critical factors threatened the viability of Roller Games. The oil crisis of 1973, which also affected Roller Derby, resulted in declining attendance at live games. Griffiths responded by adding promotions, which succeeded in some areas but not in others. Dates are a little hazy here, but shortly after the Hill-Griffiths partnership dissolved, "National Skating Derby as a league ceased to exist."[81] Griffiths kept operating Roller Games in Southern California, and John Hall took over the East Coast operations, but neither had reliable television contracts.[82] Although it must have seemed like a good sign for Roller Games, the folding of the Seltzer Roller Derby in late 1973 was the final nail in the coffin for Roller Games. "It was ironic; they couldn't live without us," Seltzer remarked.[83]

GENDER AND CLASS STEREOTYPES REDUX

As Roller Derby and Roller Games ramped up their theatrics and showmanship, the gender and sexual tensions inherent in the sport occasionally flared up in interesting ways. The roughness of the game, particularly the over-the-top fights by female skaters during the later era, continued to draw both male and female fans. When Mrs. Leslie Taylor wrote to *Roller Derby News* in May 1964 suggesting that female skaters be dropped from the game to make it more exciting, a "hot tiff" and "great debate" played out in the publication's pages over the next couple of months. In June, fans inundated the paper with responses running three to one in support of the female skaters and insisting that they were what made Roller Derby thrilling. As one fan responded,

> I think Mrs. Taylor and her friends must be nuts to suggest that the girls be thrown out of Roller Derby. They happen to be just about what makes Roller Derby a great sport. The girls help it to be great because they have short tempers and like to get even after getting hit. You never know what is going to happen while watching the girls. The boys just seem to go around the track and every once in a while there will be a good fight. The boys can hang on to their tempers longer than the girls can so it isn't as exciting watching the boys as it is watching the girls.[84]

While many loyal and supportive fans continued to love the roughness of the women, their competitive spirit, and the fact that the Roller Derby was the only sport in which they could see men and women compete under the same rules, the derby still had concerns over the skaters' reputations. How they were perceived by the general public and the sports media was a lasting concern. A reporter for the *San Francisco Chronicle* was apparently shocked when he sat down with Annis Jensen in 1958: "I fully expected her to come skating down the corridor in a red turtleneck sweater with a number on her back and her front teeth missing. I couldn't have been more wrong. She turned out to be a pleasant redhead with a beautiful tan, and wearing a light linen chemise. She looked just like a Peninsula housewife, who had been shopping in the city."[85] To counter persistent negative stereotypes, Roller Derby publications continued to describe their skaters in ways exemplified by the following from 1959: "Demure Bobby Mateer, nicely filled out to a lush 36"22"36" and looking more like a curvy siren from a James Bond movie than a Roller Derby star for the Hawaiians"; also, "Introducing Miss Jan Vallow, a shy, soft-spoken Miss who sports 130 well-proportioned pounds on her five foot six frame. With her dark brown hair, brown eyes, and warm smile, Jan is easily the finest contribution Colorado Springs has made to the world of sports."[86]

Vallow was drawn to Roller Derby because of its equality between the sexes. She told *Roller Derby News*, "I liked it because women were on an equal basis with men and I believe in that."[87] As the feminist movement gained momentum in the late 1960s and early 1970s, Roller Derby's emphasis on equality, in combination with persistent stereotypes of the female skaters, was, at least in one instance, used by a critic of the women's movement to denigrate women's libbers. As the columnist Margo (daughter of the original Ann Landers) wrote in the *Chicago Daily Tribune*, "Women's Lib is off-putting to me because many of their number remind me of roller derby dropouts. There is no chance to confuse them with your standard cream puff. They come on like ornery opportunistic militants."[88] Margo expounded on her wish to not be liberated from men, particularly men who viewed women as "delicate and fragile . . . and in need of pampering"—the opposite of both feminists and female Roller Derby skaters.

The negative connotations given to self-sufficiency, strength, and toughness—qualities that indicated women could live without men—usually led back to the longtime association of female derby skaters with lesbianism. In 1969, Candice Bergen published an article in *Esquire* magazine featuring female Roller Games skaters entitled "Little Women: What Has 40 Wheels, Seven Tits, and Fights?"[89] While detailing the culture of Roller Games and what sparked fan interest (no surprise, it was the women), Bergen also described the on-track personalities of the skaters as well as a little about their off-track lives. She described Jan Vallow (who skated for both Roller Derby and Roller Games during this era) as having "long, soft hair" and as the nicest female villain one could meet, and made sure to highlight her status as wife and mother. The skater Carolyn Moreland resented some of Bergen's other commentary about the sport. Moreland told the *Chicago Tribune* a couple years later, "She [Bergen] made us all seem like a bunch of lesbians."[90] Bergen's retelling of her visit with the skater Shirley Hardman most likely led to Moreland's accusation:

> At the moment, she was in the hospital with a back injury. A girl friend sat by her side. Shirley wore a diamond-and-gold initial ring on her pinkie. Trackside announcer Herb Roberts made it for her in his shop.

Even lying down she looked huge, albino-fair, Super Wasp, large square hands, massive muscular arms. "Why don't you ask me what I think of men?" she demanded. "What do you think of men?" She exhaled disgustedly. "What does any woman think of men?"[91]

Bergen repeatedly called the female skaters "Wonder Women" and complimented the drama of the game. The article was also steeped in familiar rhetoric that tried to simultaneously celebrate tough female competitors, denigrate the social class of the skaters and their fans, and question the female skaters' femininity. They were, as Bergen explained, "good Christians, good Americans, poor men's Raquel Welches."[92]

ROLLER DERBY AS AMERICANA

Despite its class condescension, articles like Bergen's helped roller derby, in its many incarnations, become a pop culture mainstay. The famed sportswriter Frank Deford traveled with Roller Derby on assignment for *Sports Illustrated* at the peak of the Jerry Seltzer era. He was doing a series of Americana articles for the publication, and later recalled, "The Roller Derby at that time was very popular, so it fit very much into those kind of stories that I enjoyed doing."[93] He had enjoyed watching Roller Derby on television as a young boy in the 1950s, stating, "I thought it was a hoot."[94] When he began his travels with the Roller Derby, the skaters assumed that he was writing an exposé, but he "had no interest in that whatsoever."[95] According to Deford, "What interested me was the performance and the fact that people enjoyed it . . . and beyond that what interested me more than anything else was the skaters themselves. Who were these people? That's what really intrigued me."[96]

His article "The Roller Derby" appeared in the *Sports Illustrated* issue of March 3, 1969. It describes Roller Derby as follows: "A downtown, blue-collar game that rocks and whirs on its way, exciting its own, nurturing its young, expanding all the time with hardly a care for the ordained representatives of 'respectable' sport who carefully ignore it. . . . Maybe the Roller Derby today is like all sports years ago, or maybe the Roller Derby is just something that has always been like nothing but itself."[97] Deford tapped into the pulse of the sport, its players, and its fans, and highlighted Roller Derby's appeal by emphasizing its working juxtapositions: "Roller Derby is, in fact, managed by young suburban-living executives who understand television and urban demography and know how to manipulate the realities of the '60s. At the same time Roller Derby is still a breath of the Depression, with the carnival air of the dance marathons that spawned it. It is still one-night stands and advance men, laundermats and greasy spoons."[98] He explained the combination of sport and spectacle that was Roller Derby while giving a voice to the skaters to describe their lives and experiences. Roller Derby charmed Deford in the process. Toward the end of a long and illustrious sports journalism career, Deford recalled, "I loved them. I thought they were great people. . . . I had more fun with them than with anybody I ever did a story on. Honestly!"[99] Deford turned his article into the book *Five Strides on the Banked Track: The Life and Times of the Roller Derby*, which was published in 1971. For decades, Deford's book was the preeminent historical account on the sport.

Also in 1971, Jerry Seltzer backed and presented a documentary about Roller Derby simply titled *Derby*.[100] The film, directed and photographed by Robert Kaylor and produced by William Richert, provides engaging footage of games and a glimpse into the ups and down of the skaters' personal and professional lives in locker rooms and hotel rooms, on long car drives, and at their homes.[101] It also follows a young man, Mike Snell, from Dayton, Ohio, as he plans to break into the ranks of Roller Derby. Snell, who frequently cheats on his wife, shoots pool in bars, and skips work, thinks he can become a quick star in the sport and thereby better his future.[102] Snell is described as "a true American original: a hustler, looking for angles, a ladies' man. . . . He is also engaging and smart."[103] The film morphs from a "conventional cinema verite documentary" about Roller Derby to one about the "American lower middle class" as experienced through the exploits of Mike Snell.[104]

Shown at film festivals from coast to coast and internationally, the documentary was critically acclaimed, although skaters and fans were less enthusiastic about it than anticipated, which translated into a bust at the box office.[105] Still, the movie received rave reviews from the top film critics in the country. Roger Ebert gave *Derby* four out of four stars and dubbed it "one of the most engaging movies I have seen in a long time."[106] Critics appreciated the film less for its analysis and presentation of the sport and more for opening a window into the hopes, dreams, and struggles of working-class America. Vincent Canby with the *New York Times* wrote, "Even though a lot of it is staged, it succeeds in capturing the essential truth of a time and place and state of mind that is, most often, the province of fiction. One of the reasons it is successful, I think, is that the movie itself is part of the spectacle it is documenting."[107] Canby, who rated the documentary as one of the ten best films of 1971, unequivocally believed it deserved more respect than it received at the box office. *Derby*, he wrote, "has more feeling for lower middle-class American life than any movie—documentary or fiction—made since those glorious B pictures about telephone linemen, oil field workers and what not, turned out by Hollywood in the 1930s and 1940s."[108] The world that *Derby* reveals is one "that's half hip, half square, comparatively well-informed (through television, which is never turned off) but completely unsophisticated, realistic, but full of fantasies, and always in debt. . . . As do all good movies, 'Derby' manages to say a great deal, without ever saying too much."[109] In other words, the documentary, though partly staged, presented a realistic slice of Americana, just like Roller Derby itself. The film reiterated Deford's take on the sport, whether intentionally or not.[110]

Perhaps two of the most famous examples of the popularity of roller derby came in a film and a song. In 1972, the Hollywood sex symbol Raquel Welch starred in the movie *Kansas City Bomber*, which was based on Roller Games. Welch plays a single mother and professional skater named K. C. Carr, who is starting over with a new team in Portland, Oregon. She struggles to fit in and gets involved in a romantic tangle with the owner. He wants her to lose a match race so that she can relocate with him to Chicago, but after realizing that she cannot trust him, she wins the race. Roger Greenspun, who reviewed the movie for the *New York Times*, wrote, "I can see the appeal the roller games had for a movie project like 'Kansas City Bomber.' Fast, loud, tough and violent, they provide an instant morality play with ready-made good guys, bad guys, and comic interludes, and with all the incorruptibility of Saturday-night wrestling."[111] Gene Siskel with the *Chicago Tribune* acknowledged why the film would appeal to American audiences, and he perhaps hit on the universal appeal of the sport, particularly its gender inclusiveness: "Tho the accent is on mindless fun throughout the picture, this doesn't prevent the movie from coming four square for such solid American values as playing to win, supporting one's children, male bosses mistreating female employees, and women tearing each other's hair out at the roots."[112]

Actual Roller Games skaters were hired to train Welch to skate. John Hall and Shirley Hardman, Roller Games stars, alternated the training duties until Hall and Welch had a bit of falling-out and Hall was replaced. Hall explained that whenever he trains anyone on the banked track, he trains them to "skate safely first, good secondly."[113] Part of skating safely is, perhaps paradoxically, falling safely: "One of the things you have to learn how to do is to fall correctly. When you fall correctly, you do not put your hands down. You tell them this repeatedly, you explain it to them why, you emphasize it: 'Do not put your hands down.'" Hall had trouble breaking Welch of that habit. She kept putting her hands down, which, in fairness, is the natural response, however dangerous. After practicing safely falling multiple times, Hall told Welch, "Let's try it one more time. This time, keep your hands up." He recalled,

> As she fell and started putting her hands down, I yelled, "Keep your f—— hands up, bitch!" Well, maybe I should've used my words differently. . . . She would not be talked to like that by a skater. So my team captain, Paul Rupert, took over her training. And the first day he trained her, Paul followed the safety procedures, learning to fall correctly, and she put her hands down and broke her wrist.

Shooting for the movie had to be delayed for eight weeks.[114] By the end, Hall and Welch had worked closely enough together that they were able to overcome their initial hostility. Hall ultimately complimented Welch: "She did a good job."[115]

On the heels of *Kansas City Bomber*, the folk singer Jim Croce, famous for his ballads, released the song "Roller Derby Queen" in 1973. Like the derby, Croce was a staple of Americana, and he loved the emotional interactions with his fans at concerts. One such interaction inspired "Roller Derby Queen." While playing at a local bar in Pennsylvania, Croce noticed a woman sitting about ten feet away. Every time the woman clapped, he could see the fat under her arm jiggling back and forth, and it inspired him: "It was a beautiful sight. I knew that I had to write a tune about her."[116] After talking with the woman, he learned that she was from Texas and used to be in the roller derby, but had fallen in love with a Pennsylvania state trooper and moved away. The song took five years to compose, but Croce tapped into a long history of the sport by dropping phrases, intentionally or not, such as "blond bomber," "round and round," and "Tuffy" (Toughie). Like Deford and *Derby*, Croce highlighted the appeal of the rough-edged roller derby, its participants, and Middle America.[117]

Roller derby appeared in a variety of media and films throughout the 1960s and '70s, some more popular (and appropriate) than others.[118] A 1976 *Charlie's Angels* episode was titled "Angels on Wheels," and in 1978 NBC broadcast a short-lived sitcom called *The Roller Girls*. Besides *Kansas City Bomber*, derby films included *Unholy Rollers* (1972) and the dystopian film *Rollerball* (1975). Articles on the derby appeared in *Time* and *People* magazines. There were even features on the derby in the porn magazines *Way Out* and *Inches*. Roller Derby was seemingly everywhere. Even nonfans were at least aware of its existence. But despite the rising cultural awareness and coverage, the actual organizations were struggling.

EXIT ROLLER DERBY

In December 1973, Jerry Seltzer made a cataclysmic executive decision. After an almost forty-year run, he shut down his organization. He called the skaters in for a meeting in New Haven, Connecticut, and simply said, "We just can't go on."[119] Seltzer recalled, "I don't think anybody expected it, and it really affected me for years afterwards, because you almost feel like a parent. You feel very responsible."[120] Many of the skaters had skated for the Seltzer family for decades, sometimes for more than one generation. According to Seltzer, "they kind of believed that Roller Derby was an institution—that I was the current caretaker but that somehow it was going to go on," but it did not, at least not in its customary form.[121]

The skaters' personal and professional lives were wrapped up in the sport, and this was extraordinarily difficult news to swallow. Many had never held other jobs or acquired any other professional skills. Ann Calvello had been skating since 1948, the year after she graduated from high school. She took the news hard: "What's a person to do, you know? I skated all my life."[122] She had earned good grades in school, but twenty-five years had passed since she graduated. The skaters were simply in utter disbelief. "It was like a death," explained Jan Vallow. "We were all in shock."[123]

In hindsight, the warning signs were there. Roller Derby was a cash-based institution, which never took out bank loans, and so it was subject to boom-and-bust cycles, depending on the cash flow each season. In its last few years, although still popular, the sport was not as profitable as previously and could not keep itself afloat financially. Furthermore, the quality of play had declined. Alan Ebert, a longtime fan of the game and a writer for *Roller Derby News*, was disgusted by the type of play exhibited in the derby's final years: "When I was a fan in the early days, they skated. There was none of that carnival crap that went on. . . . After a while what happened was that it became just one fight after another, and all kinds of things that just didn't exist. . . . I was embarrassed by it."[124] Seltzer corroborated Ebert's view, particularly as Roller Derby tried to keep pace with Roller Games: "As we got near the end, and we were getting more desperate, there just was—had to be a lot more activity, we felt, in terms of the presentation to the public. There were more fights. . . . We had tarnished [our image] pretty good near the end . . . trying to survive."[125]

Two direct factors contributed to Roller Derby's demise in late 1973. First, it had been broadcast on KTVU, receiving great ratings and support. But in 1971 or 1972, the station's owners hired a new program director, who hated Roller Derby. He decided to move its time slot from seven on Sunday night to four on Sunday afternoon. That switch caused ratings to plummet, which in turn affected live attendance. The second factor concerned the oil crisis of 1973. Roller Derby traveled across the country in cars and trucks, covering hundreds and sometimes thousands of miles a week. As supplies of gasoline dwindled and sometimes were cut off altogether, it became increasingly difficult to travel from arena to arena. And since the arenas were not getting the fuel they needed to stay open, many canceled their Roller Derby bookings. On top of dealing with these external issues, Seltzer explained, "We just never had that much cash to go from one year to the next."[126] There was no nest egg for the sport.

Fortunately, there was a nest egg for the skaters when the Roller Derby folded. According to Jerry Seltzer,

> The good thing was that we had done something very unusual: we had put in a profit-sharing plan so that 15 percent of what we made [every year] automatically went in. And based on [the skaters'] salary was the percentage that they got. And it had been in [existence] for over ten years, which most of them didn't believe. . . . So when we closed down, you know, they got at least $5,000. Some got as much as $60,000, which was a lot of money at that time.[127]

According to the skater Larry Smith, he and his wife, Francine Cochu, received "more than a full year's salary," which gave them options for their future that they did not have before receiving the payout.[128]

What happened organizationally after Seltzer closed his doors is a contested topic in the roller derby world. Many vehemently believe that Seltzer sold Roller Derby to Bill Griffiths of Roller Games, but Seltzer maintains that he "never sold it," as does John Hall, who was then a part owner of Roller Games.[129] Hall claims that Seltzer still had allegiance to some of his skaters; therefore, after Griffiths expressed interest in bringing them into Roller Games, Seltzer wanted to make sure they would be well taken care of. According to Hall, "That's the only cooperation I know that Griffiths and Seltzer had. There was no sale or anything else."[130] It may be that Roller Derby was never sold, but that Griffiths was given the go-ahead to pick up skaters or whole teams without any money exchanging hands.

Griffiths was incredibly interested in bringing in top-name Roller Derby skaters, but as Buddy Atkinson Jr. explained, it was not that easy: "Because all those skaters were so indoctrinated to the way they performed and how they did everything differently, the two never meshed."[131] Larry Smith, in his self-published memoir *The Last "True" Roller Derby*, confirmed this: "The National Skating Derby was a show. We were not a fast-paced sport any longer. We were told when and how to score or when to get knocked down or beaten up. The charade was a bit embarrassing for us."[132] Smith and Cochu tried to skate for Roller Games for a bit, but they could not stomach the scripted game. "We had fought the image of a fake sport for our entire careers," Smith recalled, "and now there we were, doing what we had said we would never do. . . . Roller Games had many great skaters; however, the promoters forced everyone to skate a different style of game."[133]

Whichever way Roller Derby skaters made it into Roller Games, to keep them, Griffiths paid them more. These skaters had been earning the highest salaries in Roller Derby under Seltzer, and according to Atkinson, Griffiths likewise bumped them to the top of the pay scale, which bred a lot of resentment in the other Roller Games skaters.[134] Furthermore, many of the new skaters could not or would not skate the Roller Games way, and then when they received their profit-sharing payout from Seltzer, they bolted. According to Atkinson, "Bill lost a lot of these skaters. They ended up going back to California, up to the Bay Area, where, really, most of them were from. And never came back. . . . They got their money and ran. . . . Bill Griffiths shot himself in the foot and didn't even know it."[135] Griffiths and his Roller Games organization were in trouble financially at the time, in part because of the split with Hill, the overexpansion of units, a lack of TV contracts, and, like Seltzer, the energy crisis. Griffiths was forced to shut down the Roller Games unit in California in late 1975, followed shortly by the demise of Hall's eastern Roller Games in early 1976.[136]

Throughout the next two decades, a number of roller derby organizations, some sponsored by skaters and some sponsored by sports promoters, popped up, but none lasted for a significant amount of time.[137] Yet the sport never officially died out, even if the trademarked version of Roller Derby did. Roller Games came back in a much smaller version in the late 1970s and 1980s. In the late 1990s, a revival of the sport was attempted. This time, skaters used in-line skates, the popular Rollerblades of the era, and a television series format. Dreamed up by the longtime television-producing partners Stephen Land and Ross Bagwell, the new version was called the World Skating League / Roller Jam and was featured on the television network TNN.[138] Jerry Seltzer, who served as a consultant for the league, was given the official title commissioner, and other former Roller Derby veterans such as Nick Scopas and Buddy Atkinson Jr. were hired as trainers. Like the other successor leagues, Roller Jam lasted only a couple years.[139] No one could make the sport work quite like the Seltzer family had done.

6 | DIY Roller Derby

Real. Strong. Athletic. Revolutionary.

WOMEN'S FLAT TRACK DERBY ASSOCIATION TAGLINE

Since a lot of the first [men's] teams . . . were very closely involved with area women's teams and had been helping out and had established themselves within the community as stand-up guys, it became a little bit easier to reach out and talk to the women's organizations, because we were not commodities, we weren't going to ruin anything, we weren't trying to exploit anything, and we weren't here to take anything away. . . . We were just trying to play a game that we had fell in love with.

JAKE FAHY, COFOUNDER OF PIONEER VALLEY ROLLER DERBY AND THE FIRST MEN'S ROLLER DERBY TEAM

Roller derby has always been a sport of endurance, and despite the Seltzer organization's demise in the mid-1970s, the sport has stood the test of time. The most recent (and lasting) revival of roller derby originated in Austin, Texas, in early 2001, and there are now more than 1,900 leagues across the world, nearly half of them in the United States.[1] While this version of the sport continues to evolve (as did all versions, even the Seltzers'), it has been around for nearly two decades. Thousands of amateur players skate in leagues around the world, some of which compete for international championships, so it seems safe to say that roller derby, in some form of its present-day incarnation, is here to stay.[2] Nonetheless, this version of roller derby still struggles with the battles of the past. Roller derby continues to push for the self-empowerment and the strength of its women, particularly athlete-mothers, while resisting outside attempts to control and define its athletes and beloved sport.

A rascally, barhopping promoter type originally from Tulsa named Dan Policarpo decided that his new place of residence, Austin, Texas, was ripe for a revival of the sport of roller derby. But Devil Dan, as he was nicknamed, had no intention of fulfilling Leo Seltzer's dream of bringing the derby into the mainstream athletic world as a legitimate sport. Policarpo's vision aligned more closely with that of Bill Griffiths in the later stages of Roller Games. Policarpo thought it would be fun to start a women's roller derby league that was more circus and skin than legitimate sport, and he quickly began plastering Austin with posters announcing his plan.[3] "I wanted to take a pop culture institution from the past and reload it with new information," explained Policarpo. "There were all these aggressive women running around. Some were into the whole tattooed rockabilly look, and I just thought of an all-girl roller derby league."[4] Policarpo envisioned a sort of roller derby "freak-show" and described his idea as such: "I wanted more smoke and mirrors, more like 'Rollerball' than roller derby. There was a circus in town at the time and I wanted it to be like that, but more extreme, like clowns fighting each other with knives."[5]

He recruited a group of about fifty women from the vibrant cultural scene rooted along Red River Street to meet at the bar-restaurant Casino El Camino on Sunday, January 11, 2001. He lured them in with the following speech: "The girls in this town are really angry. I want to start a Roller Derby, like a sideshow, with hot girls and fire twirlers. . . . Don't worry about knowing how to skate. The sound effects and light show will make up for it."[6] Devil Dan's vision incorporated the most outrageous and theatrical aspects of the late-1960s and 1970s Roller Derby and Roller Games (such as the use of little people for exoticism), and he placed himself firmly at the head of the whole show, Griffiths-style. The denizens of the hip underground and local music scene in Austin, as well as the bar and nightclub owners, contributed to the fund-raising for the new roller derby.[7]

At Devil Dan's suggestion, the women divided themselves into four themed teams, apparently according to the bar they patronized most often. Each team was captained by a popular Austin "scenester."[8] Roller derby was reimagined and reborn with the new teams, new captains, and new players, all of whom adopted derby pseudonyms (henceforth called derby names) that either highlighted some aspect of their personalities via a fun play on words or else served as aliases that became alter egos of a sort.[9] April Ritzenthaler, aka La Muerta, headed the Putas del Fuego; Nancy Haggerty, aka Iron Maiden, led the Hellcats; Amanda Hardison, aka Miss Information, captained the Holy Rollers; and Anya Jack, aka Hot Lips Dolly, managed the Rhinestone Cowgirls.[10] As Ritzenthaler explained, "We thought we should be larger than life. Naming yourself gave you that extra inspiration to fill out that character."[11]

The new roller derby women continued recruiting for their teams and the league in general, and many tried their hand at skating for the first time. Before the league could really take off, they needed to be financially viable, so they focused on fund-raising. But in March 2001, they realized that Devil Dan had blown all the money raised so far and then skipped town. Deeply invested in the new roller derby, the women did not want to give up on it, despite the perfidy of Devil Dan.[12] The four captains grabbed the reins of the fledgling league (with Heather Burdick, aka Sugar, replacing Amanda Hardison as captain of the Holy Rollers) and made it all up as they went along.[13]

The captains lacked knowledge of any recent roller derby model on which to base their league, and none of the leaders had any real skating skills. One original member described the league as "just party girls hanging out in bars and talking about something that may or may not happen," adding, "We did more drinking than we did skating."[14] The members had no real concept of what roller derby had been or what its new incarnation should be. According to Jennifer Barbee and Alex Cohen, the original members in essence created their own version of the sport: "From a recollection skewed by youthful idealism and media input, these pioneer skaters reincarnated the sport as a cross between the hard hits of Saturday afternoon [Joan] Weston versus [Ann] Calvello brawls and the fashion bonanza of Farrah Fawcett duking it out on skates in *Charlie's Angels*."[15]

The captains of the teams officially instituted more formal control after Devil Dan's disappearance. They formed Bad Girl Good Woman (BGGW) Productions, which stood as the "league's governing council, tasked with giving the group structure and division,"[16] but it eventually grew to be more like a business than an amateur sports league.[17] The four captains, who dubbed themselves the "She-E-Os," were determined to make roller derby succeed, but their league would reflect their own personal flair and would have no male leadership or control: "no men allowed."[18] The BGGW league initiated the do-it-yourself ethic that has since become a staple of modern roller derby, and institutionalized a culture of "sexy uniforms, skater alter egos, and new-school rules combined with unparalleled athleticism and fearlessness."[19]

It took the first league about a year and a half to research the game, revise the rules, raise money, promote the league, recruit more skaters, develop skating skills, and decide on a penalty system. By the early summer of 2002, it was ready to debut a modern flat-track roller derby.[20] As a trial run, on June 23, 2002, the BGGW held a roller derby bout at Skate World in North Austin before a crowd composed of family and friends.[21] In a result reminiscent of midcentury Roller Derby scores, the Hellcats defeated the Rhinestone Cowgirls 45–38.[22] Buoyed by the success of the bout, the BGGW held its first official public bout at the Playland Skate Center, also in North Austin, on August 22, 2002, drawing approximately four hundred fans who paid five dollars each for a ticket. By the time of its league championship in October, the BGGW had sold over 1,100 tickets. Roller derby had resurfaced in a big way.[23]

As with any young organization, particularly one with a limited structure and an unclear vision, problems quickly surfaced between the athletes and management concerning league governance. The She-E-Os retired from skating midseason during the first year to concentrate on running the league, hoping to create a profit-generating business; to the skaters, their actions looked like an attempt to consolidate control and exploit the hard work of the league members, who were paying dues but not seeing much prize money. A failed attempt to raise money by selling a league calendar featuring the skaters, along with a heated insurance controversy concerning an injured player, brought anxieties and tensions to a head. In April 2003, after an intense league meeting between the athletes and the She-E-Os failed to resolve any major issues, most of the skaters decided to break off and form their own roller derby league, the Texas Rollergirls, which was structured to be "by the skaters, for the skaters."[24] A fierce, often unpleasant rivalry developed between the two leagues. Shortly after the split, the BGGW's She-E-Os invested in an authentic banked track from the original San Francisco Bay Bombers, renamed their league the TXRD Lonestar Rollergirls, and gradually relinquished control to the skaters. The TXRD skaters eventually adopted the skater-owned-and-operated league model of their rivals—which is somewhat ironic, since the league's original structure and leadership triggered the split.[25]

Since the revival of banked-track roller derby and the institution of flat-track roller derby in Austin, amateur leagues have spread like wildfire across the country. The flat-track version is the most common form of the sport, if for no other reason than banked tracks are extremely expensive to purchase, maintain, and move. A league with a banked track needs a permanent space in which to house the track, which can be costly, particularly for non-revenue-generating teams. Only about a dozen banked-track roller derby leagues operate across the United States, whereas there are more than 800 women's flat-track leagues.[26]

WOMEN'S FLAT TRACK DERBY ASSOCIATION

In the years since the reemergence of the sport, a national volunteer, tax-exempt organization has been formed to govern the women's flat-track leagues. The Women's Flat Track Derby Association (WFTDA) describes itself as "the international governing body for the sport of women's flat track roller derby and a membership organization for leagues to collaborate and network."[27] Its mission is "to govern and promote the sport of flat track roller derby and revolutionize the role of women in sports through the collective voice of its member leagues around the world."[28] In addition, it establishes the "international standards for rankings, rules, and competition each year and provides guidance and resources to the sport of flat track derby."[29] Since 2005, the WFTDA has expanded to include 463 leagues.

The WFTDA grew out of an organization dubbed the United Leagues Coalition (ULC), which was founded in 2004 by "a handful of flat track roller derby leagues, each owned and operated by skaters sharing the singular, driving compulsion to re-imagine roller derby as a modern sport."[30] Leading the charge was the Texas Rollergirls.[31] At the ULC's first official meeting, in 2005, twenty flat-track league representatives were present. The group established the purpose, goals, and mission of its organization and voted to rename it the Women's Flat Track Derby Association. The WFTDA allowed new members to join in September 2006. In the years since then, the group has established itself as the premier governing body of the modern sport of women's flat-track roller derby.[32]

The WFTDA, run by a volunteer board of directors, a handful of paid employees, and unpaid skaters who donate their time and energy, provides a great service to the derby world, bringing it cohesion, structure, and connectivity.[33] But the association has, in many ways, been plagued by modern gender and sports politics; for a time, it was unable to duplicate Roller Derby's feat of achieving gender equality. The WFTDA is also currently facing a threat from powerful, mostly male forces challenging its official governance of the sport. The WFTDA bought into the Austin-based idea that modern roller derby was for women only—the sport, in fact, has been described as "the third wave of feminism"[34] and has ties to the woman-centered Riot Grrrl movement.[35] Most women's flat-track leagues, whether belonging to the WFTDA or not, promote their leagues as spaces for empowered women who like to work hard, challenge themselves, and enjoy teamwork.[36] For instance, the league originally called the Green Mountain Derby Dames, a WFTDA league located in Burlington, Vermont, adopted the following mission statement: "The mission of the Green Mountain Derby Dames is to empower women personally and athletically through the sport of roller derby. As a skater-owned and operated organization, it is our intention to hold ourselves to the highest standards of respect and sportswoman-ship on and off the track, uphold the rules and values of the Women's Flat Track Derby Association, and to be a positive force in our community."[37]

Women from across the country have embraced this type of athletic outlet, particularly since the male-dominated sports world has long turned a cold shoulder to women's sports, especially full-contact ones. Women-run sports organizations that focus on the empowerment of women, other than physical education departments, have been few and far between. What is particularly interesting with modern roller derby is the evolution of the WFTDA's stance regarding men's involvement in the sport and its relationship to men's roller derby. For years, a team hoping to join the WFTDA had to be a part of a league that competed only against other women, and female skaters had to own 51 percent of the league.[38] Women had finally gained control of a sport and intended to keep it. They wanted to determine the future of their sport.

While almost every league in existence nods its head to the long history of Roller Derby and pays a brief tribute to the history of the sport on its website, most leagues seem to ignore or at least to forget the fact that Roller Derby was one of the first sports to include women as equal competitors with men, from the very beginning. Women no longer wanted to include men as their partners on the track, in part for good reason, given how modern sports culture has developed since the passing of Title IX. Women's sports have often been eclipsed by their male counterparts and treated as the lesser version of the "true" male sport.[39] Once women's sports organizations gain control and experience success, they often are forced out or taken over by powerful men's organizations with longer histories, deeper pockets, and better connections.[40]

The conflict over men's roller derby has long been a problem for Pioneer Valley Roller Derby (PVRD), a co-ed league located in Northampton, Massachusetts. The PVRD, founded in 2005 by Sarah Lang and Jake Fahy, began with separate women's and men's teams that nonetheless belonged to a league whose members practiced together, like the Seltzer version of days gone by.[41] The PVRD men's team was, in fact, the first men's team created after the 2001 revival. As Fahy explained, "Really, it was just that I wanted to play. We knew that guys weren't doing it, so we knew that that would be a change or would not be usual, so to speak, but I don't know if we really thought it was that big a deal at that point."[42] Because the PVRD was owned by Lang and Fahy equally but governed by the skaters, and because its members played competitors who were not women (that is, the men's team competed against other men), the women's team was not able to join the WFTDA as its rules stood, because of this association with the men. Of course, the PVRD men's team was not eligible to join, either.[43]

The skaters at PVRD were a dedicated, innovative, and hardy group of people, so as men's roller derby continued to spread, the male skaters decided to form a men's roller derby organization. In 2007, the PVRD, along with the recently formed men's teams the Harm City Homicide, New York Shock Exchange, and the Death Quads of Connecticut, formed the Men's Derby Coalition (MDC).[44] The MDC described itself as "a loose federation of men's derby leagues [whose] primary goals were to promote men's derby through sharing resources and contributing to the derby community."[45] As men's derby continued to grow, the MDC realized it had "gained enough momentum to require national level organization and games sanctioning."[46] From the foundation laid by the MDC emerged the Men's Roller Derby Association (MRDA). The new organization, largely run by "the same passionate men and women" from the MDC, emphasized resource sharing between men's leagues but also provided specific benefits to leagues that joined the MRDA: "umbrella insurance coverage, insurance reciprocity with WFTDA, and the ability to compete in the annual MRDA Championship tournament."[47] The MRDA intended to complement the WFTDA's organizational structure, and received encouragement from the women's group, although relations were somewhat tense at the beginning while the WFTDA gauged the values, goals, and motives of men's roller derby.

Yet the MRDA's leadership formed an unofficial partnership with the WFTDA early on, and the two organizations have grown closer and more cooperative over the years.[48]

The MRDA does a fine job of governing, regulating, and promoting men's roller derby. With the WFTDA's membership limited to leagues owned and operated by female skaters, some women's teams fall through the cracks. Because of their association with men, these teams cannot join WFTDA, and because of the sex of their skaters, they cannot join the MRDA.[49] Pioneer Valley's women's traveling team, the Western Mass Destruction, was isolated in this way. There is no easy solution to this conundrum, but it can't hurt to mention that once upon a time, in a sports world largely segregated by sex (and race), men and women used to skate side by side as teammates in one organization.

It is unclear whether modern roller derby will head in the direction of the sport's more equal past or whether it will remain a sex-segregated enterprise. Developments in the last few years indicate that the WFTDA and many women's leagues are open to including men officially or partnering with men, even as they stay true to their goals of female empowerment and opportunity. For instance, the Green Mountain Derby Dames underwent a name change to Green Mountain Roller Derby in 2015 to better reflect the team's values and commitment to gender inclusion. A press release explained the reasons:

> We want our league name to reflect who we are and what we do in a concise manner. . . . Roller derby has always attracted a diverse cross-section of people—women and men, straight and LGBTQ+, those with athletic backgrounds and those without, and ages ranging from school-age to retired. We are proud to provide a safe and welcoming space for all kinds of people to grow as athletes, leaders, and more. We want the league's name to represent all of these amazing people who make roller derby happen in Vermont.[50]

Although Green Mountain Roller Derby skaters are still female identified and belong to the WFTDA, they recognize the importance of providing an open atmosphere that includes all the contributing members of their league, especially nonskaters: "We are a diverse community of people who work tirelessly to bring the empowering sport of roller derby to our state. We believe that true feminism is about being able to determine our own path and what and who we want our league to represent."[51]

SEX, POLITICS, AND DERBY

Aside from the complexities of how to govern roller derby—and there are many—gender politics has influenced the sport in other interesting ways, both positive and negative.[52] Contemporary observers, many of whom have taken to the blogosphere, have commented on the sexualization of modern roller derby skaters. Over the past decade, fishnet stockings, booty shorts, red lipstick, and sex-themed derby names have become staples of the "national punk rock derby renaissance."[53] The skaters have not only embraced this culture and their own sexuality but promoted it as well.[54] In 2009, Gotham Girls Roller Derby described its ideal skater as "an amalgam of athlete, pin-up girl, rocker and brute rolled into one badass derby girl."[55] The breathless description of the team's skaters verged on the hyperbolic: "Pretty? Hell, yeah! Tough? Of course! Badass? Always! These ladies are taking all the action and excitement of the roller derby you remember and doing it with a modern twist to keep you on your toes."[56]

This expression of a modern type of sexuality is part of a larger national conversation about feminism, sexual liberation, sexual identity, and what the writer Ariel Levy dubs "raunch feminism."[57] Are women who play a full-contact sport on their own terms and by their own rules promoting a modern feminist agenda? Does the fact that many of them do it while wearing short skirts mark their efforts as merely "a garbled attempt at continuing the work of the women's movement"?[58] Or are women simply playing a sport they enjoy, an act that has nothing to do with feminism? Is this modern sexualization of athletes merely a continuation of the emphasis on femininity that has plagued women's sports since the late nineteenth century? Is this a story of continuity or change?

There are no clear-cut answers to these questions. It is a sign of progress that thousands of women play a full-contact sport unabashedly and unapologetically. Many skaters embrace their own sexuality and legitimately enjoy wearing skimpy clothes, justifying these decisions with "post-feminist" rhetoric that insists it is their choice to wear such items and they do it for their own benefit.[59] As one Austin skater put it in 2008, "From the very beginning, the skaters embraced the attitude that we realize that we're dressing in skimpy outfits and playing up the sexiness, but we're in charge of that and we're comfortable with it. We exploit ideas about women that aren't exactly PC . . . We wear these costumes because we look good in them. This is feminist-based, and it's never about exploitation."[60] The skimpy outfits are not mandatory. Most skaters, in fact, see their clothing as liberating, as a personal expression. In my experience with the modern game, I have frequently seen average-length mesh gym shorts on female skaters, but, realistically, it is easier to skate and play roller derby in spandex. Many skaters promote women's strength and empowerment within roller derby and in their regular lives. But most skaters join roller derby leagues because the sport is fun—not to make a political statement.[61]

Yet roller derby does make a political statement, as do skaters when they publicly bout. It is hard to say what exactly that statement is, because every time roller derby is placed in a box or defined in some way, the sport changes. For instance, Gotham Girls Roller Derby skaters, who used to consider themselves "an amalgam of athlete, pin-up girl, rocker and brute rolled into one badass derby girl," now define themselves as "strong, diverse, and independent women from the world's biggest, baddest city."[62] The Gotham Girls are no longer a part of a hip, underground subculture that promoted female sexuality and toughness, but rather members of a premier amateur league "committed to fostering serious competition on a national and international level, developing amateur athletes for competition, and promoting the physical and mental strength and independent spirit of amateur female athletes."[63] The novelty of strong women hitting each other while wearing provocative clothes, if this was ever what the novelty consisted of, has passed. Roller derby is a national sport that continues to grow and evolve. It is impossible to say what it will become. Will it remain a culture-driven amateur sport, or will it, like the roller derby of the past, evolve into a paid, professional enterprise?[64] Regardless, the narrative surrounding modern roller derby is ultimately a story about female athletes struggling with their own identity, which makes it a new chapter in a continuing saga of personal and community self-identification.

FIGHTING FOR CONTROL

Without a Seltzer-type figure at the helm, it is perhaps unsurprising that not everyone agrees on what the future of roller derby should look like or what the sport should be. There are several roller derby governing organizations besides the WFTDA, although none with the strength and influence of the latter. The WFTDA is considered the preeminent ruling body of modern women's flat-track roller derby; it was the first

FIGURE 6.1. *Pioneer Valley Roller Derby skaters huddling at a bout, 2011. Photo by Lesley Arak.*

governing body, its rule set is the most widely adopted one, and it has a huge number of strong member leagues.

Another organization that developed in recent years is the Roller Derby Coalition of Leagues (RDCL). Founded in 2011 to "foster and grow the sport of banked track roller derby," the RCDL is a small organization of approximately five leagues operating under its own rule set.[65] The Modern Athletic Derby Endeavor (MADE) includes both flat- and banked-track skating and offers membership to women's, men's, and co-ed leagues. MADE, organized in 2006, emphasizes the fan experience and strives to streamline the rules of the game to allow fans "to easily follow our competitions and become enamored by our beloved sport."[66]

Since 2012, the real conflict over roller derby governance has occurred between the WFTDA, USA Roller Sports (USARS), the International Olympic Committee (IOC), the US Olympic Committee (USOC), and the Fédération Internationale de Roller Sports (FIRS).[67] This conflict is still unfolding. To be included as an Olympic sport, roller derby would have to go through the sanctioned route, following particular guidelines and rules set by national and international Olym-

Figure 6.2. *Referees checking Pioneer Valley Roller Derby gear before a bout, 2011. Photo by Lesley Arak.*

pic committees and their affiliates. For years, the WFTDA and other roller derby leagues have debated whether that status was something they even wanted for the sport. It would mean losing much of their DIY, countercultural feel—and most likely, direct control of their organizations. While skaters discussed whether the Olympics was something they wanted to try for in the future, it never seemed to be a pressing concern. In the meantime, the WFTDA fostered the growth of roller derby and began hosting international tournaments.

To be on the Olympic pathway, a sport must be recognized and sanctioned by organizations answerable to the IOC. Currently, FIRS and the USOC recognize USARS "as the National Governing Body of competitive roller sports in the United States."[68] While USARS has long governed amateur roller sports such as speed skating, figure skating, in-line hockey, and rink hockey, it was a latecomer to the roller derby scene. It began game development in 2012 when it created a rule set that resembled the original roller derby rules.[69] To reiterate the chain of command: USARS is recognized by the USOC, and the USOC and IOC recognize FIRS as the international roller sports governing body, which gives FIRS the power to oversee USARS as well. FIRS became interested in roller derby around 2012, but has taken on an increasingly aggressive tone as it attempts to consolidate power and control over the sport. This power grab comes at the expense of the WFTDA and the "for the skater, by the skater," independent, female-directed democracy that has been vital to the development of roller derby over the past fifteen years.

This move for dominance by FIRS has become increasingly apparent and threatening to WFTDA governance since 2015. According to Juliana Gonzales, aka Bloody Mary, executive director of the WFTDA from 2009 to 2015, a pivotal meeting occurred between WFTDA and FIRS representatives in Rome in February 2015. The WFTDA had been in informal contact with FIRS since late 2012 after finding out about a letter sent by FIRS president Sabatino Aracu to FIRS affiliates wherein "he ordered that roller derby be unified under the FIRS umbrella."[70] Such a state of affairs would be problematic for the WFTDA. Attendees at the Rome meeting included Juliana Gonzales, WFTDA executive director; Amanda Hull, WFTDA president; and Sabatino Aracu, FIRS president.[71] The WFTDA reps anticipated that the meeting would be mainly about rules sharing and licensing, and perhaps about FIRS's plan for the 2017 World Roller Games. But, as Gonzales explained in her recap of the meeting,

Figure 6.3. *A Pioneer Valley Roller Derby bout, 2011. Photo by Lesley Arak.*

For FIRS, the purpose of this meeting was to explore how best to "unite roller derby under the FIRS umbrella." . . . It became evident to me that FIRS was talking about a much more complete takeover. In the course of the meeting, it became clear that what they are proposing is that they move WFTDA's operations, resources, and membership into a branch of FIRS. By the end of the meeting, they acknowledged that if we follow this proposed course of action, they envision WFTDA dissolving completely within a few years, and its work being completely absorbed by FIRS.[72]

Governance by FIRS obviously would not mesh with a "by the skater, for the skater," democratic ideology. In fact, FIRS's actions validated the WFTDA's fears about aligning with traditional male sports and hierarchy. Gonzales and Hull tried to get Aracu to understand that bottom-up rule is critical to their organization and skaters: "We attempted to get across that this is a core value for us, and that far beyond our reluctance to be managed by other sports, we cannot be governed by people who are not elected by our community."[73] Aracu explained how for him and for FIRS, democracy is "an inefficient and ineffective model."[74]

The WFTDA had previously expressed some interest in pursuing an alignment with SportAccord, an international union of Olympic and non-Olympic sports organizations that allows each member sport its autonomy but also grants it important recognition.[75] Affiliation with SportAccord provides a legitimate avenue for IOC recognition.[76] Gonzales thought that perhaps she could gain FIRS's support for the WFTDA to join SportAccord, but her hopes were dashed: "It is clear from this meeting that FIRS would absolutely block any move by roller derby outside of the FIRS umbrella. . . . It is also clear that FIRS has a good relationship with SportAccord and is influential in their work. I am certain that FIRS would attempt to block our application to SportAccord, and I suspect they have the connections and influence to do that quite successfully."[77]

It was clear after the Rome meeting that FIRS wanted to bring roller derby under its control, and it wanted WFTDA's agreement to that plan. FIRS did not seem to understand either the importance of skater control in the WFTDA's democratic model or skaters' hostility to appropriation of their organization. At one point in the meeting, Gonzales recalled, "I had the opportunity to say something like 'When WFTDA's athletes look at FIRS's website, they see old white men. They don't believe that you share our 'by the skaters, for the skaters' ethic.' This made all the

FIRS people chuckle. In a way that was not actually very reassuring at all."[78] Indeed, FIRS disdained the WFTDA ethos but nonetheless wanted control of its leagues. FIRS made clear it wanted to govern roller derby officially and planned to phase out the WFTDA. WFTDA was confronted with its longtime greatest fear. Gonzales laid out the alternatives facing the association:

> They intend to pursue roller derby under their umbrella "with or without us." . . . We need to find a way to work with (or within) FIRS, or we need to assert our independence and circle up on what we do for the next decades to maintain our position. We are currently in the "friendly merger" phase of talks with an organization that is very close to the "hostile takeover" phase of actions. Straddling the collaboration line will not work much longer.[79]

By October of that year, the WFTDA publicly asserted its claim to be considered the primary governing body of roller derby and publicly rejected any such claims made by FIRS. The WFTDA sent open letters to representatives of the IOC and to President Aracu of FIRS. In the letter to Aracu, the WFTDA stated that it was happy to collaborate with FIRS to help the sport grow, but the "WFTDA will not recognize FIRS as the international governing body of roller derby, nor will we cede the authority to govern and direct the future of roller derby to FIRS."[80] The letter to the IOC provides a brief history of modern roller derby and the WFTDA's pivotal role in its development and growth. It makes the case why the WFTDA should be considered the sole governing body of the sport and why FIRS should not be: "FIRS is unknowledgeable about the sport and its community, and cannot provide any legitimate evidence of its contributions to the establishment, development or governance of flat track roller derby."[81] The WFTDA stated that it was willing to comply with IOC guidelines "so long as we are able to protect the integrity and independent governance of our sport."[82] The MRDA also sent a letter of support to the IOC, asserting the WFTDA's claim as the dominant governing body of roller derby and rejecting FIRS's actions to attempt to govern the sport.[83] As it turned out, it was not the men within the sport that the WFTDA needed to be concerned about, but rather those on the outside.

At the time of this writing, the international derby drama is still unfolding. A FIRS takeover could have deeply detrimental effects on the current democratic structure of the sport. This attempted hijacking is eerily reminiscent of the conflict in women's college sports in the 1970s and 1980s between the AIAW (Association for Intercollegiate Athletics for Women) and the NCAA (National Collegiate Athletic Association). In a nutshell, the woman-run AIAW, which governed women's sports, operated with a different ethos from the NCAA's. The AIAW emphasized academics as much as athletics and wanted to retain control of women's sports for women. Men had no interest in governing women's sports before Title IX, when there was no money or prestige attached to them. After the passage of Title IX (in 1972), and after the failure of male administrators to eliminate or even soften the law, a lot more money began pouring into women's college sports, and the NCAA took the route of co-optation: "If we can't beat 'em, let's join 'em." With its power and deep pockets, the NCAA was able to force the AIAW out of the game. The AIAW sued, claiming the NCAA had used its income from the completely separate market of men's sports to enter and dominate the women's sports market, which violated antitrust and monopoly laws. But the AIAW lost in a devastating lawsuit and was soon forced to fold.[84]

It is unclear what will happen with the WFTDA-FIRS conflict, particularly since the fall 2018 merger between FIRS and the International Skateboarding Federation, forming a new organization known as World Skate. The merger intended "to provide a more modern platform for the management of all skate disciplines."[85] World Skate, recognized by the IOC, continues to sponsor the World Roller Games, which include roller derby, and since history has shown time and again that those with power and money often get their way, the roller derby community should both beware and be vigilant if it wants history to have a different outcome this time.[86]

THE KIDS ARE ALL RIGHT

Despite these struggles and conflicts (or perhaps because of them), steps have been taken to ensure roller derby's legacy and build for its future. Junior roller derby has grown in the past seven years in a major way. The lack of a feeder system was one of the structural problems with Roller Derby. Training schools were held in the United States and Canada, but it was difficult to recruit skaters, since roller derby was not offered as a school sport or made available by groups such as the YMCA.

Modern junior roller derby emerged from skaters bringing their children to their practices, as well as from enthusiastic young fans of the women's game vying for skating opportunities. Kids would hang around to watch their family and friends practice and play, and learned the derby ropes that way. And eventually they wanted a chance to play.[87] The first junior league was the Tucson Derby Brats, which formed in 2006, followed by the Seattle Derby Brats in 2007.[88] Other junior leagues popped up across the nation, often in conjunction with an adult league. (Or at least coached by skaters or refs from established leagues.) In 2009, volunteers associated with junior leagues and teams formed the Junior Roller Derby Association (JRDA) to promote junior derby and standardize the game play and rules.[89] The JRDA was not a subsidiary of the WFTDA, despite using a modified version of the latter's rule set, nor did it belong to any other larger skating or derby organization. It simply concentrated on expanding junior roller derby for all youth.[90] The JRDA adopted a democratic ethos in determining how the organization and member leagues operated, and decisions were made by skaters, parents, coaches, and league leaders. By 2015, the JRDA had a Female Division, a Male Division, and a co-ed Open Division. The organization had grown enough by then to sponsor championships and a Junior Derby World Cup.[91]

Furthermore, in June 2015 it was announced that USARS and the Amateur Athletic Union (AAU) would host the first Roller Derby Junior Olympics, in Lincoln, Nebraska, in the summer of 2016. In December 2015, the JRDA announced that it was collaborating with USARS and the AAU on the event. The partnership emerged out of conversations about having the JRDA national championships at the same time and place as the USARS national tournament, but then addressed the possibility of the JRDA participating in the Junior Olympics, which seemed like a good opportunity for its young skaters.

The announcement stated that USARS would "define the way the sport will be represented at the event, including the team selection process, the competition structure and the requirements for participation, among other parameters."[92] Once the JRDA was officially on board, however, USARS allowed it to organize much of the event, and the JRDA made the decision to continue playing under its version of the WFTDA rule set.[93] At the time, the JRDA believed that this collaboration to include roller derby in the Junior Olympics was "taking a big step forward in the development of the sport."[94] Perhaps it was, but whether the sport, particularly the adult branch governed by the WFTDA, wanted to be included in the Olympic pipeline, even obliquely, was still a controversial topic. As seen with the FIRS conflict, which was occurring simultaneously, the skaters risked losing their DIY ethic and, ultimately, control over the game they had worked to nourish and develop. The JRDA considered its participation in the event a success and viewed it as "a good opportunity for our juniors, to showcase our juniors, and have them have that opportunity of playing in the Olympics."[95] According to the current JRDA president, Renee Miller, "The juniors have always been the main focus of any decision that the JRDA has made; it didn't have anything to do with an organization."[96] Because the JRDA exists to promote youth roller derby, it is less concerned with the politics of the adult organizations and does not strive, at least in its current form, to be the sole governing body of junior roller derby. It wants to provide opportunities for junior skaters and their families, and to try to include them in the process. Ultimately, as Miller explained, "Our only mission in life, as an organization, is to make sure that we are advancing the sport of junior roller derby and that we're doing it responsibly for our members," who are minors.

As junior derby grew, and perhaps in response to the JRDA's partnerships with USARS and the AAU and a potential hostile takeover by FIRS, the WFTDA became interested in creating a junior organization that would abide by the WFTDA mantra of "by the skater, for the skater," in order to ensure that "this philosophy will continue on in future generations of derby skaters."[97] The new organization, called the Junior Flat Track Derby Association (JFTDA), was going to be under the wing of the WFTDA's Junior Committee until the "JFTDA has a sustainable structure, at which time a Board of Directors will be voted in, and JFTDA will continue to exist as an independent organization separate from the WFTDA."[98] The program was launched in September 2015, but it never officially materialized. The JRDA, however, has kept plugging along. An important moment occurred in February 2017, when the WFTDA announced that it, the MRDA, and the JRDA were partnering on releases of roller derby rule sets. The WFTDA press release stated:

> The partnership between the WFTDA, MRDA, and JRDA will not only be to establish a standardized rule set for our sport, but to elevate the expectations of sportspersonship across roller derby and to amplify a broad message of inclusion and model it for the greater organized sport community. With the growth in worldwide participation in roller

derby, the partnership between WFTDA, MRDA, and JRDA aims to continue to make the sport as accessible as possible. The WFTDA will work with JRDA to modify the rules around contact for junior use, the standardization will allow for a united, global front—at all levels of play.[99]

Furthermore, the WFTDA noted that this new partnership with JRDA on the rules replaced the unrealized JFTDA initiative.[100] At the moment, it appears that all three organizations are pleased to work closely together to provide a smooth transition from junior derby to the WFTDA, the MRDA, or any other adult derby organization in order to keep the sport growing and strong.[101]

MODERN DERBY MOTHERS

Governance and control are not the only issues facing modern roller derby. Pregnancy and motherhood will continue to need to be addressed, as they have been since 1935. Despite often being touted as a way to see a lot of T&A (at least in the early years),[102] modern roller derby leagues have worked hard to cultivate a family atmosphere, especially at their bouts. While the sport is not conducive to pregnancy (almost none are), most leagues encourage mothers to join. Youngsters are common fixtures in roller derby practice facilities, and can be spotted playing in the stands or around the edges of the track. As mentioned earlier, it was from this family atmosphere that junior roller derby began. Most leagues provide discounted or free admission to children in an attempt to appeal to everyone.[103]

Although no official statistics have been compiled, almost all women's leagues have mothers in their ranks, and fathers are a part of the MRDA. Like the Seltzer Roller Derby, the modern derby continues to offer an athletic space for mothers, and much more so than other women's team sports. The derby community encourages mothers to return to skating as soon as possible after giving birth. Some women return to the track while still breastfeeding. In 2011, Kate Hansen, an artist and roller derby skater, posted photographs on her art blog under the title "Breastfeeding and Roller Derby." Each picture featured a roller derby skater in full derby gear breastfeeding her baby — on the team bench, in the locker room, at home, and on the edge of the track. She thoughtfully posed the question, "What is it that we find so riveting about roller derby girls breastfeeding?"[104] She answered with the following:

> Perhaps it's the contrast. The idea of roller derby, the fact it's a contact sport and a little bad-ass, combined with the soft, nurturing role of breastfeeding mother. . . . It's slightly subversive to combine the image of a full contact sport with the role of motherhood, especially breast-feeding. Even the visual contrast of the hard equipment with the soft-ness of breastfeeding is interesting. It's wonderful because it questions our notions of what women are, and what it means to be female.[105]

Hansen's last line not only highlights the contradictions of the athlete-mother but also unknowingly articulates the relationship of roller derby to the larger society. Roller derby pushes society to reassess its ideas about women's identities and physical capabilities. People are forced to confront the fact that women, even as mothers, are capable of compet-ing in a full-contact sport. Like breastfeeding, nothing could be more natural for these skaters.

This assertion is not to discount the problematic nature of preg-nancy for the committed roller derby athlete. Even those who want to be mothers struggle to align that identity with their role as a skater, especially since they are forced to take a step back from the track dur-ing the midstages of their pregnancies. Lynn Klas, aka Juke Boxx, was both a skater and a coach with the London Rollergirls when she found out she was pregnant. She and her husband, who is also a roller derby coach, wanted children but were surprised when it happened. In an article and blog post detailing how she felt upon learning of her preg-nancy, Boxx wrote, "It hit me like a train. I didn't feel a shred of excite-ment. My identity was skating, it was playing the sport, coaching, and training with my best friends."[106] She understood how pregnancy would change her career, and felt guilt for, in her mind, letting her teammates down. She researched the recommendations for how long she could continue to skate, since she was "feeling so much loss of control in my body and identity."[107] Other skaters and athletes in contact sports had played through the first trimester, and only a serious injury could poten-tially cause harm—not regular contact. Based on that information, Boxx decided to keep skating. She told her teammates about her condition and continued to play for another two and a half weeks, until, she said, "I started to just feel so tired and bloated, the idea of smashing into people sounded terrible. But in those 2+ weeks, it meant so much. I had closure, I had control, I had the choice. . . . I felt ready to partake in this next adventure, take on a new role in the team and in my life."[108]

Society, and in particular the male-dominated sports world, still views a woman's identity through the athlete-*or*-mother dichotomy and rarely celebrates or encourages the athlete-*and*-mother combination. The fact that women must stop playing temporarily because of the physical requirements of pregnancy makes it seem as if women must choose one identity over the other. Rarely have women been supported in the journey to merge or inhabit multiple identities, but historically, roller derby has understood the strength, resilience, and importance of women's many roles. There is no reason why all sports cannot do the same. Thus, the modern story of roller derby, at least in part, is a continued struggle with identity. There will not be a major shift in this mentality until women's athletics are viewed as being on par with men's and until women can gain control of leadership positions beyond the roller derby world and keep the ones they have within it — or until fatherhood is made a central feature in the sports world. Until then, roller derby will continue to engage in the legacy of female achievement, power, and motherhood and resist definition and control by the male sports world. Leo Seltzer began that fight years ago, and it is one that continues to this day.

CONCLUSION

I skated for Pioneer Valley Roller Derby for two and a half years while working on my doctorate and until I was hired for a tenure-track position to teach American history at a small college halfway across the country. PVRD has always struggled to keep players; the area has a high student population thanks to five local colleges and universities. Members often did not stay longer than a handful of years, making it difficult for PVRD to maintain momentum. Nonetheless, the skaters, refs, and volunteers formed a ready-made community, one that made you feel a part of something real, unique, empowered, and, ultimately, badass.[1] Despite being a lifelong athlete, I had never experienced that before, something that felt edgy, countercultural, and personally fulfilling.

I have never been a risk-taker or even comfortable with joining new groups or activities, so for me to try something completely out of the ordinary and out of my comfort zone was a huge step—and recall, it started with something called Fresh Meat Night. I think many skaters shared in that experience. We were different people, we came from different places, and we had different backgrounds. But there we were, skating around the track, doing something extraordinary, and when you find yourself in that situation and you understand the magic of what you are a part of, it becomes a part of you. This phenomenon seems to be as true for modern skaters as it was for those skating during the Seltzer era.

After moving to Nebraska for my new teaching job at Hastings College, I made contact with the nearest league, the Platte Valley Roller Vixens, but discovered that although they practiced occasionally in a town thirty minutes away, most often it was in a city an hour away. I skated a couple times with the league and enjoyed doing so—they seemed to be a great group of women.[2] It was also a change for me since this was

FIGURE 7.1. *Michella Marino in her Quabbin Missile Crisis uniform for a Pioneer Valley Roller Derby photo, 2012. Lynn Graves Photography.*

a women-only skater league. Alas, the demands of the job did not allow me to continue to skate, and then my own pregnancy, the birth of my son, and the distance from the practice facility prevented me from doing much except skate on my own on a local bike path.[3] Roller derby, however, is still very much a part of my identity. Working on this book kept me connected with the sport, and I have even been able to teach students about it. As far as I can tell, I taught the first college course entirely dedicated to the history of roller derby—"Hell on Wheels: Skating through Modern American History"—in January 2014. As a point of pride, at five months pregnant I was still able to skate with my students on a field trip to a local roller rink.[4] Roller derby somehow manages to always stay with you. To borrow one more line from a sports movie, this time *Love and Basketball*, "The shit just won't go away."[5]

That may be putting it crudely, but roller derby in some form has been around for approximately eighty years, and despite current tensions in the sport, I do not expect it to go away. Even more important than its longevity is what the sport offers in the way of opportunities, analysis, and sporting lessons. Roller derby, as both sport and spectacle, reveals much about American sporting values, gender relations and ideals, and the dual nature of parenthood and athletics. Roller derby constantly evolves yet continues to be popular, in part because of its co-ed nature and emphasis on contact and aggressive play. As the early decades of the Seltzer Roller Derby exemplify, the sport was novel because of its female athletes, but fans and the larger public drew multiple meanings from Roller Derby, and these meanings changed over time. Some Americans, like those in the Kratz study (see chap. 1), denounced Roller Derby for lacking social respectability, yet it was wildly popular with elite crowds in Hollywood and New York City. The sport attracted fans who identified with its countercultural nature, and simultaneously

FIGURE 7.2. *A Pioneer Valley Roller Derby bout, 2011. Photo by Lesley Arak.*

appealed to the middle and working classes, creating a lasting fan base. Fans related to Roller Derby and identified with the athletes. The drama of the sport was like the drama of their everyday lives.

Despite its popularity, Roller Derby was classified as entertainment and ostracized from the sports pages. It was not considered a true sport by the mainstream media or the larger sports world. Roller Derby was contested terrain because of the equality of the skaters — its male skaters were viewed as less masculine than other male athletes because of their association with women, and the women were viewed as unfeminine roughnecks because of their participation in a masculine, full-contact sport. Thus, Roller Derby felt the need to feminize its female skaters and legitimize its male skaters by holding queen and king contests. Bolstered by the popularity of the Miss America pageant, Roller Derby's management and female skaters understood the value of appearing feminine as a way to add respectability to the sport and its female athletes. The Roller Derby King served to highlight the Roller Derby Queen's femininity and normality while also showcasing his masculinity by emphasizing male attractiveness. This public posture was in line with postwar shifts in the imagery of masculinity that celebrated cultural representations of men as beautiful. The king contest was also used to reposition male skaters' masculinity in relation to the hegemonic masculinity of other male athletes. This gender positioning largely applied to white, supposedly heteronormative middle-class skaters. While Roller Derby practiced sexual and racial equality in regard to its skaters in general, the queens and kings outwardly reflected the all-American ideals of the mid-twentieth century in an attempt to appeal to the public.

Roller Derby's emphasis on equality among its skaters affected both the identity of the sport and its athletes, particularly the female skaters. Since masculinity and sports have long been tied together, and since sports have been used in modern society as a way for men to experience "wholeness," female athletes have been left in a no-win situation. Women have been denied the opportunity to experience wholeness through sport because most sports for women have been limited or modified by society to be deemed acceptable and respectable. Thus, it has been a continual challenge for women to reconcile a feminine identity with an athletic one. Roller Derby, though, challenged this traditional sports framework: it was (and remains) a rough, full-contact co-ed professional sport *not* modified for women. Female Roller Derby skaters came the closest to reaching the "wholeness through sport" described by Eleanor Metheny, but it was still not fully within their grasp. The irony was that within Roller Derby, skaters had more functional equality than athletes in other sports, but that equality forced them to engage in apologetic behavior and worry about their identities.

The alternate sporting model provided for Roller Derby athletes was exemplified most clearly by Roller Derby's inclusion of mother-athletes and the ways in which the sport highlighted fathers' parental roles. Roller Derby, a family affair from the start, dealt with family dynamics not seen before in a sports organization, because of its co-ed nature. After at first discouraging skaters from marrying and settling down, Leo Seltzer embraced families within his organization and refused to separate spouses. Roller Derby allowed parents to travel with their children and tried to accommodate them as best it could. Managers and skaters chose from several options for raising their children in and around the Roller Derby: some took their children on the road with them, some stayed put during the school year but traveled during the summer, some left their children with family members or friends while they traveled, and some left their children with relatives full-time while they pursued their careers. The children's experiences with Roller Derby depended on what route their parents chose. Yet in all cases, Roller Derby functioned as one big family unit. Roller Derby promoted a family atmosphere and ultimately adopted traditional values in applauding motherhood, but compared to the rest of the sports world, drew very different conclusions about what athlete-mothers could and could not accomplish.

Throughout its history, Roller Derby had a complicated relationship with television. The medium propelled Roller Derby into the limelight and forced it to relocate from its New York hub to the West Coast in the early 1950s. Leo Seltzer, tired of battling the industry, turned the organization over to his son in the late 1950s. Jerry Seltzer initiated four key changes in Roller Derby's operations that reignited interest in the sport on the West Coast and revived it as a national cultural icon. He developed the one-nighter game model; introduced a smaller, portable track; established the bicycle tape network for TV syndication; and critically analyzed market data based on television ratings and mail-in responses. The Jerry Seltzer era of Roller Derby was marked by innovation, savvy, and theatrics. Seltzer also had to deal with a new competitor during his tenure, the National Skating Derby / Roller Games. This version of roller derby evolved into a showy, scripted, and controlled game that earned an outlandish reputation for its dramatic match races and fights. Roller Derby and Roller Games became pop culture mainstays in the 1960s and early 1970s despite each organization's internal and external struggles. Both groups collapsed in the mid-1970s. Roller derby, operated by a variety of people and organizations, mostly on the West Coast as a sporting show, limped through the next three decades, but nothing was as big, popular, or lasting as the Seltzer Roller Derby.

In 2001, a modern revival of the sport surfaced in Austin, Texas. This incarnation was a feminist endeavor with a DIY ethos that continues to dominate the current roller derby world. Despite early organizational splits, this largely flat-track, female version of roller derby spread rapidly across the United States and then around the globe. The Women's Flat Track Derby Association emerged as the main governing body of the sport and has worked hard to empower its female members and to promote the kind of democratic governance reflecting its "for the skater, by the skater" mantra. Fairly early in the modern revival, men, most of whom had been involved in helping with women's roller derby, found that they too wanted to play the sport. Early men's leagues joined together to form the Men's Roller Derby Association, which, after establishing that it did not want to hijack the sport from women, has been able to forge partnerships with the WFTDA to expand the sport. Recently, the WFTDA has come under attack from powerful national and international forces that want to eliminate the self-governing structure of the sport. The WFTDA and the MRDA have united to assert the WFTDA's rightful claim to roller derby governance, but it is unclear whether it will succeed. Regardless, the WFTDA and the MRDA continue to collaborate on rules and insurance and to support the growth of the sport through junior roller derby.

At the same time, the roller derby community continues to evolve in its stance on gender politics. It has grappled with questions regarding co-ed leagues, gender inclusion, sexual expression versus exploitation, and pregnancy and parenthood. As in the Seltzer era, modern roller derby is strides ahead of the mainstream sports world in its inclusion of and openness toward, for instance, mothers, those who identify as transgender, and nonbinary people. Perhaps this is the ultimate lesson from over eighty years of roller derby history: the larger sports world must embrace women's and men's multiple roles and identities for true equality to be achieved. If roller derby can do it, even with its flaws, so can everyone else. The real question is whether they want to.

NOTES

INTRODUCTION

1. Gotham Girls Roller Derby, "About GGRD," www.gothamgirlsrollerderby .com/about, accessed March 10, 2009.

2. *Whip It* was based on a 2007 novel called *Derby Girl*, by Shauna Cross, who wrote the screenplay for the movie. The book was retitled *Whip It* when it was reissued in 2009.

3. Frank Deford, telephone interview by the author, April 18, 2011, digital audio recording, Michella Marino Oral History Collection, W. E. B. Du Bois Library, University of Massachusetts Amherst (hereafter cited as Marino Oral History Collection).

4. Susan K. Cahn, "Sports Talk: Oral History and Its Uses, Problems, and Possibilities for Sport History," *Journal of American History* 81, no. 2 (Sept. 1994): 595.

5. Sherna Berger Gluck and Daphne Patai, eds. *Women's Words: The Feminist Practice of Oral History* (New York: Routledge, 1991); Carly Adams, "(Writing Myself into) Betty White's Stories: (De)constructing Narratives of/through Feminist Sport History Research," *Journal of Sport History* 39, no. 3 (Fall 2012): 395–413; Cahn, "Sports Talk."

6. Valerie Raleigh Yow, *Recording Oral History: A Guide for the Humanities and Social Sciences*, 2nd ed. (Walnut Creek, CA: AltaMira, 2005), 5–7. For more on oral history methodology, theory, and practice, see Thomas L. Charlton, Lois E. Meyers, and Rebecca Sharpless, eds., *Handbook of Oral History* (Lanham, MD: AltaMira, 2006), and Robert Perks and Alistair Thomson, *The Oral History Reader*, 2nd ed. (New York: Routledge, 2006).

7. Kathryn Anderson and Dana C. Jack, "Learning to Listen: Interview Techniques and Analyses," in Perks and Thomson, *Oral History Reader*, 157.

8. As Kathryn Anderson and Dana C. Jack note, "A woman's discussion of her life may combine two separate, often conflicting, perspectives: one framed

in concepts and values that reflect men's dominant position in the culture, and one informed by the more immediate realities of a woman's personal experience" ("Learning to Listen," 157). Susan Cahn's oral history interviews with women athletes helped her better understand "the dynamics of power in women's sports." She discovered that contrary to official records and published sources that highlighted the inherent masculinity of sports, "oral histories pressed me to shift my vantage point, as narrators consistently described local cultures—white and black, urban working-class and rural—and peer cultures among athletes that provided alternate, far less contradictory, definitions of sport and womanhood" ("Sports Talk," 600).

9. Cheryl Cooky and Michael A. Messner, eds., *No Slam Dunk: Gender, Sport, and the Unevenness of Social Change* (New Brunswick, NJ: Rutgers University Press, 2018), 3. Also see Cheryl Cooky, Michael A. Messner, and Michela Musto, "It's Dude Time! A Quarter Century of Excluding Women's Sports in Televised News and Highlight Shows," in Cooky and Messner, *No Slam Dunk*, 209–234.

10. Paul Thompson, *The Voice of the Past: Oral History* (New York: Oxford University Press, 2000).

11. Jodi Cohen, "Sporting-Self or Selling Sex: All-Girl Roller Derby in the Twenty-First Century," *Women in Sport and Physical Activity Journal* 17, no. 2 (Fall 2008): 25.

12. They are housed in the Marino Oral History Collection: http://credo.library.umass.edu/view/collection/mums812.

13. David Ketchum, telephone interview by the author, August 16, 2016, digital audio recording, in author's possession.

14. Jerry Seltzer, quoted in Herb Michelson, *A Very Simple Game: The Story of Roller Derby* (Oakland, CA: Occasional Publishing, 1971), 171.

CHAPTER 1: FROM SPECTACLE TO SPORT

The chapter epigraph comes from Leo A. Seltzer, "The Roller Derby Story," Jerry Seltzer Collection, 1942–1997, Dolph Briscoe Center for American History, University of Texas at Austin.

1. Billy Bogash, quoted in Herb Michelson, *A Very Simple Game: The Story of Roller Derby* (Oakland, CA: Occasional Publishing, 1971), 14–15.

2. Ibid. In a six-day bicycle race, a field of two-person teams rode for six days straight, with one cyclist from each team on the track at all times; the other slept, ate, or provided entertainment from the track infield. Cyclists could gain extra laps (or, later, points) on their opponents during official periods called "sprints" or "jams." During sprints, cyclists would attempt to outlap their opponents to gain a lap advantage. At the end of the sixth day, whichever cycling duo had ridden the most laps (or earned the most points) won the race. According to the sports historian Allen Guttman, working-class women had been participating in

six-day bicycle races since the late 1880s. See "Bike Team Laps Field," *New York Times*, February 10, 1925; "Walthour-McNamara Lead," *New York Times*, February 13, 1925; "Belgian Bike Team Leads by Two Laps," *New York Times*, March 5, 1925; "Six-Day Bike Race Will Begin Tonight," *New York Times*, November 27, 1932; Keith Coppage, *Roller Derby to Roller Jam: The Authorized Story of an Unauthorized Sport* (Santa Rosa, CA: Squarebooks, 1999), 2; Allen Guttman, *Women's Sports: A History* (New York: Columbia University Press, 1991), 2, 101.

3. Bogash, in Michelson, *Very Simple Game*, 14.

4. Ibid., 14–15; Coppage, *Roller Derby to Roller Jam*, 7.

5. Frank Deford, *Five Strides on the Banked Track: The Life and Times of the Roller Derby* (Boston: Little, Brown, 1971), 75–76.

6. National Museum of Roller Skating, www.rollerskatingmuseum.org. Very few in-depth histories of roller skating exist. The official story cited by the National Roller Skating Museum is the one told above, but a mid-twentieth-century sports encyclopedia claimed that roller skating originated in Holland in the eighteenth century when an ice-skating enthusiast decided to extend the pleasure of ice-skating to the summer months. According to this version, the inventor (name unknown) "acquired large wooden spools, attached them to his shoes with strips of leather and thus the roller skating idea was born"; see Frank G. Menke, *The Encyclopedia of Sports* (New York: Barnes, 1953), 731.

7. "James L. Plimpton: Roller Skate Innovator," Smithsonian Institution, http://americanhistory.si.edu/sports/exhibit/removers/plimpton/index.cfm. But a March 1885 *Chicago Daily Tribune* article claimed that J. H. Fenton, a machine-shop employee and "fancy" ice-skater, invented the modern wooden-wheeled roller skate ("Roller-Skating," *Chicago Daily Tribune*, March 1, 1885). Other online sources indicate that Plimpton was the first to spread the popularity of skating and the quad skate. Plimpton opened the first skating rinks in America, in New York City and Newport, Rhode Island. Plimpton is also credited with founding the first roller-skating association, in 1863, the same year he patented his quad skate and opened the first rinks. But J. H. Fenton did indeed patent a version of an improved roller skate in December 1885. See "The History and Evolution of Roller Skating," http://www.mooreamy.com/evolution/history.htm; Menke, *Encyclopedia of Sports*, 731; "Roller-skate," US patent 331,291, December 1, 1885, http://www.google.com/patents/US331291.

8. Menke, *Encyclopedia of Sports*, 731.

9. "Life at Newport," *New York Times*, September 4, 1883.

10. "The Morale of Roller-Skating," *Chicago Daily Tribune*, March 8, 1885.

11. Jennifer "Kasey Bomber" Barbee and Alex "Axles of Evil" Cohen, *Down and Derby: The Insider's Guide to Roller Derby* (Berkeley, CA: Soft Skull, 2010), 11. It appears that the only claim to internationalism at this race was the appearance of a fancy skater from Japan named Miss Yeddo, who was scheduled to perform in afternoon and evening shows around the races; see "The Roller Skating Tournament," *New York Times*, February 22, 1885.

12. "The Skating Mania," *New York Times*, May 18, 1885; Barbee and Cohen, *Down and Derby*, 12.

13. "Killed by Roller Skating," *New York Times*, March 18, 1885; "Roller Skater Cohen's Death," *New York Times*, March 20, 1885; "Victim of Roller Skates," *New York Times*, April 11, 1885.

14. "Deaths from Roller Skating," *New York Times*, March 21, 1885; "Too Much Roller Skating," *New York Times*, April 24, 1885.

15. "Fascinated by Roller Skating," *New York Times*, April 5, 1885.

16. "Morale of Roller-Skating."

17. "Another Skating Tournament," *New York Times*, April 17, 1885. The National Roller Skating Congress was an organization composed of roller skate manufacturers who sought to prove to the public that roller skating was indeed beneficial and healthful if done correctly. In April 1885, the group "pledged itself to encourage the higher branches of the art . . . to be skated under the rules and according to the programme adopted by the congress." Interestingly enough, one member of the National Roller Skating Congress was J. H. Fenton, whom some sources claim invented the modern roller skate; see note 7 to this chapter.

18. "Skating Mania."

19. "Another Skating Tournament."

20. "Milwaukee Notes," *Chicago Daily Tribune*, January 13, 1886; "Morale of Roller-Skating."

21. "Night of Falls: Several Teams Suffer in Roller Skating Race," *Boston Globe*, March 21, 1907; "Loses Roller Race on Foul," *Chicago Daily Tribune*, March 23, 1911; J. G. Davis, "M'Lean Tangle Starts Trouble among Skaters," *Chicago Daily Tribune*, December 22, 1914; "First in Skating Grind: Cioni and Eglington Cover 100 Miles in 7:44:15," *Washington Post*, March 28, 1915; Barbee and Cohen, *Down and Derby*, 12.

22. Coppage, *Roller Derby to RollerJam*, viii, 2–3.

23. "West Frankfort Has Walkathon 47 Days, Nights," *Southeast Missourian*, June 20, 1934; "Stiffen Walkathon Rules," *Spokesman (WA) Review*, April 6, 1931; "Ho, Hum! Sleepy Walkathon Cast Gets Beds in Jail," *Chicago Tribune*, February 17, 1938; Barbee and Cohen, *Down and Derby*, 10; Coppage, *Roller Derby to RollerJam*, 3–4.

24. Dave Zirin, *A People's History of Sports in the United States: 250 Years of Politics, Protest, People, and Play* (New York: New Press, 2008), 65; Coppage, *Roller Derby to RollerJam*, 3–4.

25. Deford, *Five Strides*, 73; Coppage, *Roller Derby to RollerJam*, 3; "The Chicago Coliseum," South Loop Historical Society, http://southloophistoricalsociety .org/2013/10/08/the-chicago-coliseum-1513-s-wabash-ave-1900-1982, accessed July 23, 2015 (page no longer available).

26. As cited in Coppage, *Roller Derby to RollerJam*, 4.

27. Deford claims the article said that 93 percent of Americans skated, while Coppage claims the article said 97 percent skated. I have looked through the *Liter-*

ary Digest from January 1933 to December 1935 and have been unable to locate the original article. Jerry Seltzer, Leo's son, thinks his father saw the *Literary Digest* article reprinted in the *Chicago Tribune*, but I have not been able to locate it there either. Leo Seltzer told a reporter in 1950, "I read in a magazine that something like 90 per cent of Americans had roller skated at one time or another. That gave me the idea of holding races on roller skates" (Hal Boyle, "Roller Derby Gives Women Something to Yell About," *Spokane Daily Chronicle*, June 5, 1950). In an oral history interview in 1970, he told Herb Michelson, "One day I was reading in the *Literary Digest* magazine a story about participant sports. . . . This story I was reading told about how many thousands or millions of Americans played such and such sport. I was surprised, I'll tell you, to read that more people were roller skaters than anything else" (Michelson, *Very Simple Game*, 7). See also Deford, *Five Strides*, 74; Coppage, *Roller Derby to RollerJam*, 4; Jerry Seltzer, interview by the author, June 17, 2011, Sonoma, California, digital audio recording, Michella Marino Oral History Collection, W. E. B. Du Bois Library, University of Massachusetts Amherst (hereafter cited as Marino Oral History Collection).

28. "The Roller Derby," *New York Hippodrome Roller Derby Sports Program*, 1936, copy in the National Roller Derby Hall of Fame and Museum (formerly in Brooklyn, now relocated to Palm Springs, California).

29. Ibid.

30. Ibid. It was commonly acknowledged, even by Leo, that he took his cue from bike races and marathons of the 1920s and 1930s but not from similar roller-skating races (Michelson, *Very Simple Game*, 7).

31. "Roller Champs Vie for Titles in Week's Races," *Chicago Tribune*, April 23, 1922; "Marathon Race Tonight Climax for Roller Meet," *Chicago Tribune*, April 30, 1922.

32. "Marathon Race Tonight Climax for Roller Meet." Unlike the Seltzer derby, the 1922 National Roller Skating Derby was a nonprofit event sponsored by Sam Mincer and A. L. Green Sr. The National League of Roller Skaters sanctioned the event, as did the Chicago athletic commission. Seltzer was living and working on the West Coast in the early 1920s.

33. "Vintage: Roller Derby," *Chicago Tribune* Online Photograph Exhibit, http://galleries.apps.chicagotribune.com/chi-vintage-roller-derby-photos-20141105; "12,000 Fans See N.W. Skating Club Win Opal Derby Honors," *Chicago Tribune*, January 28, 1924; "Joie Ray Is Injured: Suffers Possible Fractured Skull in Roller Skate Derby," *New York Times*, February 22, 1934; "Permission Awarded for Roller Derby," *Los Angeles Times*, April 23, 1935; "Skate Derby Blanks Ready: Former A.A.U. Stars Have Entered Street Derby—Races on August 19," *New York Amsterdam News*, August 2, 1933.

34. Michelson, *Very Simple Game*, 7–8; Catherine Mabe, *Roller Derby: The History and All-Girl Revival of the Greatest Sport on Wheels* (Denver: Speck, 2007), 21–23; Deford, *Five Strides*, 74.

35. According to Coppage, 18 laps around the track equaled one mile. Sources

such as Coppage's *Roller Derby to Roller Jam*, Deford's *Five Strides*, and Margot "Em Dash" Atwell's *Derby Life* claim the participants skated approximately 4,000 miles, but if the original flat-track was 18 laps to the mile and the first skating team had to skate 57,000 laps, it would appear the winning duo skated close to 3,200 miles. Either way, it was a ridiculous amount of mileage! Coppage, *Roller Derby to Roller Jam*, 4; Deford, *Five Strides*, 74; Margot "Em Dash" Atwell, *Derby Life: A Crash Course in the Incredible Sport of Roller Derby* (New York: Gutpunch, 2015), 27.

36. Each duo-team wore a jersey with the same number on it. Even after roller derby evolved into a five-on-five team sport, each male and female on the team was partnered with someone of the opposite sex, and the partners would share a jersey number. Into the 1940s, team jerseys featured advertising logos from their sponsors, including Kool cigarettes, Pepsi-Cola, Coca-Cola, Orange Crush, the Milam Food Market, or the Ross Insulation Company, on the front. While the uniforms evolved somewhat in style, cut, and color over the decades, in general they consisted of a long-sleeved jersey with a pair of tights or leggings with built-in leather knee and hip pads, worn under a pair of satin shorts. See Coppage, *Roller Derby to Roller Jam*, 5, 14; Mary Youpelle Massro, telephone interview by the author, April 8, 2011, digital audio recording, Marino Oral History Collection.

37. Coppage, *Roller Derby to Roller Jam*, 4–5.

38. Deford, *Five Strides*, 74.

39. Ibid., 75.

40. "The Original Roller Derby," National Museum of Roller Skating, available from the Internet Archive, https://web.archive.org/web/20070222193457/http://www.rollerskatingmuseum.com/derby.htm.

41. Deford, *Five Strides*, 75.

42. Ibid., 76; Edward Burns, "Gal in Cerise Tights Leads Roller Derby, It's Rumored," *Chicago Daily Tribune*, January 5, 1936.

43. Barbee and Cohen, *Down and Derby*, 14; Deford, *Five Strides*, 77.

44. Deford, *Five Strides*, 76; Mabe, *Roller Derby*, 26; Coppage, *Roller Derby to Roller Jam*, 5.

45. Deford, *Five Strides*, 76.

46. Gene Vizena Nygra, interview by Joel Justin in a promotion for "The Roller Derby 'Wooden Wheel Wonders,'" accessed June 12, 2012, http://www.youtube.com/watch?v=4fRKxkbhyIM (video no longer available).

47. As cited in Coppage, *Roller Derby to Roller Jam*, 5.

48. Indeed, they were included in the Library of Congress's *Catalog of Copyright Entries for Pamphlets, Leaflets, Contributions to Newspapers or Periodicals, Etc., Lectures, Sermons, Addresses for Oral Delivery, Maps*.

49. Quoted in Seltzer v. Sunbrock, 22 F. Supp. 621 (S.D. Cal. 1938).

50. *Catalog of Copyright Entries*, part 1: Books, group 2, vol. 32, no. 1 (Washington, DC: GPO, 1935), 851, 1153, accessed July 30, 2015, https://ia802607.us.archive.org/3/items/catalogueofcopyr321libr/catalogueofcopyr321libr.pdf. In *Five*

Strides, Frank Deford writes that Roller Derby was copyrighted on July 14, 1935, a month before Seltzer put on his first Transcontinental Roller Derby, with the copyright number 336652 (74). It appears that Deford confused Seltzer's copyrights with his trademark or with Seltzer's first use of the term "Roller Derby." Seltzer copyrighted the two terms in 1935, but according to a 1939 court case, he was granted a trademark (no. 33,652) on the name "Roller Derby" on July 14, 1936. The earliest trademark I have been able to find of Seltzer's for "Roller Derby" was filed on November 30, 1936, with a registration date of April 27, 1937. See Seltzer v. Corem, 26 F. Supp. 892 (N.D. Ind., 1939); "Roller Derby—Trademark Details," Justia: Trademarks, https://trademarks.justia.com/713/86/roller-derby-71386128 .html; "Roller Derby" trademark, US Patent and Trademark Office, https://tsdrsec .uspto.gov/ts/cd/casedoc/sn71386128/ORC20051031194231/1/webcontent?scale=1.

51. *Sunbrock*, 22 F. Supp. 621.

52. Ibid.

53. Ibid.

54. *Corem*, 26 F.Supp. 892; Seltzer v. Corem, 107 F.2d 75, 77 (7th Cir. 1939).

55. *Corem*, 107 F.2d 75, 77. In the appeals court, Corem acknowledged that he had infringed on Seltzer's copyrights, but again held that they were invalid. He also stated that if he were prevented from holding his own planned Roller Derby, "he would not be damaged in any way," which is strange, because the point of an appeal is to show the unfairness of a previous ruling and the financial damage likely to result from it. Corem's startling admission led the judges to believe that Seltzer and Corem were in collusion. Corem's arguments were inconsistent with his evidence, as the judges picked up on, and thus they suspected that Seltzer was shopping for a new ruling. See Bruce E. Boyden, "Games and Other Uncopyrightable Systems," *George Mason Law Review* 18, no. 2 (2011): 439–479.

56. *Corem*, 107 F.2d 75, 77. What is bizarre about this scenario is that if Corem and Seltzer were working together on a shady test case, why would they appeal the district court's ruling in March? That judgment, which was in Seltzer's favor, contradicted the California ruling from 1938. A colleague of mine who is also a lawyer was likewise perplexed by Corem's appeal. We suspect that Seltzer may have sought the approval of a higher court because two district courts had rendered opposing rulings on the same question. That plan obviously did not pan out for him.

57. As mentioned, I have been unable to locate the July 14, 1936, trademark certificate mentioned in the *Seltzer v. Corem* case from March 1939. The earliest trademark I have been able to find pertaining to the use of the term "Roller Derby" was filed by Leo Seltzer on November 30, 1936, with a registration date of April 27, 1937. The serial number is 71386128 and the registration number is 0345466. This trademark notes that the first commercial use of the word mark was July 15, 1935, but it does not say when the first trademark occurred or whether this is the first one. See "Roller Derby—Trademark Details"; "Roller Derby" trademark.

58. After Jerry got out of the Roller Derby business, the trademark passed to the Oscar Seltzer branch of the family, namely, to his youngest son, Ed, who still

manages the Roller Derby Skate Company. The Roller Derby Skate Company enforces the trademark only regarding roller skates themselves. This is why the modern revival of roller derby can call itself roller derby but no business except the Roller Derby Skate Company can sell official Roller Derby skates.

59. Barbee and Cohen, *Down and Derby*, 11; Menke, *Encyclopedia of Sports*, 731.

60. "The Roller Derby," *New York Hippodrome Roller Derby Sports Program*.

61. Coppage, *Roller Derby to RollerJam*, 7.

62. Ibid.

63. Ibid.

64. Barbee and Cohen, *Down and Derby*, 14; Mabe, *Roller Derby*, 31.

65. Coppage, *Roller Derby to RollerJam*, 8; Mabe, *Roller Derby*, 31.

66. Coppage, *Roller Derby to RollerJam*, 11.

67. Michelson, *Very Simple Game*, 8; Barbee and Cohen, *Down and Derby*, 13.

68. Barbee and Cohen, *Down and Derby*, 13; see also Coppage, *Roller Derby to RollerJam*, 6.

69. This hiring practice was true for other popular marathons of the time; see Coppage, *Roller Derby to RollerJam*, 5.

70. Ibid., Mabe, *Roller Derby*, 25–26.

71. Barbee and Cohen, *Down and Derby*, 13–14; Deford, *Five Strides*, 48; Michelson, *Very Simple Game*, 16.

72. As cited in Deford, *Five Strides*, 77; see also Coppage, *Roller Derby to RollerJam*, 8.

73. Deford, *Five Strides*, 77.

74. Ibid.

75. Ibid. Given general wage levels during the Great Depression, Roller Derby paid well. Johnny Rosasco, who became a popular Roller Derby skater during the first decade of the sport, had earned thirty-five cents an hour while making golf clubs—around fifty-six dollars a month (assuming a forty-hour workweek). This was 30 percent less than the eighty dollars a month he earned with the derby; see Coppage, *Roller Derby to RollerJam*, 5. According to the US Census Bureau, hourly wages for manufacturing jobs averaged fifty-eight cents an hour in 1935, approximately ninety-three dollars a month; construction workers earned forty-nine cents an hour, approximately seventy-nine dollars a month; and those in service industries made forty-two cents an hour, approximately sixty-eight dollars each month; see "100 Years of Consumer Spending: Data for the Nation, New York City, and Boston," Bureau of Labor Statistics, US Department of Labor, 2006, http://www.bls.gov/opub/uscs/1934-36.pdf. It should be noted that many laborers were not able to work the full forty-hour workweek, since some employers reduced the number of hours each employee was allowed to work in order to avoid laying people off.

76. "The Roller Derby," *New York Hippodrome Roller Derby Sports Program*; Coppage, *Roller Derby to RollerJam*, 13.

77. Coppage, *Roller Derby to RollerJam*, 13.

78. Associated Press, "18 Die As Bus Rams Bridge and Burns Up," *Baltimore Sun*, March 25, 1937; Deford, *Five Strides*, 133.

79. Deford, *Five Strides*, 133.

80. "Bus Tragedy Laid to Tire Blowout," *Baltimore Sun*, March 26, 1937.

81. "18 Die As Bus Rams Bridge."

82. Ibid.

83. "Tire Blowout Hurls Bus against Bridge Abutment," *Daily Boston Globe*, March 25, 1937.

84. "18 Die As Bus Rams Bridge."

85. Ibid.; "18 Are Killed in Bus as Skating Troupe Crashes in Illinois," *New York Times*, March 25, 1937.

86. Deford, *Five Strides*, 133; Barbee and Cohen, *Down and Derby*, 15–16.

87. Coppage, *Roller Derby to RollerJam*, 13.

88. Ibid.

89. A popular skater named Wes Aronson recalled a remaining skater saying, "I think they would've wanted us to keep going"; Wes Aronson, interview by Joel Justin Nygra, in "The Roller Derby 'Wooden Wheel Wonders'"; Coppage, *Roller Derby to RollerJam*, 13.

90. Aronson interview; Youpelle Massro interview.

91. Youpelle Massro interview. Joe Nygra, Gene Vizena, Wes Aronson, and Tommy Atkinson had been in Chicago instead of St. Louis with the other skaters, and were scheduled to meet up with the troupe for the next race in Cincinnati. Nygra had recently purchased a new Ford, and the group drove to Cincinnati, thus avoiding the fate of their teammates who had skated in St. Louis. Joe Nygra, Gene Vizena, and Wes Aronson, interview by Joel Justin Nygra in "The Roller Derby 'Wooden Wheel Wonders'"; Joel Justin Nygra, telephone interview by the author, August 10, 2012, digital audio recording, Marino Oral History Collection.

92. As cited in Coppage, *Roller Derby to RollerJam*, 8.

93. Sources disagree about whether this Miami series took place in 1937 or 1938, but evidence suggests that contact was incorporated by the end of 1937. Roller Derby had skated in Miami, Florida, four times by 1938. There was also a race in Coral Gables, Florida, that began on December 25, 1937, and ended in January 1938. The program from Friday, December 31, 1937, mentioned a form of illegal blocking that would result in a penalty, but did not denounce blocking in general. A program from 1939 did likewise. Since blocking had definitely been incorporated into the game by 1939, the program from that year indicates that blocking was allowed in late 1937. Similarly, a program from the Coral Gables race in 1938 aligned Damon Runyon with Roller Derby, the man credited with encouraging Seltzer to add blocking. See the following programs, copies of which are in the National Roller Derby Hall of Fame and Museum: "Souvenir Program: The Roller Derby," Coral Gables Coliseum, 1938; "Transcontinental Roller Derby" program, December 31, 1937; see also "Rules of 1939," Roller Derby Program from a game

between St. Louis and Cincinnati. (A scan of the 1939 program had been posted on the Roller Derby Times online forum in Yahoo Groups, but that site was disabled on December 15, 2020.)

94. Coppage, *Roller Derby to RollerJam*, 12.

95. Ibid. Joel Justin Nygra, son of the skaters Gene Vizena and Joe Nygra, recounted a story from his mother that women started the illegal physical contact: "And during one of the [derbies], my mom, with one of the gals, locked hands with one of the other girls there, and started blocking, and wouldn't let anybody around. And the promoters, you know, just perked right up when they saw this, because nobody had, you know, thought of this aspect of the thing. And my mom was a very aggressive person." His mother told Leo Seltzer about all the cheers from the crowd when she started blocking. After her report, according to her son, "she, literally, watched [Seltzer and his business associates] walk into the manager's office . . . and they just, basically, rewrote the rules and everything right there. And that's where it, kind of, started" (Nygra interview).

96. As cited in Deford, *Five Strides*, 83; Coppage, *Roller Derby to RollerJam*, 12.

97. Deford, *Five Strides*, 83; Coppage, *Roller Derby to RollerJam*, 12.

98. Any other jammer who broke free after the jam time began had whatever time remained of that two-minute jam to score.

99. Coppage, *Roller Derby to RollerJam*, 120.

100. Ibid., 12; Barbee and Cohen, *Down and Derby*, 14. Modifications over the years have included reducing the amount of time in each period from fifteen minutes to twelve, adding a pivot player (formerly a lead blocker), mandating helmets for protection but also to officially designate the jammers, reducing the jam time to one minute, and allowing jammers to fall down without ending the jam. See Coppage, *Roller Derby to RollerJam*, 118–121; "Roller Derby History: The Rules," Loretta "Little Iodine" Behrens' Derby Memoirs, accessed January 19, 2019, http://derbymemoirs.bankedtrack.info/rules_NRD.html.

101. Mabe, *Roller Derby*, 26–27.

102. Merrie A. Fidler, *The Origins and History of the All-American Girls Professional Baseball League* (Jefferson, NC: McFarland, 2006), 33.

103. Ibid., 30–36, 48–49. The comparison between Roller Derby and the AAGPBL is to emphasize the structural and organizational differences between the AAGPBL and Seltzer's Roller Derby. The history of the league is fascinating, and I fell in love with the movie *A League of Their Own* when I was ten and then began studying the league in high school. Indeed, my first official oral history was with Dottie Collins, a Fort Wayne Daisies pitcher. This powerful interview directly sparked my interest in oral history.

104. Mary Lou Palermo, telephone interview by the author, April 7, 2011, digital audio recording, Marino Oral History Collection; Youpelle Massro interview; Coppage, *Roller Derby to RollerJam*, 18.

105. Mabe, *Roller Derby*, 33, 35; Deford, *Five Strides*, 40–41; Clifford Terry, "Elmer & Toughie & Pee Wee & Slugger," *Chicago Daily Tribune*, April 18, 1971.

106. "Skaters Dress Up," *Roller Derby News*, January 1940, copy in National Roller Derby Hall of Fame and Museum; Bert Wall, telephone interview by the author, January 25, 2012, digital audio recording, Marino Oral History Collection.

107. Seltzer interview, 2011. In 1971, Frank Deford wrote, "Slightly more than half of these [Roller Derby fans] are women, a statistic no other sport can claim" (*Five Strides*, 7).

108. Boyle, "Roller Derby Gives Women Something."

109. Wall interview.

110. L. Seltzer, "Roller Derby Story."

111. Boyle, "Roller Derby Gives Women Something."

112. Ibid.

113. Seltzer interview, 2011; Coppage, *Roller Derby to RollerJam*, 7; Mabe, *Roller Derby*, 29–31.

114. Boyle, "Roller Derby Gives Women Something."

115. Coppage, *Roller Derby to RollerJam*, 8; Mabe, *Roller Derby*, 27.

116. Mabe, *Roller Derby*, 27; Deford, *Five Strides*, 75.

117. Coppage, *Roller Derby to RollerJam*, 8; Boyle, "Roller Derby Gives Women Something."

118. Mabe, *Roller Derby*, 31.

119. Wall interview.

120. Ibid.

121. Ibid.; Frank Deford, telephone interview by the author, April 18, 2011, digital audio recording; Bobbie Mateer, telephone interview by the author, February 1, 2012, digital audio recording; Carol Meyer Roman, telephone interview by the author, July 13, 2012, digital audio recording; all interviews in the Marino Oral History Collection.

122. Boyle, "Roller Derby Gives Women Something."

123. Ibid.

124. Male sports fans, both in the United States and internationally, have a long history of acting out at sporting events. The term "hooliganism" can refer to excessively rowdy, potentially violent verbal and physical spectator behavior at a sporting event, and such conduct is often associated with men from the lower or working classes; see Allen Guttmann, *Sports: The First Five Millennia* (Amherst: University of Massachusetts Press, 2004), 309–311.

125. "A Fan Starts an Egg Roll at Roller Derby," *Chicago Daily Tribune*, April 2, 1940.

126. Robert Cromie, "It Can Happen in Roller Skate Derby Tonight," *Chicago Daily Tribune*, March 23, 1950; Loretta Behrens, telephone interview by the author, September 9, 2012, digital audio recording, Marino Oral History Collection.

127. Deford, *Five Strides*, 61.

128. Deford, *Five Strides*, 37.

129. Cromie, "It Can Happen in Roller Skate Derby."

130. "Great American Hero Segment" in "*The Great American Dream Machine*: Highlights, 1971–1972," PBS, WNET: New York, 1974, Paley Media Center, New York City. In some ways, this baby-throwing episode represents the frustrations of American mothers attempting to juggle a variety of roles. A female fan, as the primary caretaker of her child, is defined by her role as a mother, but Roller Derby got under her skin so much as a fan that she forgot her primary identity and literally threw aside her baby in the process. Upon realizing what she had done, she fainted in humiliation and fear.

131. Cromie, "It Can Happen in Roller Skate Derby."

132. "Great American Hero Segment."

133. Mateer interview.

134. Behrens interview.

135. Susan Cahn, in her article on the value of using oral history in sports history, highlights how oral histories capture the "wealth of oral lore" ("Sports Talk," 597). This incident seems a fitting example for Roller Derby, although this story is documented in varying ways in traditional sources as well.

136. Deford interview. Similarly, the skater Bert Wall described it as "a slice of American life" (Wall interview).

137. Laura Elizabeth Kratz, "A Study of Sports and the Implications of Women's Participation in Them in Modern Society" (PhD diss., Ohio State University, 1958), 3.

138. Ibid., 6.

139. Ibid., 104–107, quoted material on 106.

140. Ibid., 174.

141. Ibid.

142. Coppage, *Roller Derby to RollerJam*, 12.

143. Kratz, "Sports and Women's Participation," 293–298.

144. Susan Cahn, *Coming on Strong: Gender and Sexuality in Twentieth-Century Women's Sports* (Cambridge, MA: Harvard University Press, 1994), 111, 168–169, 184, 195–196.

145. Kratz, "Sports and Women's Participation," 174.

146. Ibid. According to Susan Cahn, the close association of bowling with "working-class pool halls, taverns, and gamblers gave it a shady reputation" before the Great Depression. The sport's appeal later broadened to include "middle-class feminine respectability," but it always retained its "blue collar appeal" (Cahn, *Coming on Strong*, 219–220).

147. Kratz, "Sports and Women's Participation," 174.

148. Ibid., 294–298.

149. Ibid., 175.

150. Coppage, *Roller Derby to RollerJam*, 23. Television coverage of the sport is discussed more extensively in chapter 5.

151. Deford, *Five Strides*, 7; Coppage, *Roller Derby to RollerJam*, 21.

152. Coppage, *Roller Derby to RollerJam*, 21–22.

153. Behrens interview; John Hall, telephone interview by the author, October 4, 2011, digital audio recording, Marino Oral History Collection; L. Seltzer, "Roller Derby Story"; Terry, "Elmer & Toughie"; Alan Ward, "The Roller Derby No Mush and Milk," *Oakland Tribune*, September 25, 1964. This is also exemplified by Roller Derby's lack of coverage in such publications as *Sports Illustrated* in the 1950s through the 1970s. When Frank Deford published his feature article on Roller Derby in the March 3, 1969, issue of *SI*, sports enthusiasts wrote in to protest it as a waste of space. R. P. Griffin Jr. from Milwaukee wrote, "Sirs: It is certainly a shame when a high-class magazine such as SPORTS ILLUSTRATED lowers itself to devoting space to a nonsport such as Roller Derby . . . Most tragic of all is the fact that Roller Derby's ridiculous 'fights,' 'grudges' and so forth eventually hurt the public's confidence in the legitimate sports." Jerry Seltzer did not care for the "extremely apologetic" language used by the magazine's publisher to explain to its readers why so much coverage was devoted to Roller Derby, so he responded with his own comments: "I do want Mr. Valk [the publisher] to know that we in Roller Derby sympathize with his situation. Many of our fans were quite upset when they heard that we were permitting SPORTS ILLUSTRATED to do a story. After all, this publication gives coverage to sissy games such as baseball and tennis." "19th Hole: The Readers Take Over," *Sports Illustrated*, March 17, 1969.

154. "They Go 'Round and 'Round and Have the Darndest Time—At the Roller Derby," *Indianapolis Star*, September 29, 1937.

155. W. Blaine Patton, "Playing the Field of Sports," *Indianapolis Star*, February 8, 1940.

156. Quotation in Frank Anderson, "Mayhem on Skates: Roller Derby Squads Follow Wrestling Cue," *Indianapolis Star*, October 31, 1954; "Three Local Skaters Seek Derby Honors," *Indianapolis Star*, May 29, 1949.

157. Deford, *Five Strides*, 7, 10; Wall interview; Lewis Burton, "Popular Derby: Leo Seltzer Sizes Up the Situation," *New York Journal American*, December 21, 1950.

158. Youpelle Massro interview; Palermo interview; "Church Finds TV Set Boon to Young and Old," *Chicago Daily Tribune*, December 3, 1949; Coppage, *Roller Derby to RollerJam*, 9.

159. "Roller Derby Scores Big Hit with Hollywood Sports Followers," *Los Angeles Times*, June 12, 1938.

160. "Betty Grable to Start Race," *Los Angeles Times*, May 23, 1938.

161. "Roller Derby Scores Big Hit."

162. Seltzer interview, 2011.

163. Ibid. Mickey Rooney later starred in a 1950 movie called *The Fireball*, based on Roller Derby, which also featured Marilyn Monroe in one of her first roles.

164. Seltzer interview, 2011.

165. In the 1930s, tickets were priced around twenty-five cents and then discounted to a dime. As prices around the country rose, so did ticket costs, but they were still discounted accordingly. By the 1950s and 1960s, tickets ran from $1 to $3 and would still be reduced significantly. A $2.50 ticket would be discounted to $1.50. See Seltzer interview, 2011; Coppage, *Roller Derby to RollerJam*, 7.

166. Seltzer interview, 2011.

167. Deford, *Five Strides*, 28.

168. Lenny Berkman, interview by the author, December 20, 2011, Amherst, MA, digital audio recording, Marino Oral History Collection.

169. Berkman interview, 8.

170. Deford, *Five Strides*, 7.

171. Michelson, *Very Simple Game*, 133.

172. Deford, *Five Strides*, 28.

173. Ibid., 39.

174. As cited in Deford, *Five Strides*, 39–40.

175. Deford interview.

176. Coppage, *Roller Derby to RollerJam*, 79–80. Coppage defines the term "red shirt" thus:

> Skater from the "visiting" team; also, skater who employs rough tactics on the track. Antics include helmet throwing, belting a skater who scores over you, blocking harder than necessary, protesting loudly to referees, yelling at the crowd. . . . Extreme situations may call for chair throwing. If the redshirt team wins, the skaters on that team must run off the track after the final whistle, partly to make them look cowardly but also for safety reasons, especially if that crowd starts to queue menacingly toward the track. "Red" usually means evil. (127)

Although many skaters had nicknames or were considered "red shirts," the Seltzer Roller Derby did not employ "alter egos," as did wrestling and the twenty-first-century version of roller derby.

177. Sometimes skaters came up with their own crowd-pleasing antics. For instance, Joel Justin Nygra recalled his father telling him about how he would sometimes hide fake blood capsules in his mouth and then would intentionally trip up another skater, who would thereafter have it out for him. Joel laughingly explained, "And they'd tumble him down, and then, of course, he would fall and fake, you know, that he didn't do it and that he got hurt. And he would bust a blood capsule in his mouth, you know." Joel described his father's actions as a method of entertaining the crowd, because if the fans loved it and kept coming back, the skaters would be paid more. But his father was reluctant to share such stories as these, because much like Leo Seltzer, he believed he was a true athlete and wanted to be remembered as such (Nygra interview).

178. Hall interview. Leo Seltzer held this view of his beloved Roller Derby from its outset to the sport's demise, in 1973.

179. Ibid.

180. In June 1949, Roller Derby brought in 55,000 fans for its World Series, held across five days at Madison Square Garden, and in 1951, 82,000 fans attended the playoffs at the same location (Coppage, *Roller Derby to RollerJam*, 20, 25).

CHAPTER 2: SKATING THROUGH
THE BOUNDARIES OF IDENTITY

1. Duncan Norton-Taylor, "Don't Beat Your Husband," *Ladies' Home Journal*, February 1938, 54.

2. Ibid., 56.

3. Ibid.

4. Ibid., 58.

5. Ibid.

6. Ibid.

7. Ibid.

8. Ibid.

9. Ibid.

10. Allen Guttman, *Women's Sports: A History* (New York: Columbia University Press, 1991), 1–4; Jaime Schultz, *Women's Sports: What Everyone Needs to Know* (New York: Oxford University Press, 2018), 41–45.

11. Susan Cahn, *Coming on Strong: Gender and Sexuality in Twentieth-Century Women's Sports* (Cambridge, MA: Harvard University Press, 1994), 217.

12. Ibid.

13. Robert Cromie, "TV's Pretty Roughnecks, the Roller Derby Queens," *Chicago Daily Tribune*, April 1, 1951.

14. Robert Cromie, "Roller Derby Often Wheels of Misfortune," *Chicago Daily Tribune*, October 31, 1952.

15. S. Andrews, Anthony Hiss, and George W. S. Trow, "Major Cultural Event No. 2," *New Yorker*, April 4, 1970.

16. Eleanor Metheny, *Movement and Meaning* (New York: McGraw-Hill, 1968), 65.

17. Benjamin G. Rader, *American Sports: From the Age of Folk Games to the Age of Televised Sports*, 3rd. ed. (Englewood Cliffs, NJ: Prentice Hall, 1996), 100.

18. Theodore Roosevelt, "'Professionalism' in Sports," *North American Review* 151, no. 405 (August 1890): 187–191; Dave Zirin, *A People's History of Sports in the United States: 250 Years of Politics, Protest, People, and Play* (New York: New Press, 2008), 30–31.

19. Roosevelt, "'Professionalism' in Sports," 187.

20. Ibid., 190. This comment shows Roosevelt's preference for amateur athletics for the masses over the professionalization of sports for a select few. Roosevelt saw sport and manliness as an integral part of American foreign and domestic policy. As the sports historian Benjamin G. Rader explained, Roosevelt and other proponents of athleticism saw sport as providing a space in which young men could "replicate the courage and hardiness" found in war and then use these "heroic virtues" to strengthen the nation (*American Sports*, 123–125).

21. Patsy Neal, *Sport and Identity* (Philadelphia: Dorrance, 1972), 14.

22. Metheny, *Movement and Meaning*, 63. Metheny was an early feminist and important physical educator who produced influential theories on human movement. For background, see Mary Leigh and Ginny Studer, "Eleanor Metheny," *Journal of Physical Education, Recreation, and Dance* 54, no. 7 (Sept. 1983): 74–77.

23. Metheny, *Movement and Meaning*, 64.

24. Ibid.; Neal, *Sport and Identity*, 14.

25. Metheny, *Movement and Meaning*, 74.

26. Ibid., 77.

27. Neal, *Sport and Identity*, 31.

28. Donna Lopiano, interview by the author, March 17, 2011, Hadley, Massachusetts, digital audio recording, Michella Marino Oral History Collection, W. E. B. Du Bois Library, University of Massachusetts-Amherst (hereafter cited as Marino Oral History Collection).

29. Mary Lou Palermo, telephone interview by the author, April 7, 2011, digital audio recording, Marino Oral History Collection.

30. Mary Youpelle Massro, telephone interview by the author, April 8, 2011, digital audio recording; Loretta Behrens, telephone interview by the author, September 9, 2012, digital audio recording; Carol Meyer Roman, telephone interview by the author, July 13, 2012, digital audio recording; all in Marino Oral History Collection.

31. Gerry Murray, telephone interview by the author, September 26, 2011, digital audio recording, Marino Oral History Collection. Usually, small high schools in rural communities offered more sports opportunities than large high schools in big cities because of female physical educators' influence there, particularly in Iowa. Murray's school appears to have been an exception to some extent; see Max McElwain, *The Only Dance in Iowa: A History of Six-Player Girls' Basketball* (Lincoln: University of Nebraska Press, 2004), 5; Cahn, *Coming on Strong*, 91.

32. Cheerleading's rise in popularity in the postwar era exemplified the "broader cultural split between male and female activities." As Pamela Grundy and Susan Shackelford notes, "With its emphasis on the female figure, on wholesome good looks and on support of male teams, cheerleading fit perfectly with the womanly ideals paraded across postwar magazine pages and television screens. . . . At many schools, a place on the cheering squad became the ultimate symbol of female success"; see Pamela Grundy and Susan Shackelford, *Shattering the Glass: The Remarkable History of Women's Basketball* (Chapel Hill: University of North

Carolina Press, 2007), 121. But as Jaime Schultz explains, the female cheerleader was a recently sanctioned phenomenon. From the late nineteenth century through World War II, cheerleading was a predominantly male activity akin to football itself. For various reasons, boys and men vacated the activity after the war, and girls and women filled the void. The shift was permanent: "Over the course of a few decades, cheerleading had transformed from a prestigious, masculine domain to what sport sociologist Laurel Davis terms a 'feminine preserve,' where girls and women could cultivate and perform a culturally sanctioned femininity"; see Jaime Schultz, *Qualifying Times: Points of Change in U.S. Women's Sports* (Urbana: University of Illinois Press, 2014), 169–175, quotation on 175.

33. Cahn, *Coming on Strong*, 218.

34. Also, as Carol Meyer Roman explained, once their clamp-on roller skates wore out, they could be appropriated for other outdoor activities: "We'd have the clamp skates, and then when the skates would get old, we'd just take them apart and then put them on coasters and ride them around" (Meyer Roman interview).

35. Meyer Roman interview.

36. Youpelle Massro interview.

37. Murray interview.

38. Meyer Roman interview.

39. Bobbie Mateer, telephone interview by the author, February 1, 2012, digital audio recording, Marino Oral History Collection.

40. Sonja Henie won gold medals at the 1928, 1932, and 1936 Winter Olympic Games. She dominated the annual world championships in figure skating from 1927 to 1936, placing first in ten straight championships, a record still unbroken. Henie pushed the bar when she shortened her skirt above the knee in order to allow her to use flexible choreography and compete more effectively. Spectators loved it. Leaving competitive skating behind in the late 1930s, Henie began a lucrative film career and earned a place among the highest-earning Hollywood stars for her work in such movies as *Thin Ice* (1937) and *Sun Valley Serenade* (1941). She further increased the popularity in America of her beloved sport of ice-skating by touring with "spectacle ice shows"; see "Sonja Henie," https://www.olympic.org/sonja-henie; Schultz, *Women's Sports*, 46.

41. Palermo interview.

42. Cahn, *Coming on Strong*, 229.

43. Behrens interview.

44. Ibid.

45. Youpelle Massro interview.

46. As cited in Susan E. Cayleff, *Babe: The Life and Legend of Babe Didrikson Zaharias* (Urbana: University of Illinois Press, 1996), 43.

47. Cahn discusses the wide variety of connotations behind the term tomboy in her chapter "Women Competing / Gender Contested" (*Coming on Strong*, 228–231).

48. Cayleff, *Babe*, 43. As Cayleff discovered, Babe Didrikson experienced this

conflict because her tomboyish persona did not wane until her late twenties (44). Alan Guttman explains that sports are often part of the *"rites de passage"* for boys at puberty, but for girls, puberty signals the "abandonment of sports" (*Women's Sports*, 3).

49. Mariah Burton Nelson, introduction to *Nike Is a Goddess: The History of Women in Sports*, ed. Lissa Smith (New York: Atlantic Monthly Press, 1998), ix.

50. Robert Cromie, "Roller Derby Combat Will Open Tuesday," *Chicago Daily Tribune*, October 16, 1949; "Girl Guerrillas," *Chicago Tribune*, June 2, 1970; Clifford Terry, "Elmer & Toughie & Pee Wee & Slugger," *Chicago Daily Tribune*, April 18, 1971; Frank Deford, "The Roller Derby," *Sports Illustrated*, March 3, 1969; Charles Bartlett, "Football? Hockey? No, Sir, It's Roller Derby Back Again," *Chicago Daily Tribune*, October 22, 1942.

51. Alan Ebert, telephone interview by the author, September 14, 2011, digital audio recording, Marino Oral History Collection.

52. Jerry Seltzer, interview by the author, June 16–17, 2011, Sonoma, California, digital audio recording, Marino Oral History Collection.

53. Behrens interview.

54. Murray interview.

55. Frank Deford, telephone interview by the author, April 18, 2011, digital audio recording, Marino Oral History Collection.

56. Jack Diamond, "Marathon of Roller Skaters Is Latest 'Bughouse' Scheme," *Washington Post*, January 20, 1936.

57. Palermo interview. This occurred when the sport was still the Transcontinental Roller Derby, and after contact was added. Mary Youpelle and her partner Joe Nygra would have to fill in for each other if either sustained injuries during the transcontinental races: "If he got hurt, I'd have to go in the boys' field and skate for him, and if I got hurt, he'd have to go in the girls' field and skate for me" (Youpelle Massro interview).

58. Palermo interview.

59. Murray interview.

60. Cahn, *Coming on Strong*, 250–252.

61. Murray interview.

62. Ibid.

63. Seltzer interview, 2011; Cromie, "TV's Pretty Roughnecks."

64. A 1949 *Chicago Daily Tribune* article placed the skaters' salaries as ranging between $3,000 and $7,000 annually (Edward Prell, "Top Skaters Eye National Roller Derby," *Chicago Daily Tribune*, March 20, 1949). A 1951 article from the same paper broke the pay down further: "All skaters, both men and women are divided into 12 classifications, which are adjusted from time to time. And salaries, paid by the association out of a 20 per cent cut of the gate receipts, range from about $3,000 plus board and room, for a beginner in Class 4C, to $10,000 with room, board, and doctor bills for a 1A wheeler" (Cromie, "TV's Pretty Roughnecks").

65. Youpelle Massro interview.

66. The three biggest stars were Joan Weston, Ann Calvello, and Charlie O'Connell.

67. Youpelle Massro interview.

68. Ibid.

69. Palermo interview.

70. Ibid.

71. Behrens interview.

72. Ibid.

73. Palermo interview.

74. Behrens interview.

75. Ibid.

76. This topic is addressed more fully in chapter 4.

77. Youpelle Massro interview.

78. Behrens interview.

79. Ibid.

80. Robert Cromie, "Fans Added Attraction at Any Roller Derby," *Chicago Daily Tribune*, February 14, 1951.

81. Terry, "Elmer & Toughie."

82. Deford interview.

83. Behrens interview.

84. Youpelle Massro interview.

85. Palermo interview.

86. Murray interview.

87. Bert Wall, telephone interview by the author, January 25, 2012, digital audio recording, Marino Oral History Collection.

88. Clifford Terry quoted a writer from the *Oakland Tribune* calling the derby "the National Enquirer of Sports," which could relate to the theatrics or the women, or most likely both—the author does not specify, but makes it clear that Roller Derby is fake or illegitimate. Terry continues, "When the newspapers do decide to give it an inch or two of coverage, the editor seems to send the last guy back from lunch" ("Elmer & Toughie").

89. He continues, "There is also no doubt that it is the girls who bring people into the arenas—even if they come to enjoy more the faster, harder men's play" (Deford, "Roller Derby").

90. Behrens interview.

91. Palermo interview.

92. Guttman, *Women's Sports*, 1.

93. The next chapter discusses in more depth how the women had to prove their femininity through apologetic behavior, particularly via beauty contests See n. 114.

94. Palermo interview.

95. Behrens interview.

96. Youpelle Massro interview.

97. Behrens interview.

98. Meyer Roman interview.

99. Mateer interview.

100. Youpelle Massro interview.

101. Ibid. This loaded comment implies that at least part of the women's personae or appearance was to suggest heterosexual availability.

102. Murray interview. Like Murray, the skater Bert Wall (who was Bobbie Mateer's husband) attempted to design a "better-looking jersey" for the women. "They hated it," he said, laughing (Wall interview).

103. Murray interview.

104. Ibid. Some of the skater trends caught on with the general public. In the 1940s and 1950s, during the height of Roller Derby's popularity, Burlington Mills manufactured Roller Derby hair bows that were "worn by the Queens of the Roller Derby." Sold for twenty-nine cents, "Gerry Murray" hair bows were a popular accessory among women and girls; Catherine Mabe, *Roller Derby: The History and All-Girl Revival of the Greatest Sport on Wheels* (Denver: Speck, 2007), 35.

105. Youpelle Massro interview.

106. Palermo interview.

107. Jennifer Barbee and Alex Cohen, *Down and Derby: The Insider's Guide to Roller Derby* (Berkeley, CA: Soft Skull, 2010), 13; Frank Deford, *Five Strides on the Banked Track: The Life and Times of the Roller Derby* (Boston: Little, Brown, 1971), 82–83.

108. Deford interview.

109. Pat Griffin, *Strong Women, Deep Closets: Lesbians and Homophobia in Sport* (Champaign, IL: Human Kinetics, 1998), 20, 54–55; Cahn, *Coming on Strong*, 164–165, 181–184.

110. Youpelle Massro interview.

111. Clifford Terry, "Elmer & Toughie."

112. Youpelle Massro.

113. Jerry Seltzer recalled that many of the male skaters during his tenure were gay, but added, "We couldn't get involved in that. . . . I didn't care" (Seltzer interview, 2011). Perhaps more importantly, both lesbians and gay men in Roller Derby challenged traditional ideas of femininity and masculinity, since they were largely indistinguishable in the ranks of the skaters, yet were participating in a full-contact sport.

114. "Apologetic behavior" is covered in depth in chapter 3. The term refers to socially acceptable behavior that is used, in a sense, to apologize for simultaneously violating a social norm. For female athletes, that usually meant wearing makeup or hair bows to emphasize their femininity while playing sports, which were seen as a masculine pastime. Jaime Schultz discusses this issue in relation to ponytails in the introduction to *Qualifying Times*: She writes, "In the world of women's sports, femininity often becomes a 'code word for heterosexuality,' and the ponytail serves as an accoutrement to one's feminine presentation of self. . . . To suggest that the ponytail is used 'for display'—as a means to moderate the muscular and athletic

body and to disassociate that body from the continued presence of the lesbian stigma in sport—implies that there is a normative, perhaps compulsory, feminine aesthetic to which many women conform" (4).

115. Palermo interview. Eigen had a television show in the late 1940s and a Chicago-based radio show that ran until 1971.

116. Ibid.

117. Youpelle Massro interview.

118. Ibid.

119. "The boys against the girls" refers to the co-ed nature of Roller Derby as opposed to the regularity of men and women skating directly against one another, although that happened upon occasion.

120. Youpelle Massro interview. Youpelle recalled a really nice "maiden" woman from Texas, whom she suspected of possibly being a lesbian, constantly sending her all sorts of homemade culinary gifts but also underwear.

121. Or, apparently, they were so famous they could not attend Roller Derby in person. According to Bobbie Mateer, Elvis Presley was a huge fan but could watch the sport only on TV, since his popularity prevented him from going anywhere public like a sports arena. She stated, "He used to rent a rink close to Graceland, and he and his buddies would play Roller Derby" (Mateer interview).

122. Youpelle Massro interview.

123. Palermo interview.

CHAPTER 3: "A VERY HANDSOME KING FOR A VERY BEAUTIFUL QUEEN"

The chapter epigraphs come from the following sources: Angie Douris, "'56 Queen Contest Begins," *Roller Derby News*, October 1956; Christy Martin, "Derby 'King' Contest Gets Rolling," *Roller Derby News*, January 1957.

1. Frank Deford, *There She Is: The Life and Times of Miss America* (New York: Viking, 1971), 193.

2. Elissa Stein, *Here She Comes . . . Beauty Queen*, foreword by Lee Meriwether (San Francisco: Chronicle, 2006), 18.

3. Deford, *There She Is*, 234–235.

4. Martin, "Derby 'King' Contest Gets Rolling," 1.

5. Angie Douris, "Miss Montague Elected by Fans '56 Roller Derby News 'Queen,'" *Roller Derby News*, December 1956.

6. Ibid., 4.

7. Stein, *Here She Comes*, 18. After winning the crown, Meriwether went on to become a successful actress, perhaps best known for her eight-year role as Betty on the CBS series *Barnaby Jones*; see "Biography" on Meriwether's website, lee meriwether.com/bio.php.

8. Douris, "Miss Montague Elected by Fans," 4.

9. Stein, *Here She Comes*, 18; Douris, "Miss Montague Elected by Fans," 4.

10. Jim Croce, "Roller Derby Queen," *Life and Times*, 1973, lyrics available from Lyrics Freak, https://www.lyricsfreak.com/j/jim+croce/roller+derby+queen _20071484.html.

11. Mary Jo Festle, *Playing Nice: Politics and Apologies in Women's Sports* (New York: Columbia University Press, 1996), 45. Jaime Schultz explains that apologetic behavior included "styling one's hair, makeup, and dress to conform to conventional beauty standards." Female athletes' compensatory acts supposedly "softened an athlete's image and assured spectators that sport participation did not threaten her femininity and, in turn, that her participation did not threaten the masculine center of sport"; Jaime Schultz, *Women's Sports: What Everyone Needs to Know* (New York: Oxford University Press, 2018), 48.

12. Festle, *Playing Nice*, 51. As discussed in chapter 2, skaters wanted to present a "ladylike" image by styling their hair in a certain way, putting on makeup before skating, or wearing gloves or scarves on the track.

13. Candace Savage, *Beauty Queens: A Playful History* (New York: Abbeville, 1998), 103.

14. Stein, *Here She Comes*, 37.

15. Savage, *Beauty Queens*, 55.

16. According to legend, a beauty contest among three Olympian goddesses led to the Trojan War. Beauty contests throughout history were generally parts of festivals in which local queens and kings were crowned as symbols of community cohesion and prosperity, or simply as competitions to select the most beautiful woman in a particular locale. See Colleen Ballerino Cohen and Richard Wilk, with Beverly Stoeltje, "Introduction: Beauty Queens on the Global Stage," in *Beauty Queens on the Global Stage: Gender, Contests, and Power*, ed. Colleen Ballerino Cohen, Richard Wilk, and Beverly Stoeltje (New York: Routledge, 1996), 3; "Paris," *Encyclopaedia Britannica*, accessed December 15, 2020, https://www .britannica.com/topic/Paris-Greek-mythology; Lois W. Banner, *American Beauty* (New York: Knopf, 1983), 250; Renee M. Laegreid, *Riding Pretty: Rodeo Royalty in the American West* (Lincoln: University of Nebraska Press, 2006), chaps. 1–3.

17. Barnum held eclectic contests that proved very popular and drew in huge numbers of paying customers to his museum. But his inaugural beauty contest, dubbed the "Handsomest Ladies," was deemed too radical by elite New Yorkers. Barnum misjudged the likelihood that the middle and upper classes would respond with vehement moral outrage. Only women "of questionable reputation" entered, and according to one contemporary report, "No mother or husband—no matter how liberal—would allow a daughter or wife to appear thus in public." See Banner, *American Beauty*, 256, 258; Savage, *Beauty Queens*, 13; Sarah Banet-Weiser, *The Most Beautiful Girl in the World: Beauty Pageants and National Identity* (Berkeley: University of California Press, 1999), 34–35.

18. Cohen and Wilk, "Introduction," 4; Banner, *American Beauty*, 262-263; Savage, *Beauty Queens*, 36-39.

19. Banner, *American Beauty*, 260.

20. Kimberly A. Hamlin, "Bathing Suits and Backlash: The First Miss America Pageants, 1921-1927," in *"There She Is, Miss America": The Politics of Sex, Beauty, and Race in America's Most Famous Pageant*, ed. Elwood Watson and Darcy Martin (New York: Palgrave Macmillan, 2004), 28.

21. Banner, *American Beauty*, 264.

22. Hamlin, "Bathing Suits and Backlash," 29.

23. Stein, *Here She Comes*, 35-37; Deford, *There She Is*, 111-113; Savage, *Beauty Queens*, 33. No women of color were eligible to participate in the Miss America pageant until the 1970s. Women of other ethnic and immigrant backgrounds were not included except in menial production roles until the 1930s and 1940s. Banet-Weiser, *Most Beautiful Girl*, 161; *Miss America*, American Experience, PBS, https://www.pbs.org/wgbh/americanexperience/films/missamerica.

24. Banner, *American Beauty*, 267; Susan Cahn, *Coming on Strong: Gender and Sexuality in Twentieth-Century Women's Sports* (Cambridge, MA: Harvard University Press, 1994), 45-51.

25. Banner, *American Beauty*, 268.

26. Ibid.

27. For instance, in a 1922 *New York Times* article, Samuel Gompers, the head of the American Federation of Labor, described Gorman as the ideal American woman: "She represents the type of womanhood America needs—strong, red-blooded, able to shoulder the responsibilities of home-making and motherhood. It is in her type that the hope of the country resides." Although the winner of the 1922 pageant looked nothing like Gorman, descriptions of her centered on her athletic build. See "'Miss Indianapolis' Is Prettiest Girl: Thelma Blossom Wins First Two Events in Atlantic City Beauty Show," *New York Times*, September 8, 1922; Banner, *American Beauty*, 269.

28. Stein, *Here She Comes*, 37; Savage, *Beauty Queens*, 61-62.

29. Banner, *American Beauty*, 269.

30. Savage, *Beauty Queens*, 62.

31. "Negress in 3d place, Beauty Contest Is Off," *New York Times*, April 5, 1924; "Beauty Contest On Again," *New York Times*, April 6, 1924; Savage, *Beauty Queens*, 62.

32. Deford, *There She Is*, 149. Slaughter was the only female pageant director in the United States in 1935. In late 1941, the Miss America organization officially appointed Slaughter its executive secretary, a position she held until 1967. She was largely responsible for the popularity and respectability of the Miss America pageant. Although the contest in many ways judged women largely on their appearance, she used the pageant to provide American women with new opportunities in employment and education. She was able to do this because pageantry fell within

a traditional female sphere, a sphere that expanded during her reign but still remained oppressive overall; see Deford, *There She Is*, 149–151.

33. Savage, *Beauty Queens*, 79–87; Deford, *There She Is*, 149–154. This ideal woman came to fruition in the person of Jean Bartel, Miss America 1943. The young, "wholesome" California co-ed provided a huge boost to the pageant's image and the American war effort. The addition of a scholarship program and the partnership with the Junior Chamber of Commerce (the Jaycees) that year solidified the respectability and increased the growing popularity of the Miss America pageant; see Deford, *There She Is*, 154–160; Savage, *Beauty Queens*, 81–83.

34. Banet-Weiser, *Most Beautiful Girl*, 2. This is particularly relevant for the 1945 winner, Bess Myerson. Myerson was the first winner of Jewish heritage. According to Banet-Weiser, "At the particular historical moment in which Myerson was crowned—1945—and in light of the racial genocide of World War II, Myerson as Miss America reaffirms the logic of assimilationist discourse: she does not threaten or disrupt, but instead represents the pluralist nation as well as American universalism" (162n).

35. Beverly Stoeltje, "The Snake Charmer Queen: Ritual, Competition, and Signification in American Festival," in Cohen, Wilk, and Stoeltje, *Beauty Queens on the Global Stage*.

36. Banet-Weiser warned of reducing beauty pageants to "obvious expressions of male dominance": "Rather than understanding beauty pageants as simple, obvious expressions of male dominance, we must begin by situating contemporary pageants within the political context" (*Most Beautiful Girl*, 21).

37. Cahn, *Coming on Strong*, 7.

38. Ibid., 19.

39. Ibid., 30.

40. Robert Cromie, "Vanities Will Open Tonight in Stadium," *Chicago Daily Tribune*, September 21, 1949.

41. Robert Cromie, "Roller Derby Combat Will Open Tuesday," *Chicago Daily Tribune*, October 16, 1949.

42. Hal Boyle, "Roller Derby Gives Women Something to Yell About," *Spokane Daily Chronicle*, June 5, 1950.

43. "Roller Derby Cheesecake!," *RolleRage*, August 1945. This is a clear example of the role conflict that female roller derby skaters, and many female athletes of the early to mid-twentieth century, faced. Allen Guttman explained, "Aggressiveness . . . has conventionally been associated more closely with men than with women. It follows, therefore, that a commitment to women's sports has almost always been to some degree problematical—in women's eyes as well as men's"; see Allen Guttman, *Women's Sports: A History* (New York: Columbia University Press, 1991), 3. Thus, women frequently engaged in apologetic behavior, or their promoters did it for them.

44. Pat Farley, "Girl Roller Derby Stars Keep Their Femininity," *Roller Derby News*, November 1958.

45. Mary Youpelle Massro, telephone interview by the author, April 8, 2011, digital audio recording, Michella Marino Oral History Collection, W. E. B. Du Bois Library, University of Massachusetts Amherst (hereafter cited as Marino Oral History Collection).

46. "Roller Derby Fans Elect Most Popular Boy and Girl Skater for 1941," *RolleRage*, February 1941, 7.

47. "Questioneer," *RolleRage*, February 1941, 8.

48. Bert Wall, telephone interview by the author, January 25, 2012, digital audio recording, Marino Oral History Collection.

49. *RolleRage*, February 1941, cover.

50. Ibid., 6.

51. Bobbie Mateer, telephone interview by the author, February 1, 2012, digital audio recording, Marino Oral History Collection.

52. Youpelle Massro interview.

53. Alan Ebert, "Skaters Can Be Ladies Too, Gloria Mack (a Lady) Insists," *Roller Derby News*, January 1959.

54. Ibid. Mack won the beauty queen competition, based on fan votes, in 1950.

55. Bernie Wayne, "There She Is, Miss America," lyrics available from Lyrics Playground, https://lyricsplayground.com/alpha/songs/t/theresheismissamerica .html; Elwood Watson and Darcy Martin, introduction to Watson and Martin, *"There She Is, Miss America,"* 7.

56. Emphasis added; Douris, " '56 Queen Contest Begins."

57. "What is the American Look? The Girls of the U.S. Have an Air All Their Own," *Life*, May 21, 1945, 87–88.

58. Ibid., 87.

59. Ibid.

60. Ibid., 88.

61. Ibid., 90.

62. "Vote Again for Derby Queen; Beauty, Not Skill, to Decide," *Roller Derby News*, November 1957.

63. Wayne, "There She Is, Miss America."

64. Savage, *Beauty Queens*, 99.

65. Cited in ibid., 99.

66. See, for example, *Roller Derby News*, October 1956.

67. Ibid., November 1957.

68. Keith Coppage, *Roller Derby to RollerJam: The Authorized Story of an Unauthorized Sport* (Santa Rosa, CA: Squarebooks, 1999), pictures on 26–27; Sandy Lepelstat, "Joan Weston Crowned Queen of Roller Derby's Universe," *Roller Derby News*, February 1958; Lepelstat, "Murray Crowned Queen of 1959 Roller Derby," *Roller Derby News*, February 1959.

69. Alan Ebert, telephone interview by the author, September 14, 2011, digital audio recording, Marino Oral History Collection.

70. "Vote Again for Derby Queen."

71. Lepelstat, "Joan Weston Crowned Queen."

72. Douris, "Miss Montague Elected by Fans."

73. Jerry Seltzer, interview by the author, June 17, 2011, Sonoma, California, digital audio recording, Marino Oral History Collection.

74. James Gilbert, *Men in the Middle: Searching for Masculinity in the 1950s* (Chicago: University of Chicago Press, 2005), 2.

75. Kenneth Krauss, *Male Beauty: Postwar Masculinity in Theater, Film, and Physique Magazines* (Albany: State University of New York Press, 2013), 8.

76. Ibid., 9. In James Gilbert's historiography and critique of the "crisis" of masculinity, he highlights Kevin White's argument that middle-class men at the turn of the twentieth century attempted to adopt the "cultural swagger of working-class men," and that persona involved heightened expectations for young men's sexual attractiveness. While Krauss demonstrates how this shift in beauty occurred in force in the postwar era, it had roots in an earlier period; see Gilbert, *Men in the Middle*, 25.

77. Krauss, *Male Beauty*, 9.

78. Ibid., 11. This emphasis on male beauty was not the most prominent new form of masculinity, but as Gilbert argues, "The absurdity of growing up in the 1950s was heightened by the reluctance—the downright opposition—of a great many cultural spokesmen to accept the changes occurring in American society . . . At the same time, there were dissenting, clear voices, proposing alternative constructions of gender that saw opportunity in those same changes" (*Men in the Middle*, 3).

79. Martin, "Derby 'King' Contest Gets Rolling."

80. Ibid.

81. Sandy Lepelstat, "Russ Massro Peoples' Choice for 1956 Roller Derby King," *Roller Derby News*, March 1957.

82. Gilbert, *Men in the Middle*, 16–17.

83. Ibid., 23–24.

84. Ibid., 10.

85. Cromie, "Roller Derby Combat." A great example from 1942 includes the following: "Enter the ladies, then, and in two minutes they make their male teammates appear to be namby-pambies who don't know the first thing about tacking or plunging on roller skates"; see Charles Bartlett, "Football? Hockey? No, Sir, It's Roller Derby Back Again," *Chicago Daily Tribune*, October 22, 1942.

86. "SERVES NOTICE," *Roller Derby News*, June 1956, 6. In a similar article in October 1956, Carol Siefert sought the title: "SEEKS TITLE—Attractive Carol Seifert, one of the outstanding young Roller Derby stars, is seeking to capture the title of 'Queen of the Roller Derby' this year. The attractive skating star has always been close but never has won the coveted title."

87. Angie Douris, "'Queen' Balloting Heavy and Close; Porter Leading," *Roller Derby News*, November 1956; "Doss Leads for Rink Queen," *Roller Derby News*, December 1957; "Weston Ahead in Close Vote," *Roller Derby News*, January 1958.

88. To be clear, women were included in this type of coverage as well; see "Balloting Continues: 3 Qualify for Hall of Fame," *Roller Derby News*, May 1956; "Joan Weston Paces Derby All-Star Balloting: Red Smartt Leads Men; Braves List 7 Skaters," *Roller Derby News*, September 1956; "Fans, Skaters Pick Red Smartt as Derby Tops," *Roller Derby News*, October 1957; "Red Smartt Leads All Star Balloting," *Roller Derby News*, September 1957; "Rookies Brewer, Frame, Copeland Lead Fans' Poll," *Roller Derby News*, June 1957.

89. Farley, "Girl Roller Derby Stars."

90. R. W. Connell, *Masculinities*, 2nd ed. (Berkeley: University of California Press, 2005), 54.

91. See chapter 2 for more on this idea.

92. Billy Bogash, quoted in Herb Michelson, *A Very Simple Game: The Story of Roller Derby* (Oakland, CA: Occasional Publishing, 1971), 16.

93. "Roller Derby Girls Play Rough," *Burlington (NC) Daily Times-News*, January 6, 1949.

94. C. J. Pascoe and Tristan Bridges, *Exploring Masculinities: Identity, Inequality, Continuity, and Change* (New York: Oxford University Press, 2016), 3; Connell, *Masculinities*, 76–81.

95. Michael Messner, *Out of Play: Critical Essays on Gender and Sport* (Albany: State University of New York Press, 2007), 32.

96. Connell, *Masculinities*, 77.

97. Messner, *Out of Play*, 33.

98. Seltzer interview, 2011.

99. Jerry Seltzer's tenure lasted from 1959 until 1973. Here he referred to the skaters' sexualities or sexual preferences.

100. Seltzer interview, 2011. If their homosexuality had been openly acknowledged or widely known, they would have been further subordinated within the masculine gender order; see Connell, *Masculinities*, 78.

101. Cahn, *Coming on Strong*, 203.

102. Ibid., 186.

103. Loretta Behrens, telephone interview by the author, September 9, 2012, digital audio recording, Marino Oral History Collection.

104. Seltzer interview, 2011.

105. Ibid.

106. Frank Deford, telephone interview by the author, April 18, 2011, digital audio recording, Marino Oral History Collection.

107. I was unable to procure an interview with any openly gay Roller Derby skaters from the Seltzer era. The inclusion of such voices would add depth to the history of Roller Derby.

108. In the 1930s and 1940s, lesbian and gay communities burgeoned, particularly in large cities. Gay and lesbian bars played an important part in this development. Although unable to change the stigma of homosexuality, lesbians and gay men of the time were able to meet and socialize with others like themselves.

As more women entered the workforce and gained a measure of independence, lesbians became harder to identify and thus had more freedom to be seen in public spaces. Unfortunately, the conservative backlash of the 1950s reimposed traditional gender norms with a vengeance and established a climate that was openly hostile to gays and lesbians. Homosexuals continued to organize socially and politically, but the gay rights revolution did not emerge until the 1970s. See Lillian Faderman, *Odd Girls and Twilight Lovers: A History of Lesbian Life in Twentieth-Century America* (New York: Penguin, 1992); Madeline D. Davis and Elizabeth Lapovsky Kennedy, *Boots of Leather, Slippers of Gold: The History of a Lesbian Community* (New York: Penguin, 1994); Marcia M. Gallo, *Different Daughters: A History of the Daughters of Bilitis and the Rise of the Lesbian Rights Movement* (Emeryville, CA: Seal, 2007).

109. Youpelle Massro interview.

110. Youpelle Massro interview. I address the larger debate about why lesbians are not classified as feminine, which Youpelle indicates here, later in the book.

111. Behrens interview.

112. Deford interview; Seltzer interview, 2011.

113. Youpelle Massro interview.

114. Behrens interview; Mateer interview; Carol Meyer Roman, telephone interview by the author, July 13, 2012, digital audio recording, Marino Oral History Collection; Mary Lou Palermo, telephone interview by the author, April 7, 2011, digital audio recording, Marino Oral History Collection; Gerry Murray, telephone interview by the author, September 26, 2011, digital audio recording, Marino Oral History Collection.

115. Palermo interview.

116. Mateer interview.

117. Behrens interview.

118. Ibid. The term "butch" has been used by both gays and straights to describe lesbian women who adhere to a more traditional masculine appearance and behavior, but within the lesbian community, the term can refer to specific identity roles and behavior codes; see Faderman, *Odd Girls and Twilight Lovers*, 59–60, 126.

119. Behrens interview.

120. Ibid.

121. Murray interview.

122. Seltzer interview, 2011.

123. Ibid. There is one exception to this. According to Jerry Seltzer, the famous skater Ann Calvello, known for her shock tactics and blunt manner, accused Jerry of putting her on a team largely composed of lesbians. She stated, " 'You made my team all nellies!' " Seltzer recalled that the term "nelly" referred to the attractive, pretty lesbians, whereas traditionally masculine lesbians were referred to as "bull dykes."

124. Coppage, *Roller Derby to RollerJam*, 50. Several Black women, including Toni Stone, the first Black woman to play in the Negro leagues, wanted to play

professional baseball for the All-American Girls Professional Baseball League but were either denied tryouts or were not asked to join the teams. Local newspapers reported that at least three Black players tried out for the South Bend Blue Sox in the early 1950s. According to the minutes of postseason league board meetings in 1951, board members discussed in depth whether to include Black players, and representatives from different cities disagreed on how to proceed: "The consensus of the group seemed to be against the idea of colored players, unless they would show promise of exceptional ability, that in the event a club did hire one of them, that none of the clubs would make her feel unwelcome." No club hired a Black female baseball player. See Merrie A. Fidler, *The Origins and History of the All-American Girls Professional Baseball League* (Jefferson, NC: McFarland, 2006), 190; Martha Ackmann, *Curveball: The Remarkable Story of Toni Stone* (Chicago: Lawrence Hill, 2010), 109.

125. Victoria Wolcott, *Race, Riots, and Roller Coasters: The Struggle over Segregated Recreation in America* (Philadelphia: University of Pennsylvania Press, 2012), 17, 66–72.

126. "Ex-Ben Franklin Athlete on Wheels," *New York Age*, January 24, 1953.

127. A. Ebert interview. An article published in 1958 in the *New York Amsterdam News* mentions John "Hank" Hershey, a Black referee and trainer who had been with Roller Derby since 1951. According to the article, "Hank is one of the best liked referees in the game. He has officiated or worked as a trainer since 1951." I located no other references to Hershey, and no skaters mentioned him in their interviews. Although not a skater, it is possible that Hershey was the first Black person involved with the sport in some capacity.

128. Sources including major newspapers and some skaters claim that either Darlene Anderson or George Copeland was the first Black skater in Roller Derby. Although Maurice Plummer did not leave an outstanding skating legacy, he was in fact the first Black skater; see A. Ebert interview.

129. Coppage, *Roller Derby to RollerJam*, 50.

130. George Banner, "One in 1958, Now 11 Are Starring in Roller Derby," *New York Amsterdam News*, April 30, 1960.

131. "Simply Darlene," Darlene Anderson, as told to Jim Greene, Loretta "Little Iodine" Behrens' Derby Memoirs, http://derbymemoirs.bankedtrack.info/Anderson_Darlene.html.

132. Seltzer interview, 2011; Meyer Roman interview.

133. Deford interview.

134. Seltzer interview, 2011.

135. Deford interview.

136. Ronnie Robinson, quoted in Michelson, *Very Simple Game*, 109.

137. Ibid.

138. The historian David R. Roediger, who grew up in St. Louis, Missouri, in the 1960s, recalled similar instances of sports fans' colorblindness regarding race. He described the contradictions between theoretical racism and cultural anti-

racism: "We all hated Blacks in the abstract, but our greatest heroes were the Black stars of the great St. Louis Cardinals baseball teams of the sixties. The style, as well as the talent, of players like Lou Brock, Bob Gibson and Curt Flood was reverenced. More grudgingly, we admired Muhammad Ali as our generation's finest sportsman"; see David R. Roediger, *The Wages of Whiteness: Race and the Making of the American Working Class*, rev. ed. (New York: Verso, 2003), 4.

139. Jason Lewis, "Darlene Anderson Broke Roller Derby Color Barrier in 1958," *Los Angeles Sentinel*, January 20, 2011, https://lasentinel.net/darlene-anderson-broke-roller-derby-color-barrier-in-1958.html.

140. John Hall, telephone interview by the author, October 4, 2011, digital audio recording, Marino Oral History Collection.

141. Coppage, *Roller Derby to RollerJam*, 50.

142. Ibid., 51. This was mostly likely in 1959 or 1960. Coppage cites Ronnie Robinson for this detail, and Robinson joined Roller Derby in 1959.

143. Coppage, *Roller Derby to RollerJam*, 51–52.

144. Meyer Roman interview.

145. As cited in Coppage, *Roller Derby to RollerJam*, 51.

146. Wall interview.

147. Coppage, *Roller Derby to RollerJam*, 50.

148. Deford, *Five Strides*, 156.

149. This is clearly seen in the Roller Derby Queen and King contests and the coverage of skaters in their own publications.

150. Watson and Martin, *"There She Is, Miss America,"* 2.

151. Maxine Leeds Craig, *Ain't I a Beauty Queen: Black Women, Beauty, and the Politics of Race* (New York: Oxford University Press, 2002), 5, 7, 10, 19, 30.

152. Ibid., 7.

153. Ibid.

154. Palermo interview; Ebert, "Skaters Can Be Ladies."

155. Craig, *Ain't I a Beauty Queen*, 94.

156. Ibid., 24; Valerie Felita Kinloch, "The Rhetoric of Black Bodies: Race, Beauty, and Representation," in Watson and Martin, *"There She Is, Miss America,"* 94–95.

157. Kinloch, "Rhetoric of Black Bodies," 94. As Sarah Banet-Weiser explained in her book on beauty pageants and national identity, the Miss America pageant used whiteness as "an explicitly racialized category" to develop an imagined community that "has historically maintained dominance precisely by erasing its racial distinctiveness" (*Most Beautiful Girl*, 154). In the search for the "ideal" American woman, whiteness became a crucial element, since it "defines typicality according to white, middle-class norms." Sarah Banet-Weiser, "Miss America, National Identity, and the Identity Politics of Whiteness," in Watson and Martin, *"There She Is, Miss America,"* 69; Banet-Weiser, *Most Beautiful Girl*, 156.

158. Banet-Weiser, "Miss America, National Identity," 103.

159. Kinloch, "Rhetoric of Black Bodies," 98–99.

160. Lepelstat, "Joan Weston Crowned Queen."

161. Farley, "Girl Roller Derby Stars"; Kinloch, "Rhetoric of Black Bodies," 97.

162. Jerrilyn McGregory, "Wiregrass Country Pageant Competitions, or What's Beauty Got to Do with It?," in Watson and Martin, *"There She Is, Miss America,"* 128; see also Laegreid, *Riding Pretty*, 43.

163. Seltzer interview, 2011.

164. McGregory, "Wiregrass Country Pageant," 128.

165. A. Ebert interview.

166. Ibid.

167. Ebert, "Skaters Can Be Ladies."

168. Pascoe and Bridges, *Exploring Masculinities*, 18.

CHAPTER 4: DIAPER DERBIES

The epigraphs to this chapter come from the following sources: Mary Youpelle Massro, telephone interview by the author, April 8, 2011, digital audio recording, Michella Marino Oral History Collection, W. E. B. Du Bois Library, University of Massachusetts Amherst (hereafter cited as Marino Oral History Collection); Bert Wall, telephone interview by the author, January 25, 2012, digital audio recording, Marino Oral History Collection; Buddy Atkinson Jr., telephone interview by the author, August 23, 2016, digital audio recording, interview in author's possession.

1. National Roller Derby yearbook, 1952, copy in the National Roller Derby Hall of Fame and Museum, Palm Springs, California.

2. "Shadows of the Future," National Roller Derby yearbook, 1952.

3. Keith Coppage, *Roller Derby to RollerJam: The Authorized Story of an Unauthorized Sport* (Santa Rosa, CA: Squarebooks, 1999), 21; *RolleRage*, August 1945; *National Roller Derby Official Program*, 1951; *Roller Derby News*, June 1956; *Roller Derby News*, January 1958. Oscar eventually bought out Leo's shares in the skate company: Jerry Seltzer, interview by the author, September 20, 2015, digital audio recording, in author's possession.

4. Coppage, *Roller Derby to RollerJam*, 19.

5. Youpelle Massro interview.

6. Coppage, *Roller Derby to RollerJam*, 7–8; Catherine Mabe, *Roller Derby: The History and All-Girl Revival of the Greatest Sport on Wheels* (Denver: Speck, 2007), 27–31.

7. Mary Lou Palermo, telephone interview by the author, April 7, 2011, digital audio recording, Marino Oral History Collection.

8. As cited in Frank Deford, *Five Strides on the Banked Track: The Life and Times of the Roller Derby* (Boston: Little, Brown, 1971), 81.

9. Gerry Murray, telephone interview by the author, September 26, 2011, digital audio recording, Marino Oral History Collection.

10. As cited in Deford, *Five Strides*, 82–83.

11. Loretta Behrens, telephone interview by the author, September 9, 2012, digital audio recording, Marino Oral History Collection.

12. Youpelle Massro interview.

13. Bobbie Johnstone Atkinson, quoted in Herb Michelson, *A Very Simple Game: The Story of Roller Derby* (Oakland, CA: Occasional Publishing, 1971), 43.

14. Youpelle Massro interview.

15. Murray interview; Coppage, *Roller Derby to RollerJam*, 6; Deford, *Five Strides*, 81.

16. Murray interview. This also underscores the value of the female skaters to the organization.

17. As cited in Deford, *Five Strides*, 81.

18. Gene Vizena Nygra, interview by Joel Justin, in a promotion for "The Roller Derby 'Wooden Wheel Wonders,'" accessed June 12, 2012, http://www.youtube.com/watch?v=4fRKxkbhyIM (video no longer available).

19. Murray interview.

20. Deford, *Five Strides*, 81.

21. Bobbie Mateer, telephone interview by the author, February 1, 2012, digital audio recording, Marino Oral History Collection.

22. Coppage, *Roller Derby to RollerJam*, 17.

23. Clip included in *Demon of the Derby: The Ann Calvello Story*, dir. Sharon Rutter, prod. Christine Murray, Fireproof Productions, 2010, DVD.

24. As cited in Deford, *Five Strides*, 137.

25. Ann Calvello, quoted in Michelson, *Very Simple Game*, 69.

26. Mateer interview.

27. Jerry Seltzer, interview by the author, June 17, 2011, Sonoma, California, digital audio recording, Michella Marino Oral History Collection.

28. Deford, *Five Strides*, 29; Seltzer interview, 2011. See chapter 5 for more on how and why certain cities were chosen for the tour.

29. Mateer could not remember the exact date they played in Chicago in 1950 but believed it was either late March or the first week of April (Mateer interview).

30. Ibid.

31. Ibid.

32. Seltzer interview, 2011.

33. Murray interview.

34. Carol Meyer Roman, telephone interview by the author, July 13, 2012, digital audio recording, Marino Oral History Collection.

35. Ibid.

36. Stephanie Coontz, *The Way We Never Were: American Families and the Nostalgia Trap* (New York: Basic Books, 2000), 24–25; Elaine Tyler May, *Homeward Bound: American Families in the Cold War Era* (New York: Basic Books, 1999), 50–51, 98–99, 165–166.

37. Ruth Rosen, *The World Split Open: How the Modern Women's Movement*

Changed America (New York: Penguin, 2000), 18–19, 51–53; Beth Bailey, *Sex in the Heartland* (Cambridge, MA: Harvard University Press, 1999), 6–12.

38. Alan Ebert, telephone interview by the author, September 14, 2011, digital audio recording, Marino Oral History Collection.

39. Ibid.

40. Seltzer interview, 2011. This is reminiscent of the modern "cougar" mentality, whereby older single women try to date younger men.

41. Ken Monte, quoted in Michelson, *Very Simple Game*, 52. Midge's first husband, Bill Golba, was a referee when Ken Monte joined the derby, but Golba had previously been a skater and skated under the name "Bill Roskoff."

42. Ibid., 53.

43. Deford, *Five Strides*, 55.

44. Mateer interview.

45. Ibid.

46. Ibid.

47. Seltzer interview, 2011.

48. Deford, *Five Strides*, 138.

49. Ibid., 55.

50. Seltzer interview, 2011.

51. Mateer interview.

52. Behrens interview.

53. Ibid.

54. Ibid.

55. Ibid. Behrens's understanding that pregnancy and motherhood would alter her skating career exemplifies the fact that "childbirth is more than a biological event in women's lives." As the historian Judith Walzer Leavitt explained, "It is a vital component in the social definition of womanhood"; see Judith Walzer Leavitt, *Brought to Bed: Childbearing in America, 1750–1950* (New York: Oxford University Press, 1986), 3. Childbirth and pregnancy have not remained static, and as the historian Rickie Solinger pointed out, "Pregnancy has carried different meanings depending on the age of a girl or woman and also depending on her race and on whether she is rich or poor or in the middle." "The meaning of a pregnancy," wrote Solinger, "can also be determined by the historical moment in which it occurs"; see Rickie Solinger, *Pregnancy and Power: A Short History of Reproductive Politics in America* (New York: New York University Press, 2005), 1.

56. Mari Jo Buhle, Teresa Murphy, and Jane Gerhard, *A Concise Women's History* (Boston: Pearson, 2015), 473. This has deep Cold War implications as well, which May's *Homeward Bound* covers.

57. Susan J. Douglas and Meredith W. Michaels, *The Mommy Myth: The Idealization of Motherhood and How It Has Undermined All Women* (New York: Free Press, 2004), 33.

58. As Stephanie Coontz demonstrates in her important work *The Way We Never Were*, not only was this mother idealized, but the entire idea of the 1950s tra-

ditional middle-class nuclear family has been romanticized and mythologized, too. In addition, the family dynamics of that era have been removed from the economic, racial, and political context in which they existed. It is important to note that the ideal family and the values that come along with it were new phenomena. Indeed, "at the time, most people understood the 1950s family to be a new invention" (Coontz, *Way We Never Were*, 26). In her pivotal book *Homeward Bound*, Elaine Tyler May hits on this very issue: "The depression of the 1930s and World War II laid the foundation for a commitment to a stable home life, but they also opened the way for a radical restructuring of the family. The yearning for family stability gained momentum after the war, but the potential for restructuring the family withered as the powerful ideology of domesticity was imprinted on everyday life. Ironically, traditional gender roles became a central feature of the 'modern' middle-class home" (14). These traditional gender roles led to the feminine mystique and "the problem that had no name"; see Betty Friedan, *The Feminine Mystique*, ed. Kirsten Fermaglich and Lisa M. Fine (1963; New York: Norton, 2013), 9.

59. Buhle, Murphy, Gerhard, *Concise Women's History*, 473.

60. Douglas and Michaels, *Mommy Myth*, 34–35.

61. Ibid., 35.

62. Buhle, Murphy, and Gerhard, *Concise Women's History*, 475.

63. In other words, women's domestic labor allowed their spouses and children to participate in sports; see Shona M. Thompson, *Mother's Taxi: Sport and Women's Labor* (Albany: State University of New York Press, 1999), 3.

64. Mateer interview.

65. Murray interview.

66. Ibid.

67. Glenda Riley, *Inventing the American Woman: An Inclusive History*, vol. 1, *To 1877*, 4th ed. (Wheeling, IL: Harlan Davidson, 2007), 235.

68. Linda Gordon, *The Moral Property of Women: A History of Birth Control Politics in America* (Urbana: University of Illinois Press, 2007), 111–118, 286–288; Rosen, *World Split Open*, 52, 55; Bailey, *Sex in the Heartland*, 1–3; Solinger, *Pregnancy and Power*, 71–79, 169–174, 230. For more on this topic, see Ellen Chesler, *Women of Valor: Margaret Sanger and the Birth Control Movement in America* (New York: Simon and Schuster, 1992).

69. Leavitt, *Brought to Bed*, 4.

70. A. Ebert interview.

71. Ibid.

72. Ibid. While other skaters acknowledged the lack of birth control and described the dating scene in Roller Derby, no skaters discussed abortion as an option. In response to the pile-up abortion statement, Gerry Murray claimed, "I never heard of anything like that!" (Murray interview).

73. Seltzer interview, 2011.

74. Youpelle Massro interview.

75. Ibid.; Deford, *Five Strides*, 132–133.

76. Youpelle Massro interview.

77. Deford, *Five Strides*, 132.

78. Ibid.

79. Ibid.

80. Youpelle Massro interview.

81. Seltzer interview, 2011.

82. Ibid.

83. Jerry Seltzer, "Derby's Golden Age . . . for me," *Roller Derby Jesus* (blog), January 14, 2012, accessed April 24, 2017, https://rollerderbyjesus.com/2012/01/14/derbys-golden-age-for-me. Joe DiMaggio was a star in baseball, Red Grange in football, and Hank Luisetti in basketball.

84. Mateer interview; Murray interview. Other skaters such as Bobbie Johnstone, Monta Jean (Kemp) Payne, Toughie Brasuhn, and Mary Youpelle also made this decision (Palermo interview; Youpelle Massro interview).

85. "Mike Gammon's Biography," Mike Gammon's personal website, accessed June 11, 2012, www.mikegammon.com.

86. Murray interview.

87. In her interview, Murray put the date of her marriage to Gene in either 1944 or 1945, but their marriage certificate shows it took place on February 17, 1948. Gammon and Murray marriage certificate, February 17, 1948, available on Ancestry.com (registration required).

88. Murray interview.

89. Ibid.

90. Ibid.

91. Mateer interview.

92. Wall interview.

93. Mateer interview.

94. Ibid.

95. Ibid.

96. Ibid.

97. Further exemplifying Roller Derby's family atmosphere, Loretta Behrens encouraged Palermo to travel to California to skate, and she opened her home to Palermo and her daughters. Palermo fondly recalled, "It was Loretta that got me to come out there . . . the first time . . . She had two little ones. And I had my two. So we'd stay there and we'd skate, and we'd take care of the kids. And she called me her husband's 'summer wife.'" Another time, Loretta was asked to skate in Hawaii when Palermo and her girls were already staying with them in California for the summer. Palermo encouraged her to go ahead and take the opportunity and offered to help Loretta's husband, Phil, babysit her son and daughter. She told her, "Well, go ahead. I'll watch the kids; Phil and I will watch the kids. [But] Phil got a little antsy, so he took his son and he went to Hawaii, so I had [all] the girls. But we

worked it out really, really well. And Loretta—Loretta's a hell of a gal" (Palermo interview).

98. Ibid.

99. Ibid.

100. Ibid. Sometimes the travel could wear on the young girls, especially around the holidays. Palermo had a Christmas tradition of taking her girls to see Santa Claus at Marshall Field's Walnut Room when they were at home in Chicago. One December, she told the girls to get ready for their annual Santa excursion. But this time the girls asked, "Why? We seen him in Pittsburgh."

101. Cliff Butler, telephone interview by the author, May 25, 2016, digital audio recording, in author's possession.

102. Ibid. Cliff admitted that as a California man, he was equally enchanted by the snow.

103. Youpelle Massro interview.

104. Ibid.

105. Palermo interview.

106. Ibid. Similarly, Bobbie Mateer and her husband, Bert Wall, decided to continue skating until their daughter Deborah started school. Mateer retired at thirty-one and settled down into the role of housewife and mother while their daughter was still young: "I was involved in community organizations and PTA and ran school carnivals and just the typical things that anybody would do in the neighborhood" (Mateer interview). Although Mateer no longer skated, she took up sports such as bowling, skiing, and tennis, which were more compatible with her new life.

107. Meyer Roman interview.

108. Phil Berrier, "Ann Calvello," Loretta "Little Iodine" Behrens' Derby Memoirs, accessed June 14, 2012, http://derbymemoirs.bankedtrack.info/mem_Calvello_ann.html; *Demon of the Derby*.

109. *Demon of the Derby*.

110. Calvello, quoted in *Demon of the Derby*.

111. Gloria "Miffy" Mifsud, interview in *Demon of the Derby*.

112. Calvello, in *Demon of the Derby*.

113. Ibid.

114. Ibid.

115. Ibid.

116. Gloria Mifsud, also a single parent, had to move in with her parents because she could not afford an apartment on her salary (*Demon of the Derby*).

117. A lack of work experience outside Roller Derby was a problem for Calvello and other longtime skaters when Roller Derby shut down in 1973. They had been skating all their adult lives and did not know what else to do.

118. Calvello, in *Demon of the Derby*.

119. Teri Ann Conte interview, in *Demon of the Derby*.

120. Ibid. Teri experienced a real relationship with her mother only as an

adult. She never lived with her mother as a young child and spent time with her only at Christmas and Easter and possibly for a couple weeks in the summer if Calvello was not skating abroad. Teri has no childhood memories of bonding with her mother because it never happened. She never scraped her knees as a young girl and ran to her mother for comfort. She simply was not there. But her grandmother and great-grandmother did not speak ill of Calvello. No one ever discussed why their situation was the way it was. They simply told Teri that her mother was skating, that Teri was there with them, and that was it. Calvello always seemed bigger than life to Teri. She remembers her mother's outrageous clothes, shoes, and hair. When not on the track, Calvello usually wore miniskirts and sky-high heels. Her multicolored bouffant hairstyle always stuck out in a crowd. Calvello constantly told her daughter to sit up straight and to "put her tickets out," meaning to put her breasts forward. Teri's memories consist of tagging along behind her mother as she purposefully strutted around in tight dresses and pointy bras.

121. Calvello, quoted in Michelson, *Very Simple Game*, 70.

122. Ibid. Calvello took great pride in her daughter's manners and responsibility but also her independence: "I'm very lucky with my daughter about this kinda thing. I just happen to have a daughter who calls me when she's five minutes late, and I thank God every night, believe it or not" (68). Calvello appreciated the compliments she received on her daughter's good behavior: "When we go to a soda fountain for some sodas after the game, they'll come up to me and say 'Ann, your daughter's so well-behaved and such a lady and everything.' You know, to me this is a great compliment because I tried to bring her up this way" (69).

123. Ibid., 69.

124. Ibid., 70.

125. Ibid.

126. Mateer interview.

127. This meant that these skating parents did not go on tour across the United States after the home season ended. They remained tied to one city and might skate when Roller Derby came back through that city during the tour. But because of their school-age children, they were not willing to go on the road during the school year.

128. Mateer interview.

129. As stated previously, Paul Milane was Mike Gammon's biological father, but after marrying Gerry Murray, Gene Gammon helped raise Mike, and Mike later took his stepfather's last name.

130. Murray interview.

131. Ibid.

132. As cited in Coppage, *Roller Derby to RollerJam*, 83.

133. Murray interview.

134. Ibid.

135. Atkinson interview.

136. Ibid.

137. See chapter 5 for more on Roller Derby's relocation to the West Coast.

138. Atkinson interview.

139. Ibid.

140. Ibid.

141. "Shadows of the Future," Roller Derby Program, 1953, binder 1952–1955, National Roller Derby Hall of Fame and Museum.

142. Murray interview.

143. As cited in Coppage, *Roller Derby to RollerJam*, 83.

144. Atkinson interview.

145. Jeane Hoffman, "The Fan Club Comes of Age," National Roller Derby Official Program 1951, 5; copy in author's possession.

146. Ibid.

147. Meyer Roman interview.

148. Lenny Berkman, interview by the author, December 20, 2011, Amherst, MA, digital audio recording, Marino Oral History Collection.

149. David Ketchum, telephone interview by the author, August 16, 2016, digital audio recording, in author's possession.

150. *Roller Derby News*, May 1956.

151. Sandy Lepelstat, "Trackside Chatter," *Roller Derby News*, June 1956.

152. Sylvia Henley, "Editorial," *Roller Derby News*, March 1957. Youpelle returned to skating after the birth of her second child (Youpelle Massro interview).

153. Lepelstat, "Trackside Chatter," *Roller Derby News*, August 1956.

154. Henley, "Editorial."

155. *Roller Derby News*, November 1939.

156. *Roller Derby News*, June 1956.

157. Palermo interview.

CHAPTER 5: CALIFORNIA OR BUST

The chapter epigraphs are taken from Buddy Atkinson Jr., telephone interview by the author, August 23, 2016, digital audio recording, interview in author's possession; and John Hall, telephone interview by the author, October 4, 2011, digital audio recording, Michella Marino Oral History Collection, W. E. B. Du Bois Library, University of Massachusetts Amherst (hereafter cited as Marino Oral History Collection).

1. Jerry Seltzer, interview by the author, June 17, 2011, Sonoma, California, digital audio recording, Marino Oral History Collection. Seltzer calls Jacobs "Lou," but he was referring to Mike Jacobs; see "Mike Jacobs," International Boxing Hall of Fame, ibhof.com/pages/about/inductees/nonparticipant/jacobsmike .html. The date for this contact comes from Stephen Miller, "Ivy King, 90, Roller Derby Queen," *New York Sun*, July 20, 2006.

2. Seltzer interview, 2011; "Where and What Was the Hippodrome?" (video),

New-York Historical Society Museum and Library, http://www.nyhistory.org/com munity/hippodrome.

3. Seltzer interview, 2011.

4. Keith Coppage, *Roller Derby to RollerJam: The Authorized Story of an Un-authorized Sport* (Santa Rosa, CA: Squarebooks, 1999), 19; Frank Deford, *Five Strides on the Banked Track: The Life and Times of the Roller Derby* (Boston: Little, Brown, 1971), 90. The Roller Derby Hall of Fame's website states that the first tele-vised game in New York occurred in 1946 at the Polo Grounds, but it was not until the November 1948 broadcast at the armory that public attention caught on; see "Roller Derby Timeline," National Roller Derby Hall of Fame and Museum, roller-derbyhalloffame.com/id3.html. Footage from the Polo Grounds game is available online from the 1946 AP Archive.

5. Coppage claims that 500 spectators were in attendance that Monday night, 400 of whom had received free tickets (*Roller Derby to RollerJam*, 19). Deford claims there were closer to 1,000 people there, and the *New York Times* reported a precise attendance figure of 2,231 (William J. Briordy, "Teams of 10 Begin Derby on Rollers," *New York Times*, November 29, 1948). Varying figures notwithstanding, the point is that few fans showed up for the Sunday-night game. But significantly more came the second night, which was the first night of the live broadcast, and for the next few games, attendance skyrocketed. Eventually, Roller Derby filled the armory to capacity. Deford, *Five Strides*, 91.

6. "New York Skaters Win, 15–11," *New York Times*, December 4, 1948; De-ford, *Five Strides*, 90; Coppage, *Roller Derby to RollerJam*, 19.

7. Deford, *Five Strides*, 93.

8. Jerry Seltzer, cited in Coppage, *Roller Derby to RollerJam*, 23.

9. Deford, *Five Strides*, 95. Seltzer also moved his base of operations to offices in Madison Square Garden; see Coppage, *Roller Derby to RollerJam*, 21.

10. Coppage, *Roller Derby to RollerJam*, 21; Deford, *Five Strides*, 100.

11. Coppage, *Roller Derby to RollerJam*, 23.

12. Ibid., 23–24.

13. Clifford Terry, "Elmer & Toughie & Pee Wee & Slugger," *Chicago Daily Tribune*, April 18, 1971.

14. Coppage, *Roller Derby to RollerJam*, 23–25; Deford, *Five Strides*, 97–100; Margot "Em Dash" Atwell, *Derby Life: A Crash Course in the Incredible Sport of Roller Derby* (New York: Gutpunch, 2015), 31–32.

15. Coppage, *Roller Derby to RollerJam*, 29.

16. Ibid., 31–32.

17. Ibid., 32–34. This is the return to New York that Buddy Atkinson men-tions in chapter 4, when his parents rejoined Roller Derby, prompting him to fol-low them.

18. Coppage, *Roller Derby to RollerJam*, 34; Seltzer interview, 2011.

19. Seltzer interview, 2011; Coppage, *Roller Derby to RollerJam*, 35.

20. Seltzer interview, 2011.

21. Coppage, *Roller Derby to RollerJam*, 33.

22. Seltzer interview, 2011; Coppage, *Roller Derby to RollerJam*, 34.

23. Seltzer interview, 2011.

24. Ibid.; Atwell, *Derby Life*, 33.

25. Seltzer interview, 2011.

26. Ibid.

27. Ibid.

28. Ibid.

29. Ibid.

30. When Roller Derby was headquartered in the Los Angeles area in the 1950s, the Bay Bombers team consisted of skaters from the LA area who went to San Francisco to skate. The Bay Bombers became an official team in 1954, and when Roller Derby left the LA area for the Bay Area in 1958, the San Francisco Bay Bombers became Roller Derby's main team; see Jerry Seltzer and Keith Coppage, *Images of America: Bay Area Roller Derby* (Charleston, SC: Arcadia, 2012), 28–31.

31. Seltzer interview, 2011.

32. Ibid.

33. Ibid.

34. Coppage, *Roller Derby to RollerJam*, 38.

35. Ibid.

36. Ibid.

37. Seltzer interview, 2011.

38. Ibid.

39. Coppage, *Roller Derby to RollerJam*, 40.

40. Seltzer interview, 2011.

41. Ibid.

42. Ibid.

43. Ibid.

44. Jerry Seltzer, email to the author, May 31, 2017.

45. Hall interview.

46. Atkinson interview.

47. Hall interview.

48. Jerry Seltzer, email to the author.

49. Seltzer interview, 2011.

50. Ibid.

51. Ibid.

52. Atkinson interview. To be fair, even if final scores mattered, surely Atkinson would have had trouble recalling them, since he skated in over 3,300 games throughout his career, an amazing feat.

53. Seltzer interview, 2011.

54. Ibid.

55. Atkinson interview.

56. Seltzer interview, 2011.

57. Atkinson interview.

58. Neither this new organization nor any outlaw unit could directly call itself "Roller Derby," since Seltzer had trademarked the name in the 1930s. The National Skating Derby / Roller Games underwent multiple name changes, but whatever its official title, skaters usually referred to it as Roller Games or just National.

59. Hall interview.

60. Ibid.

61. Atkinson interview.

62. Hall interview.

63. Ibid.

64. Hall interview.

65. Ibid.

66. Big names from Roller Derby went over to Roller Games in later years, including Buddy Atkinson Jr., Judy Arnold, Mike Gammon, and Judi McGuire ("Roller Derby Timeline").

67. Hall interview.

68. Ibid.

69. Ibid.

70. Ibid.

71. Atkinson interview.

72. Deford, *Five Strides*, 124–125; Frank Deford, telephone interview by the author, April 18, 2011, digital audio recording, Marino Oral History Collection.

73. Hall interview.

74. Atkinson interview.

75. Seltzer interview, 2011; Atkinson interview; Steve Chawkins, "Bill Griffiths Dies at 91; Promoter Brought Glitz to Roller Derby," *Los Angeles Times*, April 7, 2015.

76. Hall interview.

77. Ibid.; Atkinson interview.

78. Hall interview; "Roller Derby at Comiskey," *Chicago Tribune*, chicagotribune.com/photos/chi-080806-roller-derby-photogallery-photogallery.html.

79. Hall interview.

80. Ibid.

81. Ibid.

82. Online sources claim that Griffiths changed the name of the National Skating Derby to the National Roller League. It is unclear whether this happened before Hill got out or after the National Skating Derby dissolved. Units that retained the "Roller Games" name continued to operate until 1976. An undated T-bird program (probably from the 1972 season) states that the team is in the National Roller League, which was formerly called the Roller Games Annual, but it was still under the auspices of the National Skating Derby, Inc.

83. Seltzer interview, 2011.

84. "Should They Be Dropped? Hot Tiff Rages on Girl Issue," *Roller Derby News*, June 1964.

85. Terrance O'Flaherty, "Annis Surprises Coast Reporter," *Roller Derby News*, August 1958 (reprinted from the *San Francisco Chronicle*).

86. Alan Ebert, "Tomboy Jan Vallow Buys Sex Equality on Wheels," *Roller Derby News*, June 1959.

87. Ibid.

88. "Margo," *Chicago Daily Tribune*, June 2, 1970.

89. Candice Bergen, "Little Women: What Has Forty Wheels, Seven Tits, and Fights?," *Esquire*, May 1, 1969.

90. Terry, "Elmer & Toughie."

91. Bergen, "Little Women,"104.

92. Ibid., 106.

93. Deford interview.

94. Ibid.

95. Ibid.

96. Ibid.

97. Frank Deford, "The Roller Derby," *Sports Illustrated*, March 3, 1969, 61.

98. Ibid.

99. Deford interview.

100. Jerry Seltzer, "*Derby* (1971) Trailer — Ok, I made a film I loved . . . but what about the skaters and fans?," *Roller Derby Jesus* (blog), January 21, 2014, https:// rollerderbyjesus.com/2014/01/21/%E2%96%B6-derby-1971-trailer-youtube.

101. *Derby*, dir. Robert Kaylor (Cinerama Releasing Corp., 1971), included in *The Roller Derby Chronicles* (Video Service Corp, 2009).

102. Robert Lipsyte explained that the filmmakers did not start the project intending to document Mike Snell's journey with Roller Derby: "According to producer William Richert the filmmakers joined the troupe in Dayton, Ohio, and met Snell by happenstance. Later they decided to go back and thread the film with Snell's hope of bettering his life by joining the Derby"; Robert Lipsyte, "Derby's Snell Rides with the Tides," *New York Times*, April 15, 1971.

103. Roger Ebert, review of *Derby*, June 15, 1972, RogerEbert.com, rogerebert .com/reviews/derby-1972.

104. Ibid.

105. Seltzer, "*Derby* (1971) Trailer."

106. Ebert, review of *Derby*.

107. Vincent Canby, "Sure, Hollywood Is Collapsing, But . . . ," *New York Times*, May 2, 1971.

108. Vincent Canby, "Critic's Choice — Ten Best Films of '71," *New York Times*, December 26, 1971.

109. Canby, "Sure, Hollywood Is Collapsing."

110. In 1971, the same year that Deford's *Five Strides on the Banked Track* and

the film *Derby* came out, Roller Derby released an in-house book titled *A Very Simple Game: The Story of Roller Derby*. Jerry Seltzer commissioned the book to support the movie, although it was a separate enterprise. Its author, Herb Michelson, noted, "The book was never intended as a Valentine for Jerry . . . In the Summer of 1970, [Jerry] asked for a history of the game from someone who had written around it but never about it" (iv). Michelson, who had formerly worked as a reporter and editor of *Roller Derby News*, compiled brief oral histories of skaters and other Roller Derby personnel into a history of the sport. The book, more so than the film, was popular with the sport's fans.

111. Roger Greenspun, "Instant Morality: 'Kansas City Bomber' Stars Raquel Welch," *New York Times*, August 3, 1972.

112. Gene Siskel, "The Movies: 'K.C. Bomber,'" *Chicago Tribune*, August 8, 1972.

113. Hall interview.

114. Dave Anderson, "'A Batchy, Sweaty, Funky Life,'" *New York Times*, July 30, 1972.

115. Hall interview.

116. *Have You Heard: Jim Croce Live* (Shout Factory, 2013), DVD; Dave Thompson, "Jim Croce: Biography," Jim Croce official website, http://jimcroce .com/?page_id=773#sthash.VteTkmf1.dpbs.

117. Croce worked on the song for so long because the former roller derby skater and her husband, a police officer, lived in his township in Pennsylvania. He was terribly afraid of insulting the husband.

118. One of the most famous roller derby movies came out in 1950 at the peak of Leo Seltzer's time in New York, when "Roller Derby was one of TV's most watched programs." Titled *The Fireball*, the film starred Mickey Rooney and Pat O'Brien and featured an early performance by Marilyn Monroe. *The Fireball*, dir. Tay Garnett, featuring Mickey Rooney and Pat O'Brien (Twentieth Century Fox, 1950), DVD (Warner Bros., 2010).

119. Seltzer interview, 2011.

120. Jerry Seltzer, in *Demon of the Derby*.

121. Seltzer interview, 2011.

122. Calvello, in *Demon of the Derby*.

123. Jan Vallow, in *Demon of the Derby*.

124. Alan Ebert, telephone interview by the author, September 14, 2011, digital audio recording, Marino Oral History Collection.

125. Seltzer interview, 2011.

126. Ibid.

127. Ibid.

128. Larry Smith, *The Last "True" Roller Derby* (Bloomington, IN: iUniverse, 2016), 176.

129. Buddy Atkinson Jr., Larry Smith, and Gerry Murray are among the many

skaters who believe that Seltzer sold Roller Derby to Griffiths. As stated above, Seltzer denies he sold anything, as does John Hall; see Hall interview; Atkinson interview; Murray interview; Smith, *Last "True" Roller Derby*, 148.

130. Hall interview.

131. Atkinson interview.

132. Smith, *Last "True" Roller Derby*, 175.

133. Ibid, 176–177.

134. Atkinson interview.

135. Ibid. In his autobiography, Smith acknowledged that he was paid more. He and Francine quit Roller Games after receiving their portion of the profit sharing, although Francine had some doubts about giving up the sport. A few days after they left, the Canadian promoter of their former team called and "offered us double and then triple our weekly salary" if they would come back for the road trip, which they agreed to. According to Smith, "when we returned, the animosity of the other skaters was clear" (*Last "True" Roller Derby*, 176).

136. Hall interview.

137. Roller Games in its original form outlasted Roller Derby by only a couple of years, but units operating under the "Roller Games" name resurfaced throughout the 1970s and 1980s. It is difficult to follow the names of the teams, units, and leagues that cropped up in the late 1970s and 1980s; many were interchangeable. See the website of the National Roller Derby Hall of Fame and Museum for more details, rollerderbyhalloffame.com.

138. Coppage, *Roller Derby to RollerJam*, 98–103.

139. "Roller Derby Timeline." Ann Calvello, at age seventy-one, appeared in an episode to skate a match race (*Demon of the Derby*).

CHAPTER 6: DIY ROLLER DERBY

The second chapter epigraph comes from Jake Fahy, telephone interview by the author, September 14, 2012, digital audio recording, Michella Marino Oral History Collection, W. E. B. Du Bois Library, University of Massachusetts Amherst (hereafter cited as Marino Oral History Collection).

1. "List of Roller Derby Leagues," DerbyListing.com, http://derbylisting .com/dl/grid. Although this website lists 1,911 active roller derby leagues worldwide and 879 American leagues (as of June 12, 2019), new leagues are constantly cropping up, and older leagues sometimes split into two leagues or die out. It is therefore difficult to get a precise figure for the number of leagues. This list appears to be the most up-to-date and accurate one currently available. For a brief discussion of the quick international spread of the sport, see Maddie Breeze, *Seriousness and Women's Roller Derby: Gender, Organization, and Ambivalence* (Basingstoke, UK: Palgrave Macmillan, 2015), 12.

2. Then again, I am not the first to claim that roller derby in a particular version is here to stay. The Seltzers thought the same throughout their tenure with the sport, and Brian Hughes, the vice president of TNN, which sponsored Roller Jam, insisted, "It's here to stay. Absolutely." See Keith Coppage, *Roller Derby to Roller-Jam: The Authorized Story of an Unauthorized Sport* (Santa Rosa, CA: Squarebooks, 1999), 116. Roller Jam folded after a couple of years.

3. Apparently Devil Dan overheard someone talking about some form of roller derby one night in Austin, and he "co-opted the brainstorm and ran with it"; see Melissa "Melicious" Joulwan, *Rollergirl: Totally True Tales from the Track* (New York: Simon and Schuster, 2007), 53.

4. Michael Corcoran, "Return of the Roller Derby: Revival with Roots in Austin Has Been Bruising on Track and Off," May 30, 2008, www.austin360.com, available at https://www.michaelcorcoran.net/roots-of-the-roller-derby-revival.

5. Ibid. Directed by Norman Jewison and starring James Caan, *Rollerball* (1975) was a futuristic sci-fi action movie. The film takes place in a corporate-run society that has replaced war with the sport of Rollerball, which a reviewer for the *New York Times* described as "a combination of the kind of roller skating you see in a roller derby, professional wrestling and pinball, and it's supposedly so brutal, vicious and exciting that it works off all aggressions"; see Vincent Canby, "Film: Futuristic World of 'Rollerball,'" June 26, 1975; *Rollerball* (1975), IMDb, imdb.com /title/tt0073631.

6. As cited in Joulwan, *Rollergirl*, 53; Jennifer Barbee and Alex Cohen, *Down and Derby: The Insider's Guide to Roller Derby* (Berkeley, CA: Soft Skull, 2010), 32–33.

7. Joulwan, *Rollergirl*, 53.

8. Ibid.; Barbee and Cohen, *Down and Derby*, 33.

9. Barbee and Cohen, *Down and Derby*, 33.

10. Ibid.; Joulwan, *Rollergirl*, 53.

11. Barbee and Cohen, *Down and Derby*, 157–158. At the beginning of the revival, many women adopted derby names not only because they enjoyed having aliases, but also because they did not necessarily want their real names tied to the alternative and somewhat controversial sport of roller derby for professional or personal reasons.

12. Devil Dan has a slightly different version of events, claiming the girls took the money and refused to return his calls. "I picked the four captains based on how strong they were, but they went behind my back, trashed my name, and decided to do it without me," alleges Dan. The captains "dispute this, saying they never again heard from Policarpo." He had left Texas for Tulsa by August 2001; see Corcoran, "Return of the Roller Derby."

13. Joulwan, *Rollergirl*, 54; Barbee and Cohen, *Down and Derby*, 34–37; Catherine Mabe, *Roller Derby: The History and All-Girl Revival of the Greatest Sport on Wheels* (Denver: Speck, 2007), 61.

14. As cited in Barbee and Cohen, *Down and Derby*, 35.

15. Ibid. A December 1976 *Charlie's Angels* episode entitled "Angels on Wheels" featured the Angels going undercover in the derby after a star skater was killed during a game; see the entry on IMBd.com, https://www.imdb.com/title/tt0539193/?ref_=ttep_ep13.

16. Barbee and Cohen, *Down and Derby*, 36.

17. This vision for the sport did not sit well with many of the BGGW skaters as the months wore on, and it eventually led to a split in the league.

18. Mabe, *Roller Derby*, 61.

19. Ibid. It is important to note that the game is currently evolving away from the "showier" aspects of roller derby (e.g., sexy uniforms and skater names). Many teams are adopting more standard sports uniforms, and more players are skating under their own names, although most derby leagues still operate under a DIY, punk-rock-type ethos. See Travis D. Beaver, "Roller Derby Uniforms: The Pleasures and Dilemmas of Sexualized Attire," *International Review for the Sociology of Sport* 51, no. 6 (2016): 639–657; Travis D. Beaver, " 'By the Skaters, for the Skaters': The DIY Ethos of the Roller Derby Revival," *Journal of Sport and Social Issues* 36, no. 1 (2012): 25–49; Breeze, *Seriousness and Women's Roller Derby*, 17–19.

20. Using a flat track was a major change from the banked-track roller derby days, but as noted later in this chapter, it was cheaper and easier to use a flat track than a banked track. It also meant skating could occur practically anywhere that duct tape sticks. It is important to note that the branch of the Seltzer family that is descended from Oscar Seltzer (Leo's brother and Jerry's uncle), which still owns and operates the Roller Derby Skate Corporation, technically holds the trademark on the term "Roller Derby," but has no interest in enforcing it where the name of the sport is concerned. The company does enforce the trademark on skating products, since that is what it continues to sell.

21. Barbee and Cohen, *Down and Derby*, 42. Under the Seltzers' Roller Derby, when teams competed against each other, they were called games, the term used in most team sports. But in the modern roller derby world, games are now called "bouts," like boxing matches. April Ritzenthaler, one of the skaters involved in the creation of the new sport, had been involved with boxing, so she decided to use the term "bout" instead of "game." The description stuck, and thus roller derby skaters no longer play games but rather have bouts. See Jerry Seltzer, "Springtime for Roller Derby," *Roller Derby Jesus* (blog), August 5, 2011, http://rollerderbyjesus.com/2011/08/05/springtime-for-roller-derby.

22. Barbee and Cohen, *Down and Derby*, 42.

23. Corcoran, "Return of the Roller Derby"; Joulwan, *Rollergirl*, 3–13; Barbee and Cohen, *Down and Derby*, 42. Corcoran lists the date of their first public bout as August 4, but Barbee and Cohen give it as August 22.

24. Joulwan, *Rollergirl*, 82.

25. Barbee and Cohen, *Down and Derby*, 47; *Hell on Wheels*, dir. Bob Ray, CrashCam Films, 2007, Indie Pix, 2009, DVD.

26. This number too is hard to pinpoint, but by checking the rule sets on

DerbyListing.com (http://derbylisting.com/dl/grid), combined with information from the Roller Derby Coalition of Leagues (http://therdcl.com/about-rdcl) and online forums such as Reddit (see the subreddit r/rollerderby: https://www.reddit .com/r/rollerderby/comments/9i607s/banked_track_question), it appears that the number of banked-track leagues ranges from nine to twelve.

27. Women's Flat Track Derby Association, https://wftda.com.

28. Women's Flat Track Derby Association, "About WFTDA," https://resour ces.wftda.org/about-wftda.

29. Ibid.

30. Women's Flat Track Derby Association, "WFTDA History," https:// wftda.org/history.

31. Barbee and Cohen, *Down and Derby*, 61.

32. Women's Flat Track Derby Association, "WFTDA History."

33. I have tried at least twice over the years of working on this project to sched-ule an oral history with a representative of the WFTDA, to no avail.

34. As cited in Corcoran, "Return of the Roller Derby." The use of wave meta-phors is highly debatable, but that does not diminish the ties of roller derby to feminism in general.

35. Adele Pavlidis, "From Riot Grrrl to Roller Derby? Exploring the Rela-tions between Gender, Music, and Sport," *Leisure Studies* 31, no. 2 (2012): 165–176. The Riot Grrrl movement, according to Pavlidis, "started around 1992, emerging from the punk and independent music communities of Olympia, Washington, and Washington, DC. Riot Grrrl encouraged women and girls to take control of the means of cultural production" (167). See also Adele Pavlidis and Simone Fulla-gar, *Sport, Gender, and Power: The Rise of Roller Derby* (Burlington, VT: Ashgate, 2014), about modern Australian roller derby. This physical-culture study draws on feminist theory to explore how female skaters in Australia have negotiated modern gender contradictions through roller derby; it also "provide[s] an account of the sport that can take into consideration the multiple ways the sport is being played, represented, developed, governed, and experienced" (12).

36. Carolyn E. Storms, "'There's No Sorry in Roller Derby': A Feminist Ex-amination of Identity of Women in the Full Contact Sport of Roller Derby," *New York Sociologist* 3 (2008): 68–87; Pavlidis, "From Riot Grrrl to Roller Derby." While most female leagues have allowed only women to skate, Patrick Kegan Flem-ing notes that men have been active in these leagues as referees, volunteers, or babysitters from the beginning. The leagues did not rely on these men to operate, but benefitted from their labor. See Patrick Kegan Fleming, "A Man in a Woman's World: Male Support Networks in Women's Flat Track Roller Derby" (master's thesis, University of North Carolina at Greensboro, 2016), 86–90.

37. Green Mountain Derby Dames, "About," accessed September 6, 2012, gmderbydames.com/about-gmdd.html. The Green Mountain Derby Dames are now known as Green Mountain Roller Derby; for its "About" page, see http:// gmrollerderby.com/about/history.

38. "How to Join WFTDA," WFTDA Roller Derby, accessed January 5, 2021, https://resources.wftda.org/membership/join. The WFTDA has recently expanded its gender definitions regarding who is eligible to join the organization, but member leagues must be "managed by at least 67% league skaters who identify as women or gender expansive, as detailed in the WFTDA Gender Statement [and] 51% owned by league skaters who identify as women or gender expansive, as detailed in the WFTDA Gender Statement."

39. Men and women need not necessarily skate together on the track, of course. Nonetheless, for the most part, men and women no longer belong to the same teams or the same leagues, although this has begun to shift slightly in the last few years. Also, both men and women now serve on the WFTDA and the MRDA boards of directors.

40. This has happened a couple times in the history of basketball, notably with the NCAA's hijacking of the AIAW (Association for Intercollegiate Athletics for Women) and the NBA and WNBA's conflict with the ABL (American Basketball League, a women's league).

41. This is the league I joined, but because I had been studying the co-ed Seltzer Roller Derby, I did not fully understand the unique (and even controversial) nature of the PVRD's league structure until later.

42. Jake Fahy, telephone interview by the author, September 14, 2012, digital audio recording, Marino Oral History Collection.

43. In the fall of 2012, Fahy stated, "I would like to see our women be eligible to join if that is their choice. I personally would like to see a change made in that particular language" (ibid.).

44. Erich Bennar, telephone interview by the author, September 13, 2012, digital audio recording, Marino Oral History Collection; Fahy interview; Barbee and Cohen, *Down and Derby*, 215.

45. Men's Roller Derby Association, "About MRDA," accessed September 10, 2012, http://www.mensderbycoalition.com/aboutmdc (website discontinued).

46. Ibid.

47. Ibid.

48. Ibid.; Bennar interview; *This Is How I Roll*, dir. Kat Vecchio (Fork Films, 2012), DVD; Breeze, *Seriousness and Women's Roller Derby*, 45–47.

49. The issue of transgendered skaters has raised questions of gender politics. The WFTDA worked for three years to develop a transgender policy that reflected its identity as a "female-oriented" sport and also its "value of inclusivity." The gender policy, effective January 1, 2012, allowed transgendered females to compete. The WFTDA has continued to refine its gender policy, and in the past couple of years has expanded it to include not only trans women but also intersex and gender-expansive individuals. See "Women's Flat Track Derby Association Statement about Gender," https://resources.wftda.org/womens-flat-track-derby-association-statement-about-gender. The MRDA similarly has a flexible gender policy and refuses to differentiate between members who identify as male and those

who identify as nonbinary. The MRDA "does not and will not set minimum standards of masculinity for its membership or interfere with the privacy of its members for the purposes of charter eligibility"; see "MRDA Non-Discrimination Policy," https://mrda.org/resources/mrda-non-discrimination-policy.

50. Green Mountain Roller Derby, "The Premiere of Green Mountain Roller Derby," press release, May 17, 2015, http://www.gmrollerderby.com/the-premier-of -green-mountain-roller-derby.

51. Ibid. Patrick Fleming addresses the role of male volunteers in women's roller derby as well as the alternative femininities and masculinities that create "respectful working relationship[s]" within a feminist space ("Man in a Woman's World," 86–91).

52. This includes roller derby's #MeToo movement, which demonstrates that even feminist, empowered, and inclusive spaces have not been safe. These incidents have caused shockwaves and backlash in the WFTDA, the MRDA, and the Junior Roller Derby Association (JRDA) communities, and prompted those governing bodies to revise their codes of conduct so that they can take swift action when offenders are brought to their attention. See Sara Morrison, "First Came Roller Derby's Own #MeToo Moment, Then Came the Backlash," Jezebel, June 1, 2018, https://jezebel.com/first-came-roller-derbys-own-metoo-moment -then-came-t-1826447452. Members of the derby community have started a blog as a "safe space for members of the derby world to share their experiences of rape, sexual assault, and non-sexual harassment and bullying within the community"; see *It Happens in Derby* (blog), accessed June 17, 2019, www.ithappensinderby .com/about (the blog has moved to Facebook).

53. Gotham Girls Roller Derby, "About GGRD," accessed March 10, 2009, www.gothamgirlsrollerderby.com/about. For the GGRD's current mission statement, see https://www.gothamgirlsrollerderby.com/mission.

54. Beaver, "Roller Derby Uniforms."

55. Gotham Girls Roller Derby, "About GGRD."

56. Ibid.

57. Ariel Levy, *Female Chauvinist Pigs: Women and the Rise of Raunch Culture* (New York: Free Press, 2005), 74.

58. Ibid., 75.

59. Beaver, "Roller Derby Uniforms," 647–651.

60. As cited in Storms, "No Sorry in Roller Derby," 80.

61. While no official nationwide polls exist concerning the topics in this paragraph, my own experiences with the sport, my professional discussions with current players, my search through current league websites, and my general research on the sport led me to this conclusion. Maddie Breeze's description of her experience with forming a league in the UK highlights these issues (*Seriousness and Women's Roller Derby*, 11).

62. Just as importantly, they describe themselves as "New York City's only skater-operated roller derby league for cisgender, transgender and intersex women

and gender non-conforming participants"; see Gotham Girls Roller Derby, "Mission."

63. Gotham Girls Roller Derby, "About GGRD."

64. Roller derby skaters disagree among themselves about the future direction of the sport. According to the first president of the WFTDA, Jennifer Wilson, aka Hydra, surveys and member meetings "show that people's ideas are all over the map. . . . It's the same situation in almost every sector of the association and impossible to find a direction that satisfies everyone" (Barbee and Cohen, *Down and Derby*, 66; see also Breeze, *Seriousness and Women's Roller Derby*, 2–3, 8).

65. Roller Derby Coalition of Leagues, "FAQ," accessed June 14, 2017, rollerderbycoalitionofleagues.com/faq (page no longer available); Roller Derby Coalition of Leagues, "About Us," http://therdcl.com/about-rdcl; Roller Derby Notes, "About RCDL," rollerderbynotes.com/tag/rdcl; RDCL, "Rules," http://therdcl.com/rdcl-rules-banked-track-roller-derby; Margot "Em Dash" Atwell, *Derby Life: A Crash Course in the Incredible Sport of Roller Derby* (New York: Gutpunch, 2015), 107.

66. Modern Athletic Derby Endeavor, "Our Story," skatemade.org/ourstory. MADE's style of play has been described as a "modernized, legitimate version of the traditional 1960s-1970s style of roller derby"; see Roller Derby Notes, "About MADE," rollerderbynotes.com/tag/made. MADE was organized in 2006 by a handful of leagues that for one reason or another did not find other governing bodies or rule sets that fit their needs. In May 2015, MADE had thirty-five full-member leagues in the United States and abroad, along with thirteen affiliated partial-member leagues.

67. FIRS recently underwent a name change to World Skate.

68. Team USA: USA Roller Sports, "Resources," http://teamusa.org/usa-roller-sports/resources.

69. Note: this was a decade after the WFTDA's rule sets were instituted; see Atwell, *Derby Life*, 106; Team USA: USA Roller Sports, "Resources."

70. Juliana Gonzales, "Recap and Thoughts," talk delivered at a meeting of the Fédération Internationale de Roller Sports (FIRS), Rome, February 3, 2015. A link to a PDF of the transcript is in Steven Rodriguez, "Pivotal Meeting with FIRS Leads WFTDA to Seek IOC Recognition for Roller Derby," Roller Derby Notes, November 2, 2015, http://www.rollerderbynotes.com/2015/11/02/pivotal-meeting-with-firs-leads-wftda-to-seek-ioc-recognition-for-roller-derby.

71. Also present were Alessandra Lunadei, FIRS general affairs; Laura Morandi, FIRS vice secretary-general; and Roberto Marotta, FIRS secretary-general.

72. Gonzales, "Recap and Thoughts."

73. Ibid.

74. Ibid.

75. Ibid.; Rodriguez, "Pivotal Meeting with FIRS."

76. Rodriguez, "Pivotal Meeting With FIRS."

77. Gonzales, "Recap and Thoughts."

78. Ibid.

79. Ibid.

80. WFTDA Board of Directors to President Aracu, October 7, 2015, https://static.wftda.com/letters/WFTDA-Response-to-FIRS-October-2015.pdf.

81. WFTDA to the International Olympic Committee, October 7, 2015. https://static.wftda.com/letters/WFTDA-Letter-to-IOC-October-2015.pdf.

82. Ibid.

83. Ibid.

84. Donna A. Lopiano, interview by the author, March 17, 2011, Hadley, MA, digital audio recording, Marino Oral History Collection; Allen Guttman, *Women's Sports: A History* (New York: Columbia University Press, 1991), 212–214; Pamela Grundy and Susan Shackelford, *Shattering the Glass: The Remarkable History of Women's Basketball* (Chapel Hill: University of North Carolina Press, 2007), 179–181. Something similar occurred with the ABL and the NBA when women's professional basketball was on the rise in the mid to late 1990s.

85. World Skate, "FIRS Evolves into World Skate to Support Growth on the Road to the Tokyo 2020 Olympic Games and Beyond," October 27, 2017, world-skate.org/skateboarding/news-skateboarding/1525-firs-evolves-into-world-skate-to-support-growth-on-the-road-to-the-tokyo-2020-olympic-games-and-beyond.html.

86. The World Roller Games, which included a roller derby competition, took place in 2017 in Nanjing and in July 2019 in Barcelona. World Skate still claims, as does the WFTDA, to be the international governing body of roller derby; see World Skate, "Roller Derby," worldskate.org/roller-derby.html.

87. Renee Miller and Marc Golas, joint interview by the author, digital audio recording, June 19, 2017, in author's possession.

88. Tucson Derby Brats, "About Us," tucsonderbybrats.com/about.html; Seattle Derby Brats, "A Brief History of the Seattle Derby Brats," seattlederbybrats.com/history.

89. Miller and Golas interview.

90. Steven Rodriguez, "WFTDA to Launch Independent Junior Roller Derby Coalition," Roller Derby Notes, September 9, 2015, rollerderbynotes.com/2015/09/09/wftda-to-launch-independent-junior-roller-derby-association.

91. Ibid.

92. "Roller Derby welcomed to the AAU Junior Olympic Games," Team USA: Roller Sports, June 12, 2015, https://www.teamusa.org/USA-Roller-Sports/Features/2015/June/12/Roller-Derby-welcomed-to-the-AAU-Junior-Olympic-Games.

93. Steven Rodriguez, "JRDA Partners with USARS, AAU for First Roller Derby Junior Olympics," Roller Derby Notes, January 3, 2016, rollerderbynotes.com/2016/01/03/jrda-partners-with-usars-aau-for-first-roller-derby-junior-olym

pics. There appears to be some overlap in organizational personnel. At the time, Chris Hunter was a member of the USARS Roller Derby Sport Committee as well as senior vice president of the JRDA.

94. Andrew Mc, "JRDA and AAU Are Proud to Present the Inaugural Junior Olympics Roller Derby Tournament!," Junior Roller Derby Association, December 4, 2015, juniorrollerderby.org/news_article/show/585668?referrer_id=2371162.

95. Miller and Golas interview.

96. Ibid.

97. "JFTDA FAQ," accessed June 12, 2017, https://wftda.org/faq/jftda-faq (page no longer available).

98. Ibid.

99. Women's Flat Track Derby Association, "WFTDA, MRDA, and JRDA Announce Partnership on The Rules," February 6, 2017, https://wftda.com/wftda-mrda-jrda-rules.

100. Ibid.

101. Ibid.

102. Tits and ass.

103. Mabe, *Roller Derby*, 65.

104. Kate Hansen, "Breastfeeding and Roller Derby," *Kate Hansen Art* (blog), http://www.katehansen.ca/the-artful-mother/breastfeeding-and-roller-derby.

105. Ibid.

106. Juke Boxx, "I'm a Pregnant Roller Derby Athlete," https://coachjukeboxx.tumblr.com/post/160748644612/im-a-pregnant-roller-derby-athlete-part-one.

107. Ibid.

108. Ibid. Boxx posted a refreshingly honest account of the birth of her daughter that underscores the complexities of motherhood and how society uses the identity of mother to define women and delegitimize their human responses to the process of giving birth and raising children; see Juke Boxx, "I'm a Pregnant Roller Derby Athlete, Part Five: My Birth Story," https://coachjukeboxx.tumblr.com/post/177462906882/im-a-pregnant-roller-derby-athlete-part-five-my.

CONCLUSION

1. This is not to say that there was not drama among league members—far from it—but a strong derby community still existed.

2. After a solid run of eight years, the Platte Valley Vixens dissolved in December 2019; "Formal Announcement of Dissolution," accessed December 23, 2019, www.rollervixens.com (page no longer available).

3. I have moved back to my home state of Indiana. I have not yet returned to skating, but I also haven't ruled out the possibility, since Indianapolis has two solid leagues and I skated a couple of times years ago with the Circle City Derby Girls.

4. My students got plenty of exposure to the derby apart from class meet-

ings. The Platte Valley Roller Vixens allowed them to attend a scrimmage, and two league members spoke on a panel I hosted (Steph Gallaway, aka Florence Welts, and Sara Thomas, aka Dame Von Slapavitch). A skater (Andrea Tarnick) from No Coast Roller Derby in Lincoln drove down to sit on the panel, as did a former teammate of mine from the PVRD (Diane Williams, aka Lady Hulk) who drove six hours from Iowa City. And Jerry Seltzer Skyped in to talk with my students. The roller derby community is a giving one.

5. *Love and Basketball*, dir. Gina Prince-Bythewood (40 Acres and a Mule Filmworks, 2000).

INDEX